T0217128

Lecture Notes in Artificial Intelligence 1159

Subseries of Lecture Notes in Computer Science
Edited by J. G. Carbonell and J. Siekmann

Lecture Notes in Computer Science

Edited by G. Goos, J. Hartmanis and J. van Leeuwen

Springer
Berlin
Heidelberg
New York
Barcelona
Budapest
Hong Kong
London
Milan
Paris
Santa Clara
Singapore
Tokyo

Díbio L Borges   Celso A.A. Kaestner (Eds.)

Advances in Artificial Intelligence

13th Brazilian Symposium
on Artificial Intelligence, SBIA '96
Curitiba, Brazil, October 23-25, 1996
Proceedings

 Springer

Series Editors
Jaime G. Carbonell, Carnegie Mellon University, Pittsburgh, PA, USA
Jörg Siekmann, University of Saarland, Saarbrücken, Germany

Volume Editors

Díbio L. Borges
Celso A.A. Kaestner
Centro Federal de Educação Tecnológica, Depto. de Informática
Av. 7 de Setembro, 3165, 80230-901 Curitiba PR/Brazil

Cataloging-in-Publication Data applied for

Die Deutsche Bibliothek - CIP-Einheitsaufnahme

Advances in artificial intelligence : proceedings / 13th Brazilian
Symposium on Artificial Intelligence, SBIA '96, Curitiba,
Brazil, October 1996. Díbio L. Borges ; Celso A. A. Kaestner
(ed.). - Berlin ; Heidelberg ; New York ; Barcelona ; Budapest ;
Hong Kong ; London ; Milan ; Paris ; Santa Clara ; Singapore ;
Tokyo : Springer, 1996
  (Lecture notes in computer science ; Vol. 1159 : Lecture notes in
  artificial intelligence)
  ISBN 3-540-61859-7
NE: Borges, Díbio L. [Hrsg.]; Brazilian Symposium on Artificial
  Intelligence <13, 1996, Curitiba>; GT

CR Subject Classification (1991): I.2

ISBN 3-540-61859-7 Springer-Verlag Berlin Heidelberg New York

© Springer-Verlag Berlin Heidelberg 1996
Printed in Germany

Typesetting: Camera ready by author
SPIN 10558110   06/3142 – 5 4 3 2 1 0   Printed on acid-free paper

Preface

The Brazilian Symposium on Artificial Intelligence has been organized by the interest group in Artificial Intelligence of the Brazilian Computer Society since 1984. In order to promote research in Artificial Intelligence and scientific interchange among Brazilian AI researchers and practitioners, an their counterparts worldwide, it is being organized as an international forum.

Continuing with the effort to make the SBIA symposia an international forum of high standard, the XIIIth SBIA has expanded the number of members of the program committee from the international community, it has used blind reviewing and discussion for the submitted papers, and it has published the proceedings through Springer-Verlag to make them available worldwide.

We have received 66 papers, distributed as follows: Brazil 47, Portugal 6, France 4, USA 2, Mexico 2, Germany 2, Belgium 2, and United Kingdom 1. From this total 23 papers were accepted and are included in this volume.

We would like to thank and congratulate all the program committee members, and the other reviewers, for their work in reviewing and commenting on the submitted papers. We would also like to thank CNPq, CAPES, Banco Bamerindus, FINEP, and IBM Brazil in their role as the main sponsors of the symposium in Curitiba.

Curitiba, October 1996

Díbio Leandro Borges
Celso Antônio Alves Kaestner

Program Committee Members

L. Valéria R. Arruda	(Federal Center for Education in Techology, Brazil)
Bert Bredeweg	(University of Amsterdam, The Netherlands)
Díbio Leandro Borges *	(Federal Center for Education in Technology, Brazil)
Yves Demazeau	(LEIBNIZ/IMAG, France)
Edson C. B. Carvalho Filho	(Federal University of Pernambuco, Brazil)
Robert Fisher	(University of Edinburgh, United Kingdom)
Hector Geffner	(University Simon Bolivar, Venezuela)
Malik Ghallab	(LAAS, France)
Kaoru Hirota	(Tokyo Institute of Technology, Japan)
Décio Krause	(Federal University of Paraná, Brazil)
Soundar Kumara	(Pennsylvania State University, USA)
José Gabriel P. Lopes	(New University of Lisbon, Portugal)
Maria Carolina Monard	(University of Sao Paulo - Sao Carlos, Brazil)
Eugénio Oliveira	(University of Porto, Portugal)
Cécile L. Paris	(ITRI, United Kingdom)
Armando Rocha	(State University of Campinas, Brazil)
Donia Scott	(ITRI, United Kingdom)
Flávio S. Correa da Silva	(University of Sao Paulo, Brazil)
Sheila Veloso	(Federal University of Rio de Janeiro, Brazil)
Rosa Viccari	(Federal University of Rio Grande do Sul, Brazil)
Jacques Wainer	(State University of Campinas, Brazil)

* Program Chair

Local Organization Committee Members

In alphabetical order: Paulo R. I. Adriano, Luiz Alberton, L. Valéria R. Arruda, Díbio Leandro Borges, Flávio Bortolozzi, Celso A. Alves Kaestner **, Vera Lúcia Delfino, Myriam R. Delgado, José Rank Filho, Hélic H. Duarte Marques, Júlio César Nievola, Júlio César Nitsch, all from CEFET-PR, and Milton Pires Ramos from TECPAR.

** Conference General Chair

Reviewers

Contents

Nonmonotonic Reasoning

Planning, Learning and Heuristic Search

Distributed AI and Multi-Agent Systems I

Genetic Algorithms

Natural Language Processing

Vision and AI Applications

Logic Programming, Temporal Reasoning and Belief Functions

Distributed AI and Multi-Agent Systems II

Abstracts of Tutorials and Invited Lectures

An Argumentation Based Framework for Defeasible and Qualitative Reasoning

Nikos I. Karacapilidis   Dimitris Papadias   Thomas F. Gordon

Artificial Intelligence Research Division
Institute for Applied Information Technology
GMD - German National Research Center for Computer Science
Schloss Birlinghoven, 53754 Sankt Augustin, Germany
e-mail: {karacapilidis, papadias, gordon}@gmd.de

Abstract. Multiagent settings are usually characterized by numerous goals, diverse opinions and conflicts of interest. In order to reach understanding and achieve cooperation, agents need a means of expressing their individual arguments which may contain explanations, justifications or any other kind of information. Furthermore, existing information may usually be incomplete, inconsistent and expressed in qualitative terms. In this paper, we present an argumentation-based framework that supports defeasible and qualitative reasoning in such environments. An interval-based qualitative value logic is applied, together with an inference mechanism in order to refine agents' knowledge, check consistency and, eventually, conclude the issue. The model is currently under development in Java, the aim being to deploy it on the World Wide Web.

1   Introduction

The argumentation component of the interaction between agents seems to attract the interest of researchers from various well-established areas, such as Distributed AI, nonmonotonic reasoning, decision theory, legal reasoning, as well as linguistics, philosophy, psychology and cognitive science. Stemming from legal reasoning procedures, argumentation has become an appropriate means of interaction in order to handle problematic instances, like normative conflicts and nonmonotonicity. Our goal is the development of a computational model of argumentation, by which groups of natural or artificial agents can express their claims and judgements, aiming at informing or convincing, depending on the kind of interaction. Such a model has to support rational, effective and fair decision making in ill-defined cases, where information is limited and/or not precisely known, and conflicts among agents are common. In this paper, we present a framework for defeasible argumentation and negotiation under the above conditions. It can be used in any kind of group decision making processes, and is able to handle inconsistent, qualitative and incomplete information in cases where one has to weigh reasons for and against the selection of a certain course of action.

We view such a framework as only a part of a mediating system for collaborative decision making and problem solving (see [14] for an extensive discussion on it). More specifically, the overall system also consists of a *Logic Layer*, where the notions of necessary *consequence* and *contradiction* are defined, a *Speech Act Layer*, where the space of possible kinds of actions an agent may perform is defined, and a *Protocol Layer*, where norms and rules about duties and rights of agents are specified (see also [8] and [19] for discussions on two slightly different approaches).

Formal models of argumentation have been built on various logics (see for example: [7] reconstructing Rescher's theory of formal disputation [21]; [18] based on Reiter's default logic [20]; and [12] using Geffner and Pearl's concepts of conditional entailment [11]). Whether it makes sense to use nonmonotonic, inductive or analogical logics at the logic layer is extensively discussed in [19]. In this paper, we shall not strictly specify the logic we intend for the system. The formalization of the other (more higher) layers should not assume any particular choice on the underlying logic. Similar models of defeasible argumentation have also left the subject unspecified (e.g., [26]).

The next section introduces the concepts involved in our argumentation framework and defines preference relations among competing statements. The argumentation concepts at this level result in a non-monotonic formalism founded on argumentation principles. Section 3 illustrates the procedure of concluding an issue together with the associated inference mechanisms that refine agents' knowledge and check consistency. Related and future work is discussed in Section 4.

2 The Argumentation Based Framework

2.1 Elements

Our terminology is based on that of issue-based information systems (first introduced in [15]; used in the IBIS system [27]). The argumentation elements presented below are the position, issue and argument (pro and contra)[1].

Positions are considered to be the basic objects in our framework. Any kind of data an agent wants to assert during an interaction can be used in order to represent a position. These data may have been brought up to declare alternative solutions, justify a claim, advocate the selection of a specific course of action, or avert the agents' interest from it. A position can be (or become) true or false, important or irrelevant for the corresponding problem, and may finally become acceptable or not.

Issues correspond to decisions to be made, or goals to be achieved. They consist of a set of alternative positions and a set of constraints that hold among them. An issue can be interpreted as which alternative position to prefer, if any. We don't allow more than one alternative position of an issue to be selected. At any stage of the argumentation process, an issue may be either inconsistent (due to inconsistency in the associated set of constraints), able to recommend a

---

[1] Due to space limitations, the formal definitions of the argumentation framework elements have been omitted in this version of the paper

solution (position) for its conclusion, or not. In fact, the last case indicates that none of the alternative positions of the issue is recommended.

Arguments are assertions about the positions which speak for or against them (multiple meanings of the term *argument* are discussed in [19]; various application areas are presented in [2]). An argument links together two positions of different issues. Agents can put forward arguments to convince their opponents or to settle an issue via a formal decision procedure. We distinguish between supporting arguments (pro) and counterarguments (con). Besides, we assume that arguments are refutable (see also [5], [6]), and two conflicting arguments can simultaneously be applied.

Various notions of an argument have been suggested in the literature. In [9], an argument consists of a *support base*, that may contain formulas which speak for or against a certain position, and a *conclusion*. A similar notion of argument has been given in [3]. All the above notions are extensions of the one proposed in [23]. Our definition differs from the above in that it does not presume that the support base of an argument is minimal. That is, a strict subset of the support base of an argument can be the support base of another argument with the same conclusion.

In most cases, we have to compare arguments in favor of the same conclusion, as well as, arguments leading to contradictory conclusions. The subjects of priority relationships and preference orders between arguments have been handled through quantitative approaches. For example, [16] and [22] have used the concepts of *penalty logic* (cost of not taking a premise into account) and *confidence factors*, respectively. Unfortunately, well defined utility and probability functions regarding properties or attributes of alternative positions (used, for instance, in traditional OR approaches), as well as complete ordering of these properties are usually absent. On the other hand, non-monotonic formalisms have defined preference relations on subtheories in various ways (see for example the concepts of *preferred subtheories* [5], *conditional entailment* [11] and *prioritized syntax-based entailment* [4]).

An argumentation system is usually defined given a set of arguments equipped with a binary relation holding among them. Since decision making and problem solving are evolving and theory-construction procedures, and also due to the problems mentioned above, an argumentation framework should allow for "weak" commitments on such relations. It is up to the agents to strengthen eventual weak relations, by providing the appropriate argumentation, and achieve the desired results.

2.2 Preference relations

Argumentation can be viewed as a special form of logic programming. As shown in [10], an argumentation system may be considered as consisting of two parts: an argument generation unit and an argument processing unit. The second one is a logic program consisting of the clauses: (i) $\mathbf{acc(x)} \leftarrow \neg\mathbf{defeat(x)}$ and (ii) $\mathbf{defeat(x)} \leftarrow \mathbf{attack(y,x), acc(y)}$, where (i) means that an argument is acceptable if it is not defeated, and (ii) means that an argument is defeated if it is attacked by an acceptable argument.

A first sketch of an appropriate underlying logic for such an argumentation framework, namely *Qualitative Value Logic*, was first proposed in [8]. This logic aims at relieving the users of the necessity of specification of exact cost values on subtheories, while offers them the possibility to reason about preferences (see also [13] exploring it together with abilities of constraint satisfaction formalisms). In this paper, we enhance this logic, in order to address the following problems that usually appear in real decision making instances: (i) A complete preference ordering among statements is not always attainable. There may be some formal properties such as transitivity and non-circularity, but still a partial ordering is what we are able to achieve. (ii) There is not always complete information for each alternative position of an issue regarding the attributes asserted by the arguments. In other words, the union of the support bases of each alternative position in an issue is not common. For instance, in order to conclude an issue with two alternative positions p_1 and p_2, we may know that "p_1 has the attributes a and b", while "p_2 has the attributes a, c and d", but no information regarding the ordering of b, c and d has been given.

We need a means for comparing alternative positions in an issue, taking into account the argumentation which has been put forward by the agents. We compare positions according to the value of their importance for the agents taking place in the communication process. The *importance value* of a position may range from $-\infty$ to $+\infty$. However, in most real world decision making instances, asking agents to attach a numeric weight or a certainty factor to default rules seems rather utopian (see also [2]). We associate with each position an *interval of importance*. Positions with (only) positive or negative importance may consist of the support base of a supporting argument or a counterargument, respectively. Note that, by using intervals, the framework also allows for a certain value of importance to be asserted (when the first and last points of the interval coincide). In other words, with such an interval-based value logic, our framework covers the cases where importance is interpreted as having either a certain value or a range of consecutive values.

A *preference relation* is a formula that relates two arguments[2]. Preference relations provide a qualitative way to weigh reasons for and against the selection of a certain course of action. Note that preference relations are also considered to be defeasible and subject to debate. We introduce the following preference relations between arguments: *SMP (strongly more preferable), SLP (strongly less preferable), EQP (equally preferable), WMP (weakly more preferable)* and *WLP (weakly less preferable)*. The key difference between strong and weak preference is that in the former case the existing argumentation allows us to draw a distinction considering the entire support bases of the arguments under consideration, where

---

[2] To be more precise, we should say the support bases of two arguments. As mentioned above, an argument links two positions of two different issues, a support base and a conclusion; our framework allows "actions" on arguments implicitly, i.e., through their support bases.

in the latter only some parts of them[3] The above relations form two pairs of inverse relations ($SMP(p, q) \equiv SLP(q, p)$ and $WMP(p, q) \equiv WLP(q, p)$). The disjunction of all the above relations, usually known as the *universal* relation, will be denoted as *UNK* (it can be interpreted as *unknown* in our framework, since any of them may hold).

In addition, preference relations may be asserted independently of the position they refer to, i.e., independently of the conclusions of the related arguments (e.g., distinguish between the argument stating that speed is more important than price for any type of car, and another one arguing the same, but only for a particular car model).

3 Concluding an issue

As discussed above, our argumentation framework allows for defeasible reasoning in agent communication; that is, further information can trigger another course of action to appear more preferable than what seems best at the moment. Agents can put forward new preference relations at any time. Whenever that happens, the model infers all consequences by computing the transitive closure of the associated preference relations. This procedure is similar to the one first proposed in [1]. Briefly, a new relation adds a constraint in the relevant issue, which may in turn introduce new constraints between other arguments through the transitivity rules that hold among these relations. These rules are summarized in Figure 1.

	SMP	SLP	EQP	WMP	WLP
SMP	SMP	UNK	SMP	SMP	UNK
SLP	UNK	SLP	SLP	UNK	SLP
EQP	SMP	SLP	EQP	WMP	WLP
WMP	SMP	UNK	WMP	WMP	UNK
WLP	UNK	SLP	WLP	UNK	WLP

Fig. 1. The transitivity rules for the preference relations.

3.1 Inference mechanism

A constraint satisfaction problem is implicitly deployed. The corresponding constraint graph is being formed as the communication evolves. Each issue is actually a complete sub-graph of it. Applying path consistency algorithms together

---

[3] Formal definitions of these relations have been also left out in this version of the paper. However, informally speaking, $WMP(p, q)$ should be interpreted as "p could be better than q (we doubt due to lack of the appropriate information), but q could never be better than p"; $SMP(p, q)$ should be interpreted as "p is always better than q".

with the transitivity rules shown in Figure 1, we refine the agents' knowledge about the preference relations and check consistency. Initially (with no constraints yet asserted), all pairs of positions in each issue "receive" the *UNK* relation. When a new preference relation is brought up, all consequences are computed (through the computation of the transitive closure of the associated preference relations, for more details see [1]). Let $R(p_k, p_i) \otimes R(p_i, p_j)$ denote the composition function for lists of preference relations holding among (p_k, p_i) and (p_i, p_j), and *CheckQueue* denote a queue of "tests" to be done. The path consistency algorithm is as follows:

```
for each pair of positions (pi,pj)
        push (pi,pj) to CheckQueue
end-for
while not-empty-CheckQueue
        pop-CheckQueue (pi,pj);
                for each position pk such that pk ≠ pi and pk ≠ pj
                        NewRel(pk,pj) = R(pk,pj) ∩ (R(pk,pi) ⊗ R(pi,pj))
                        if NewRel(pk,pj) = ∅
                                then return inconsistency;
                                else if    NewRel(pk,pj) ⊂ R(pk,pj)
                                           and not-in-CheckQueue(pk,pj)
                                                   then push-CheckQueue(pk,pj);
                        NewRel(pi,pk) = R(pi,pk) ∩ (R(pi,pj) ⊗ R(pj,pk))
                        if NewRel(pi,pk) = ∅
                                then return inconsistency;
                                else if    NewRel(pi,pk) ⊂ R(pi,pk)
                                           and not-in-CheckQueue(pi,pk)
                                                   then push-CheckQueue(pi,pk);
                end-for
end-while
```

Finally, what is needed is a classification of the positions in each issue. Aggregating the final set of preference relations, i.e., the one resulting after the application of the path consistency algorithm, we can eventually draw some comparisons among positions, and assign a *qualification label* to each of them. We allow for the labels *SBTA* (strongly better than all), *SBTS* (strongly better than some), *WBTA* (weakly better than all), *WBTS* (weakly better than some), *ETA* (equal to all), *SWTS* (strongly worse than some), *SWTA* (strongly worst than all), *WWTS* (weakly worse than some), and *WWTA* (weakly worst than all). Similar ideas are discussed in [9], based on a classification of arguments to those with an *empty support*, those which are not *rebutted*, and those which are not *undercut* by another argument.

3.2 Examples

In this section we present two examples in order to demonstrate the features of our framework. First consider the following: the goal at a part of a discussion is to find a constructor for a part of a car engine. Assume the following three alternatives: *C1*, *C2* and *C3*. The asserted attributes concern the quality, service, delivery time and cost that each of the alternatives provide. Figure 2 illustrates the discussion graph: positions are denoted with ellipses, issues with rectangles and arguments with straight lines (counterarguments are distinguished with a small horizontal line crossing the diagonal ones). The shadowed position of each issue is the system-recommended one. Figure 3a summarizes the existing knowledge about the attributes that each alternative has (or not). Assume also that the following preference relations have been asserted so far:

```
SMP(fair cost, good quality), and
SLP(meet due date, fair cost).
```

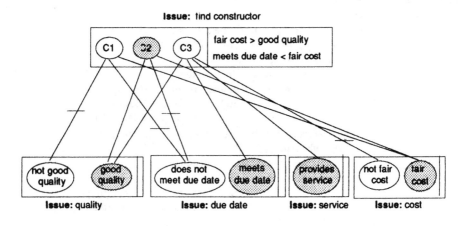

Fig. 2. Utility example.

As shown, there is not a complete linking between each alternative of an issue and every asserted attribute. For instance, there is no argumentation at the moment about the service provided for the *C1* and *C2* alternatives. The preference relations between the alternative constructors, resulting after the application of the inference mechanism illustrated above, are given in Figure 3b. One can see that *C2* is the recommended solution of the "find constructor" issue (*WBTA(C2)*). *C1* is strictly less preferable than each of *C2*, *C3*, i.e., *SLP(C1, C2)* and *SLP(C1, C3)*, while *C2* is weakly more preferable than *C3*, i.e., *(WMP(C2, C3)*.

The second example is a slightly modified version of the classical Tweety one. The example demonstrates how our framework can handle *specificity*. The existing argumentation, which has been brought up by two interacting agents (N and T are their names), is given in Figure 4, together with the corresponding discussion graph.

Experiments with examples from diverse types of communication indicate that, according to their content, we can distinguish between two types of issues:

	good quality	meets due date	service provided	fair cost			C1	C2	C3
C 1	no	no	??	yes		C 1	EQP	SLP	SLP
C 2	yes	no	??	yes		C 2	SMP	EQP	WMP
C 3	yes	yes	yes	no		C 3	SMP	WLP	EQP
	(a) data						**(b) results**		

Fig. 3. Utility example data and results.

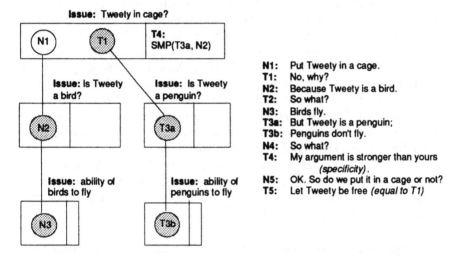

Issue: Tweety in cage?

N1:	Put Tweety in a cage.
T1:	No, why?
N2:	Because Tweety is a bird.
T2:	So what?
N3:	Birds fly.
T3a:	But Tweety is a penguin;
T3b:	Penguins don't fly.
N4:	So what?
T4:	My argument is stronger than yours *(specificity)*.
N5:	OK. So do we put it in a cage or not?
T5:	Let Tweety be free *(equal to T1)*

Fig. 4. Tweety example.

(i) *boolean* issues, in which only a position and its negation can be included. However, it is not obligatory that both of them will be included, since there is not always an automatic insertion of the position $\neg p$ after the assertion of p (consider the issues "Tweety in cage?" and "Is Tweety a bird?" in the second example, and "quality"[4], "due date", etc. in the first example); (ii) Selection issues, in which alternative positions can be included and no alternative is the negation of another one (consider the issue "find constructor" in the first example).

4 Discussion

Approaches to reasoning in the presence of inconsistency can be distinguished to these based on the notion of *maximal consistent subbase*, where coherence is restored by selecting consistent subbases, and those based on *argumentation principles*, where inconsistency is "accepted" by providing arguments for each

---

[4] The reader should interpret "quality" as an abbreviation title for the issue "what kind of quality does Constructor Cx provides?", while $x=1,2,3$. In fact, our model retains three "copies" of this issue, one for each Constructor.

conclusion [9]. Non-monotonic inference relations are basically used in the first category, defined by methods of generating "preferred" belief subbases and classical inference [5]. The second category, inspired from work done on AI and Law, views the validity and priority of belief bases as subject to debate. The role of agents here is to construct theories, that are robust enough to defend a statement. Throughout this paper, we have taken into account belief bases that have been explicitly stated by an agent.

Among related, well-tried concepts and theories that have addressed the problems of practical and substantial reasoning, we only mention here Toulmin's early *second theory of argumentation* that considers logic as generalized jurisprudence [25], Pollock's OSCAR model of defeasible reasoning [17], Rescher's theory of *formal disputation* [21], Sycara's PERSUADER model of *goal conflict resolution* [24], and the IBIS *rhetorical method* developed at MCC [27]. These approaches have been attempting to account for how humans combine deductive, defeasible, inductive and probabilistic reasoning. The main target of our approach is to jointly exploit the linguistic model of argumentation, as it has been evolved among logicians and computer scientists, with quantitative models coming from disciplines like Game Theory and Operations Research.

The model presented is currently under development in Java. We experiment with various user interfaces on the World Wide Web, the target being a high quality visualization of the structure of the communication as it evolves, and the easy retrieval and contribution of information.

Acknowledgements: The authors thank Gerhard Brewka, David Kerr, Kia Toubekis and Hans Voss for helpful discussions on various topics of this paper. This work was partially funded by the European Commission (DG XIII), under the GEOMED project. Dimitris Papadias is financed by the Commission of the European Communities through the ERCIM Fellowship Programme.

References

1. Allen, J.F.: Maintaining Knowledge about Temporal Intervals. *Communications of the ACM* 26 (11), 1983, pp. 832-843.
2. Bench-Capon, Tr.: Argument in Artificial Intelligence and Law. In J.C. Hage, T.J.M. Bench-Capon, M.J. Cohen and H.J. van den Herik (eds.), *Legal knowledge based systems - Telecommunication and AI & Law*, Koninklijke Vermande BV, Lelystad, 1995, pp. 5-14.
3. Benferhat, S., Dubois, D., Prade, H.: How to infer from inconsistent beliefs without revising? In *Proceedings of the 14th IJCAI*, Montreal, 1995, pp. 1449-1455.
4. Benferhat, S., Cayrol, C., Dubois, D., Lang, J., Prade, H.: Inconsistency Management and Prioritized Syntax-Based Entailment. In *Proceedings of the 13th IJCAI*, Chambery, 1993, pp. 640-645.
5. Brewka, G.: Preferred Subtheories: An extended logical framework for default reasoning. In *Proceedings of the 11th IJCAI*, Detroit, 1989, pp. 1043-1048.
6. Brewka, G.: Reasoning about Priorities in Default Logic. In *Proceedings of the 12th AAAI*, Seattle, 1994, pp. 940-945.

7. Brewka, G.: A Reconstruction of Rescher's Theory of Formal Disputation Based on Default Logic. In *Working Notes of the 12th AAAI Workshop on Computational Dialectics*, Seattle, 1994, pp. 15-27.

8. Brewka, G., Gordon, T.: How to Buy a Porsche: An Approach to Defeasible Decision Making. In *Working Notes of the 12th AAAI Workshop on Computational Dialectics*, Seattle, 1994, pp. 28-38.

9. Cayrol, C.: On the Relation between Argumentation and Non-monotonic Coherence-Based Entailment. In *Proceedings of the 14th IJCAI*, Montreal, 1995, pp. 1443-1448.

10. Dung, P.M.: On the acceptability of arguments and its fundamental role in non-monotonic reasoning and logic programming. In *Proceedings of the 13th IJCAI*, Chambery, 1993, pp. 852-857.

11. Geffner, H., Pearl, J.: Conditional Entailment: Bridging two Approaches to Default Reasoning. *Artificial Intelligence* 53 (2-3), 1992, pp. 209-244.

12. Gordon, T.: The Pleadings Game: An Exercise in Computational Dialectics. *Artificial Intelligence and Law* 2(4), 1994, pp. 239-292.

13. Karacapilidis, N.I.: Planning under Uncertainty: A Qualitative Approach. In C. Pinto-Ferreira and N.J. Mamede (eds.), *Progress in Artificial Intelligence*, Lecture Notes in Artificial Intelligence 990, Springer-Verlag, 1995, pp. 285-296.

14. Karacapilidis, N.I., Gordon, T.: Dialectical Planning. In *Proceedings of the 14th IJCAI Workshop on Intelligent Manufacturing Systems*, Montreal, 1995, pp. 239-250.

15. Kunz, W., Rittel, H.W.J.: Issues as Elements of Information Systems. Working Paper 131, Universität Stuttgart, Institut für Grundlagen der Plannung, 1970.

16. Pinkas, G.: Propositional Non-Monotonic Reasoning and Inconsistency in Symmetric Neural Networks. In *Proceedings of the 12th IJCAI*, Sydney, 1991, pp. 525-530.

17. Pollock, J.: Defeasible Reasoning. *Cognitive Science* 11, 1988, pp. 481-518.

18. Prakken, H.: Logical tools for modelling legal argument. Ph.D. Dissertation, Free University of Amsterdam, 1993.

19. Prakken, H.: From Logic to Dialectics in Legal Argument. In *Proceedings of the 5th International Conference on AI and Law*, ACM Press, 1995, pp. 165-174.

20. Reiter, R.: A Logic for Default Reasoning. *Artificial Intelligence* 13, 1980, pp. 81-132.

21. Rescher, N.: *Dialectics: A Controversy-Oriented Approach to the Theory of Knowledge*. State University of New York Press, Albany, 1977.

22. Sian, S.S.: Adaptation based on cooperative learning in multi-agent systems. In Y. Demazeau and J.P. Müller (eds.), *Decentralized AI 2*, Elsevier Science Publishers B.V., 1991, pp. 257-272.

23. Simari, G.R., Loui, R.P.: A Mathematical Treatment of Defeasible Reasoning and its Implementation. *Artificial Intelligence* 53 (2-3), 1992, pp. 125-157.

24. Sycara, K.: Resolving Goal Conflicts via Negotiation. In *Proceedings of the 7th AAAI*, Saint Paul, Minnesota, 1988, pp. 245-250.

25. Toulmin, S.E.: *The Uses of Argument*. Cambridge University Press, 1958.

26. Vreeswijk, G.: Studies in Defeasible Argumentation. Ph.D. Dissertation, Free University of Amsterdam, 1993.

27. Yakemovic, K.C.B., Conklin, E.J.: Report on a Development Project Use of an Issue-Based Information System. In F. Halasz (ed.), *Proceedings of CSCW 90*, LA, 1990, pp. 105-118.

Well-Behaved IDL Theories *

Ana Teresa C. Martins**, Marcelino Pequeno and Tarcísio Pequeno

Laboratório de Inteligência Artificial
Departamento de Computação
Universidade Federal do Ceará
P.O.Box 12166, Fortaleza, CE 60455-760 Brasil
e-mail: {ana, marcel, tarcisio}@lia.ufc.br

Abstract. The field of nonmonotonic logic, sixteen years old now, is devoted to solve the problem of reasoning under incomplete knowledge, whose good understanding is essential to the construction of AI as a science and whose relevance reaches far beyond AI applications. During these years, many insights have been accumulated in the form of desirable properties the proposed formalisms should exhibit and of criticisms on the available solutions. This paper takes advantage on this experience to derive from them a sort of canon to be imposed to nonmonotonic formalisms. This canon is translated as a set of etiquette rules guiding knowledge representation into theories framed within the *Inconsistent Default Logic*, IDL. It is then established the important result that IDL produces a unique extension for a theory constructed according to these rules. This result calls forth IDL as an interesting alternative to credulous common sense reasoning formalization fulfilling many desired properties.

Key words: knowledge representation, nonmonotonic reasoning, default logics, paraconsistent reasoning.

1 Introduction

The field of nonmonotonic reasoning in artificial intelligence is sixteen years old, a teenager, now. During this time, many logical apparatus, more or less formal, have been proposed to achieve the task of reasoning under practical conditions, i.e., to perform sensible inferences on the basis of realistically incomplete knowledge. How successful has been the field in accomplishing its duty is a disputable matter. However, since reasoning under incompleteness is the kind of problem that has to be faced if a science of artificial intelligence is ever to be constructed, a fair judgement on the matter can only be done in comparison with the achievements in other areas of AI where this problem is approached by different methods. Seeing in this realistic way, the situation by the nonmonotonic barracks does not look that desperate. It is not the purpose of this paper

---

* research partially sponsored by PICD/CAPES and CNPq.
** PhD student at Federal University of Pernambuco, e-mail: atcm@di.ufpe.br

to perform this sort of analysis or comparison but it aims to increase the hope that a real logical solution, facing the subtleties of this problem, is at sight. The core of this paper is to demonstrate how the *Inconsistent Default Logic*, IDL, proposed in [11], can be used to treat successfully most of these problems. In order to do so, it should be equipped with a sort of 'etiquette', a set of rules of good usage to be adopted for the formulation of well behaved IDL theories. This is what this paper is about.

As a fact of life, the adoption of nonmonotonic rules of reasoning, by achieving conclusions that are only partially supported, may, unfortunately, lead to the achievement of contradictions. So, attempts to retain consistency has been one of the main concerns in the field. Two general attitudes towards this problem have been proposed as solutions. One has been called a *credulous* attitude, which accepts all the achieved conclusions, by splitting them, when contradictory, into self consistent, deductively closed, subsets, called extensions, as in [14]. The other alternative, called *skeptical*, simply rejects all conflicting conclusions, as in [9]. An alternative way of treating the credulous attitude is adopted in IDL ([11],[12]): keeping all conclusions, no matter if contradictory, into a single theory. Of course this will cause some trouble because inconsistent theories are also trivial meaningless theories. Well, classically speaking, that is so. The question is: who says we should remain classical in a situation like that? Classical logic has been created to work under very clearly defined conditions and, from the beginning, these conditions do not fit the problem we are facing here. So, what is the point in trying to remain faithful to classical logic upon tricky expedients such as the splitting into multiple extensions? By this and some other reasons, the idea that the deductive part of nonmonotonic reasoning should be performed by classical logic should not be taken for granted. In fact, it is much more natural to assume that a peculiar kind of reasoning like this one would require a peculiar logic all over. Such a logic has been thus presented, in order to support the above alternative. It is a paraconsistent logic, i.e., a logic which does not collapse in face of contradictions of a certain kind [2]. In our case, contradictions among defeasible partial conclusions. This logic, specially designed to perform sound reasoning under conditions of relative ignorance, is called the *Logic of Epistemic Inconsistency* (LEI) [12]. LEI is the monotonic basis for IDL, instead of classical logic.

IDL provides a default rule, Reiter's like [14], but suitably modified to implement the above policies. It follows the pattern $\frac{\alpha:\beta;\gamma}{\beta?}$ where 'α' is known as *prerequisite*, 'β' as *normal justification*, 'γ' as *seminormal justification* and '$\beta?$' as the *consequent* of the default rule.

There are two main differences from IDL default rule and Reiter's one. The first one is the additional ?-mark suffixing plausible formulae. It is a form to distinguish the different epistemic status of irrefutable, monotonic formulae from refutable, nonmonotonic ones. Such symbol can be interpreted as a modal operator used to emphasise the existence of evidences, or some points of view, in supporting the formula it suffixes.

A second difference consists in the distinct treatment given to the normal and the seminormal part of the justification of the default rule. To inhibit the application of an IDL rule you must either derive a strong conclusion '$\neg\beta$', or merely a plausible conclusion '$(\neg\gamma)$?'. Such different treatment of the seminormal part of the default rule justification implies a preferential order between defaults by giving priorities to exceptions, represented in the seminormal justification. This order reflects the *exception first* principle [10]. This is a key issue in performing correct reasoning in some sort of problems, for instance, the famous *Yale Shooting* problem ([5]), where other nonmonotonic logics fail by deriving anomalous extensions. Another example of the same sort of problem is the following which, if translated to DL, will produce an anomalous extension where, from the simple fact that 'Tweety is a bird', 'it does not fly'. In IDL, the intended extension, where 'winged(tweety)?' and 'fly(tweety)?' hold, is the only one derived.

Example 1. $D=\{\dfrac{animal(x):\neg fly(x);\neg winged(x)}{(\neg fly(x))?}, \dfrac{bird(x):winged(x)}{winged(x)?}\}$
$W=\{winged(x) \to fly(x), bird(x) \to animal(x), bird(tweety)\}$

The following example shows the complementary role of paraconsistency to nonmonotonic reasoning. Instead of Reiter's solution, which splits the conflicting plausible conclusions in two extensions, IDL keeps them paraconsistently into the same extension until forthcoming evidence gives support to decide which one must be retained.

Example 2. $D=\{\dfrac{republican(x):\neg pacifist(x)}{(\neg pacifist(x))?} \dfrac{quaker(x):pacifist(x)}{pacifist(x)?}\}$
$W=\{republican(Nixon) \wedge quaker(Nixon)\}$

The approach of keeping two opposite plausible formulae together allows an inner logical treatment to this problem, without appealing to external procedures to handle multiple extensions. Although IDL puts all opposite possibilities together in a single theory, LEI, its deductive support, does not mix them up and so, unreasonable conclusions are not reached.

IDL presents some nice properties. It embodies a powerful formalism, which is responsible for its superior discriminative skills. On the other hand, this power may also be misused, bringing about unpleasant effects, such as incoherent (zeroextensions) theories or multiple extensions theories, which represents an inconvenient, and perfectly avoidable, kind of IDL theory. In fact, unrestricted IDL generalizes Default Logic. So, everything that is derived in Reiter's logic may also be derived in IDL. To achieve nice formulated, single extensioned, IDL theories, some restrictions must be imposed in the use of the language resources, analogously to restrictions that have been set in the design of well structured programs on the usage of programming language. *Ergo*, our aim here is to introduce a sort of 'etiquette', or a set of rules of style, to enable the formulation of well written IDL theories. The following section will be devoted to discuss some current criticisms on default logics, in general, and to examine IDL natural properties under the same optics. The idea is to try to extract from this criticism a canon against which rules of usage for IDL could be justified. These rules are formulated in section 3. Whether this standardization really succeeds is analyzed on section 4.

2   Criticisms on Default Theories

Since its introduction in 1980 [14], Reiter's Default Logic (DL) has suffered intense criticism. Many drawbacks and malfunctions have been diagnosed and some suggestions to circumvent them were forwarded [3], giving rising to many variants for Reiter's logic ([6], [1] and [15]). Furthermore, some desirable properties that nonmonotonic logics should obey were introduced and compliance with these properties were the leitmotif for some proposed variants.

These analyses focused mainly in technical and syntactical aspects of the logical representation and power of inference while semantic concerns have systematically been neglected. With this in mind, it is shown that some proposed variants for DL fix problems which, in reality, do not exist. Semantic considerations on the representation and formalization of common sense constitute the core of the ideas suggested in this paper.

Few researchers are aware to the semantic difference between evidence to the denial of the conclusion of a default rule and evidence for the non-applicability of the rule. John Pollock in [13] has been the first to explicitly point out this distinction calling them *rebutting* and *undercutting defeaters*, respectively. In general, the AI community has labelled both cases as exceptions and has, accordingly, treated them equally.

From semantic perspective, the properties of *semimonotonicity* and *orthogonality of the extensions* should not be required. Notice that, undercutting defeatears (or exceptions) are represented in the same normal part of a default justification. Therefore, consistency of the justification (the exception is absent) implies the applicability of the default. Now, if new defaults are added in such a way that the justification is no longer consistent (the exception is now derived), then the application of the default should be precluded. This is just the opposite of what the semimonotonicity property asserts. On the other hand, defaults might conflict (generating multiple extensions) in the sake of their conclusions or justifications. When the conflict involves the justification of a default, one should not expect extensions to be inconsistent with each other, the opposite of what the orthogonality property claims. Both properties were proposed for normal default theories where rebutting defeaters are the only representation for exceptions but they have been extended to seminormal default theories, what is a rather strange.

M. Pequeno claims that, in common sense reasoning, priority is given to the derivation of exceptions to default rules (see example 1). This important fact has been neglected in the main trend of nonmonotonic reasoning research in despite of not complying with the exceptions-first criterion [10] be a reason for the *anomalous unintended extensions* nonmonotonic logics produce. IDL and DLEF (Defeasible Logic with Exceptions First [10]) are the first nonmonotonic logics to attend to this principle.

Paraconsistency is another unique feature of IDL. IDL takes full advantage of this particularity splitting conclusions from defaults apart. Thus, *commitment to assumptions* gains a new significance in IDL theories. Default conclusions which, according to this property, should be separated in multiple extensions are kept apart in the same IDL extension.

Although essentially dealing with inductive reasoning[3], nonmonotonic logics were designed to be as close to the deductive paradigm as possible. Existence of pre-requisites on default rules diminishes the power of inference of the DL when compared with a corresponding deductive theory. Thus, DL does not allow *reasoning by cases*, the *contrapositive* of a default is not valid, etc. Even the property of *cautious monotonicity* would be acquired by adopting a pre- requisite free default language using only normal/seminormal defaults. This is exactly what is recommended in the next section.

The *existence of extensions* being not generally assured in DL has always been pointing out as a major drawback. Unrestricted, unmotivated language is again one of the reasons for this deficiency. Nonnormals defaults are anomalous and defective in essence. Its use either brings anomalies or it is superfluous [10]. So, only allowing seminormal (including normal) defaults would prevent some idiosyncratic representation of default theories.

However, the main reason for the non-existence of extensions lays elsewhere. Self-exclusion and mutual exclusion of defaults (see section 3.2) are unnatural. It means that a default indirectly gives support to its own exception or gives support to the exception of other and vice-versa. Theories presenting these patterns are incoherent (have no extension) or present multiple extensions. The patterns themselves are defectives and should be avoided. A suitable ordering on defaults may detect this phenomenon. Ordered theories will thus be free of self or mutual excluding defaults. They are coherent, well-behaved (assuming all etiquette rules outlined in the next section are complied with) and, in IDL, they have a unique extension. This is the main achievement of this paper.

3   Well-Behaved IDL Theories

The guidelines outlined here add a semantic concern to the syntactical representation of knowledge. They take full advantage of the distinctive characteristics of IDL: the discernment between defeasible knowledge from the unquestioned one, compliance with the exceptions-first criterion and the paraconsistent treatment of defeasible contradictions. An IDL theory, designed according to the following strictures, will be very well behaved, producing a single extension deductively handle in LEI.

Two kinds of constraints should be introduced: individual and global ones. The first ones are syntactical restrictions applied to formulae and defaults, and the second ones have the form of constraints over the structure of the theory.

---

[3] [10] presents a comprehensive comparison between inductive and nonmonotonic reasoning

3.1 Individual Rules

The fundamental principle is to translate DL into IDL rules, respecting original IDL motivation. It is possible, but not desirable, a straightforward translation of a DL rule $\frac{\alpha:\beta\wedge\gamma}{\beta}$ to an IDL rule $\frac{\alpha:\beta\wedge\gamma}{\beta?}$. Normal and seminormal justifications must have a distinct treatment to perform nonmonotonic reasoning properly. This attitude is syntactically reflected in IDL through the introduction of ';' in the default rule. The new symbol ';' splits the justification condition into normal and seminormal part to emphasize that different treatment. Thus, the DL rule should have the proper IDL translation as $\frac{\alpha:\beta;\gamma}{\beta?}$.

The use of '?' must be parsimonious: '?' must neither appear in W nor in default justifications. ?-mark was included in the original language to distinguish monotonic, irrefutable conclusions, from nonmonotonic, defeasible ones, derivable directly from default conclusions. Nevertheless, it is desirable the interaction among default conclusions and other (monotonic or default) theorems. The monotonic and paraconsistent IDL basis, the Logic of Epistemic Inconsistency (LEI), govern the use of '?' and its interaction face to other logical constants through proper axiomatics. In fact, '?' appears in the deductive closure of W by the use of the schema $\alpha \rightarrow \alpha?$, e.g., but should not appear in the original W, taken as the expression of irrefutable facts and relations. On the other hand, a default must be understood as an inference rule, where its justification consists of meta provisos about its applicability. Thence, what really matters, is how and what conditions are stipulated. The presence of ?-formulae in the justification brings about some ambiguity for the reading and understanding of defaults.

Only seminormal defaults, including normal ones as a particular case, should be used in nonmonotonic IDL theories. Nonnormal defaults, i.e., $\frac{A:B}{C}$ where C is not a deductive logical consequence of B, are counterintuitive as they do not check for the consistency of their conclusions.

Pre-requisite free defaults are also fundamental to attain a maximal approximation of LEI theorems. IDL seminormal default $\frac{\alpha:\beta;\gamma}{\beta?}$ can be translated to labelled implicational defaults $(\alpha \rightarrow \beta;\gamma)/(\alpha? \rightarrow \beta?)$, where $(\alpha \rightarrow \beta;\gamma)$ are referred as the (supporting) label. Labelled formulae belong to the object language and they obey the same LEI operational rules (which ignore labels), allowing to reason about defaults whenever these additional meta provisos, recorded in their labels and managed by proper (structural) rules, were respected.

3.2 Global Rules

For a faithful modelling of a given epistemic situation by a nonmonotonic logic it is very important to guarantee that all information in hand is rightly represented. A common mistake is to subsume or not explicitly represent in the codification the potential exceptions to the defaults. Another important issue is to distinguish between 'exceptions' and 'conflicting evidences'. Exceptions are here taken as statements or conditions under which a default rule does not apply and must be considered before its application. Conflicting evidence is an indication for the denial of the conclusion of the default and may be paraconsistently tolerated.

In building a nonmonotonic theory two problems should be avoided: a default that supports its own exception (self-exclusion) and defaults which supports exceptions to each other, simultaneously (mutual exclusion). These cases lend a cyclic character to the default theory, with no intuitive ground for them. An order on the LEI literals for the IDL theory is introduced below as an adaptation of Etherington's one to DL [4] to capture such cycles. Other relations are also introduced to characterize self and mutual exclusion in IDL theories. Definitions of LEI Clausal Form, other related terms and main theorems in concern with this subject are in [7].

Definition 1. ($\leqslant$, $\prec$ and $\prec_e$). Let $\Delta_{\rightarrow}=(D_{\rightarrow},W)$ be a closed, seminormal, IDL default theory with implicative defaults. Without loss of generality, assume all formulae in W are in LEI Clausal Form. Assume, also, from the individual rules above, that formulae in W and formulae in the justification of default rules are all ?-free. The partial relations '$\leqslant$', '$\prec$' and '$\prec_e$', on (LEI Literals $\times$ LEI Literals), are defined as follows:

1. If $\alpha \in W$, then $\alpha = \alpha_1 \vee \ldots \vee \alpha_n$. For all $\alpha_i, \alpha_j \in \{\alpha_1, \ldots, \alpha_n\}$, if $\alpha_i \neq \alpha_j$, let $\sim (\alpha_i) \leqslant \alpha_j$.
2. If $\delta \in D_{\rightarrow}$, then $\delta = (\alpha \rightarrow \beta; \gamma)/\alpha? \rightarrow \beta?$, Let $\alpha_1, \ldots, \alpha_r$, $\beta_1, \ldots, \beta_s$, and $\gamma_1, \ldots, \gamma_t$ be the LEI literals obtained from the LEI clausal forms of α, β, and γ, respectively. α, β and γ are ?-free formulae, by the above assumption. Note that the external ? in $\alpha?$ and $\beta?$ are not essential to this analysis, so they are ignored. Then:
   (a) If $\alpha_i \in \{\alpha_1, \ldots, \alpha_r\}$ and $\beta_j \in \{\beta_1, \ldots, \beta_s\}$, let $\alpha_i \leqslant \beta_j$.
   (b) If $\alpha_k \in \{\alpha_1, \ldots, \alpha_r\}$, $\gamma_i \in \{\gamma_1, \ldots, \gamma_t\}$, $\beta_j \in \{\beta_1, \ldots, \beta_s\}$, let $(\neg\gamma_i)? \prec (\sim \alpha_k)$ and $(\neg\gamma_i)? \prec \beta_j$.
   (c) Also, $\beta = \beta_1 \wedge \ldots \wedge \beta_m$, for some m$\geq$1. For each i$\leq$m, $\beta_i = (\beta_{i,1} \vee \ldots \vee \beta_{i,m_i})$, where $m_i \geq 1$. Thus, if $\beta_{i,j}, \beta_{i,k} \in \{\beta_{1,1}, \ldots, \beta_{m,m_m}\}$ and $\beta_{i,j} \neq \beta_{i,k}$, let $\sim \beta_{i,j} \leqslant \beta_{i,k}$.
3. The following relationships holds for $\leqslant$, $\prec$ and $\prec_e$:
   (a) If $\alpha \leqslant \beta$ and $\beta \leqslant \gamma$, then $\alpha \leqslant \gamma$.
   (b) If ($\alpha \prec \beta$ and $\beta \leqslant \gamma$) or ($\alpha \leqslant \beta$ and $\beta \prec \gamma$), then $\alpha \prec \gamma$.
   (c) If $\alpha \prec \beta$, then $\alpha \prec_e \beta$.
   (d) If $\alpha \prec \beta$, $\beta \prec \gamma$ and $\gamma \prec_e \delta$, then $\alpha \prec_e \delta$.
   (e) If $\alpha \prec_e \beta$, $\beta \prec \gamma$ and $\gamma \prec \delta$, then $\alpha \prec_e \delta$.

Definition 2. (theories with self-exclusion): A seminormal default theory has a self-exclusion iff there is α, such that '$\alpha \prec_e \alpha$'.

Definition 3. (theories with mutual-exclusion): A seminormal default theory has a mutual-exclusion iff there are α and β such that '$\alpha \prec_e \beta$' and '$\beta \prec_e \alpha$'.

Definition 4. (ordered theories): A seminormal default theory is said to be ordered iff this theory has neither self-exclusion nor mutual exclusion.

Example of self-exclusion $W=\{\}, D=\{(A; \neg B)/A?, (B; \neg C)/B?, (C; \neg A)/C?\}$

Example of mutual exclusion $W=\{\}$, $D=\{(A; \neg B)/A?, (B; \neg A)/B?\}$

It is important to notice that, in DL, self-exclusion implies the incoherence of the theory, but mutual exclusion (albeit unordered) yields multiple extensions, a normal occurrence for default theories. Self-exclusion theories have too little extensions (none), and mutual exclusion theories have too much (more than one). Ordered theories rules out both defective cases. Nevertheless, IDL offers an extra criterion for being well-behaved: the existence of a unique extension. This will be explored in the next section.

4   Resulting IDL Properties

Criticisms to DL will be, now, revisited through the use of IDL, taken with restrictions on the light of the etiquette rules presented above.

The parsimonious use of ? in IDL axiomatic base $< W, D >$ and the elimination of self-exclusion of defaults in IDL ordered theories have cut out incoherent theories assuring the *existence of extensions*. As a matter of fact, ordered theories also remove mutual exclusion from defaults. Fortunately, IDL ordered theories has only a unique extension in accordance with its initial motivation of maintaining all partial conflicts in a sole extension.

Theorem 5. *If an IDL theory is ordered, then it has a unique extension.*

Considering only IDL ordered theories, at least one extension is secured. Coherent DL normal theories may have multiple extensions. Coherent IDL normal theories, though, have always one extension where partial conflicts are paraconsistently tolerated. Multiple extensions are possible in IDL only by the use of seminormal defaults (considering that parsimonious use of ?). However, the split in multiple extensions occurs, in IDL, when two defaults may be simultaneously triggered and one supports the proof of the exception condition of the other and conversely. This is exactly the mutual exclusion problem that is ruled out by ordered theories. The detailed proof is in [8].

The *uniqueness of extension* is a much cherished result since IDL, for being paraconsistent, has no need to pull apart conflicts. Relevant properties for Default Logic concerning the multitude of extensions like the *orthogonality of extensions* simply do not apply for the uni-extensional IDL. *Commitment to assumptions*, on the other hand, is not solved through the use of multiple extensions. IDL commits to their assumptions into a same extension using ? to encapsulate defeasible conclusions from different DL extensions, which can not be mixed up to derive further conclusions.

Semimonotonicity does not hold in IDL as such. Indeed, it was intentionally rejected from the beginning. As pointed out in [1], semimonotonicity destroys default expressiveness. The exception first criterion, which allows to establish priorities between defaults, are no more reflected in a semimonotonic logic. CDL (*Cumulative Default Logic*) [1], for instance, is semimonotonic, and to recover that expressiveness, Brewka proposes CDL$_F$ [1] which keeps the priority preserving extensions by the subsequent use of filters on the resulting extensions. In [16], an alternative definition of CDL$_F$ is proposed by a direct quasi-inductive characterization where filters are no more essential. IDL keeps priorities between defaults also directly through its definition.

Semimonotonicity is not ruled out in IDL, though. A restricted version of semimonotonicity does hold: IDL is semimonotonic if an order of choice between default applicability is obeyed [7]. The elected order, already presented in section 3, preserves the advantages of semimonotonicity without loosing expressiveness.

Cumulativity (*cut* and *cautious monotonicity*) are trivially obtained in IDL by the use of (pre-requisite free) labelled default formulae [7]. Any (nonmonotonic) theorem, a derived default, added to premises does not change the theory previously obtained without it. They hold whenever their support (label) holds, which are inherited from their parent labels.

Reasoning about defaults is also possible in IDL: *reasoning by cases* and *contrapositive* are now obtained by the use of defaults in the implicational form. Contrapositive, however, is only possible with constraints: the proof of that scheme involves *reductio ad absurdum* which is not satisfied by a paraconsistent negation. However, IDL keeps contraposition to its classical negation.

5 Conclusions

The modelling of practical reasoning is an eluding task which is here faced by taking full advantage of the nonmonotonic paraconsistent logic IDL. Some guidelines to the faithful management of such epistemic situation were here outlined. Following some proposed etiquette rules, the well-behaved IDL will always produce one, and only one, coherent extension. The intended extension, indeed. This is very much in tune with IDL philosophy, since there is no need to break an IDL theory into many extensions, sometimes anomalous. IDL accommodates conflicting evidences into a single extension, without being trivialized. Hence, some desired features concerning multiple extensions and which have caused problems to DL simply do not apply for the uni-extensional IDL.

A cumulative IDL version is straightforward attained by the use of labelled implicative defaults, which allows to handle defaults in the object language, accumulating derived ones in the same extension. A restricted form of semimonotonicity is also achieved if the proposed order between defaults is respected whenever they are applied.

A difficult problem still remains, unfortunately. Defeasible conclusions, in a same IDL extension, are not adjunctive and it is exactly what is expected if they are considered as from different original DL extensions. The IDL commitment to its assumptions comes straightforward from that. However, there are situations where defeasible conclusions belong to the same original DL extension and they may be combined. Such combinations are not possible in IDL, unless previously anticipated, what is really hard. It is a promise point for further investigations.

References

1. Brewka, G. 'Cumulative Default Logic: in defense of nonmonotonic inference rules'. *Artificial Intelligence*, 50(2):183-205, July, 1991.
2. da Costa, N.C.A. 'On the Theory of Inconsistent Formal Systems.' *Notre Dame Journal of Formal Logic*, 15. 1974. pp.497-510.
3. Delgrande, J.P. & Jackson, W.K. 'Default Logic revisited'. In:*Proc. of the 2nd KR'91*, J.A. Allen, R.Fikes and E.Sandewall, editors, pp.118-27. San Mateo, CA, Apr. 1991. Morgan Kaufmann Publishers Inc.
4. Etherington, D.W. 'Formalizing Nonmonotonic Reasoning Systems'. *Artificial Intelligence*, 31:41-85, 1987.
5. Hanks, S. & McDermott, D. 'Nonmonotonic Logic and Temporal Projection.' *Artificial Intelligence*, 33:27-39, 1980.
6. Lukaszewicz, W. 'Considerations on default logic — an alternative approach'. *Computational Intelligence*, 4:1-16, 1988.
7. Martins, A.T.C. & Pequeno, T. 'A Meta Axiomatics for the Inconsistent Default Logic'. *Journal of the IGPL*. Oxford University Press. Submitted.
8. Martins, A.T.C. 'Sequent Calculi for the Logic of Epistemic Inconsistency and for the Inconsistent Default Logic'. Qualification Exam. DI-UFPE. To be submitted.
9. McCarthy, J. 'Circumscription — a form of nonmonotonic reasoning'. *Artificial Intelligence*, 28:89-116, 1986.
10. Pequeno, M. 'Defeasible Logic with Exception First'. PhD Thesis, Imperial College, London. 1994.
11. Pequeno, T.H.C. 'A Logic for Inconsistent Nonmonotonic Reasoning.' Technical Report 90/6. Department of Computing, Imperial College. London. 1990.
12. Pequeno, T.H.C. & Buchsbaum, A.R. 'The Logic of Epistemic Inconsistency'. In: Proc. of the *2nd KR'91*. J.A. Allen, R.Fikes and E.Sandewall, editors, pp 453-60. San Mateo, CA, Apr. 1991. Morgan Kaufmann Publishers Inc.
13. Pollock, J.L. 'Defeasible Reasoning'. *Cognitive Science*, 11:481-518, 1987.
14. Reiter, R. 'A Logic of Default Reasoning.' *Artificial Intelligence*, 13:81-132, 1980.
15. Schaub, T. 'Assertional Default Theories: a semantical view'. In: *Proc. of the 2nd KR'91*, J.A.Allen, R.Fikes and E.Sandewall, editors, pp. 496-506, San Mateo, CA, Apr. 1991. Morgan Kaufmann Publishers Inc.
16. Zaverucha, G. 'A Prioritized Contextual Default Logic: Curing Anomalous Extensions with a Simple Abnormality Default Theory'. In: *Proc. KI-94*, Nebel and Dreschler-Fischer, eds, Saarbrucken, LNAI 861 (Springer 1994) 260-271.

Epistemic Conditional Logics

Ana Maria Monteiro and Jacques Wainer
{anammont,wainer}@dcc.unicamp.br

Instituto de Computação, UNICAMP

Abstract. This paper develops two conditional logics that allows one
to reason about the belief of another agent (which reasons in conditional
logic himself). The desirable properties of such logics that reason about
the beliefs of another non-monotonic agent are discussed and the two
logics proposed here are shown to have those properties.

1 Introduction

An intelligent system sometimes must interact with other intelligent systems to
accomplish a task or a goal. If that is the case, it may be important for the
system to represent the knowledge of the other agents with whom it interacts.
For example, a tutoring system may find it is important to explicitly represent
and reason about the knowledge of agent being taught. Or, an intelligent system
may find it necessary to reason about the knowledge of the other agents in order
to effectively communicate with them.

On the other hand, it is widely assumed that intelligent reasoning must include a component of non-monotonicity. Thus many non-monotonic logics have
been proposed to model different aspects of intelligent reasoning. This paper
deals with the intersection of the two issues above: the proposal of a non-
monotonic logic that not only models the agent reasoning (non-monotonically)
about the world, but also reasoning about the knowledge of other agents.

There are in principle two approaches to developing multi-agent non-monotonic
logics: to develop new logics or to adapt some of the existing ones. This paper
follows the latter approach: we will propose an extension of two conditional logics of normality proposed in [Bou94], so that the extended logics can represent
and reason about formulas that contain reference to the knowledge of another
agent. This is only a first step in developing full multi-agent conditional logics.
The logic presented here will be called epistemically extended conditional logic
(following [Wai93]): the logic allows the system being modeled to reason about
the knowledge of just another agent, but that agent does not reason about the
system's knowledge. Furthermore, the logic assumes the system's point of view
(what [Lev90] calls an internal perspective) since that is the approach taken by
the majority of the non-monotonic logics (with the exception of [Lev90, Lak93]).

We will first present an an overview of the two conditional logics on which
we base this work.

2 Conditional Logics of Normality

Recent work in non-monotonic reasoning has led to the development of some conditional theories of default inferencing such as the logic N [Del87], ϵ-entailment [Pea88], preferential entailment [KLM90], CT4O and CO [Bou94] among others. These conditional logics have a minimal set of properties that ought to be common to all non-monotonic inference systems and that constitue, as has been suggested by Pearl [Pea89], a "conservative core" of non-monotonic reasoning. The properties are related to the fact that these approaches:

- provide a more natural representation of defaults than the traditional formalisms, such as default logic [Rei80], autoepistemic logic [Moo85] or circumscription [McC80],
- do not have problems with fixed points or multiple extensions,
- deal satisfactorily with the specificity of defaults.

Because of their clear semantics, we chose CT4O and CTO [Bou94] as the base of our work.

2.1 The CT4O logic

The language of CT4O, $\mathcal{L}_C$, is that of the classical propositional logic (CPL) formed from a set of atomic sentences $\mathbf{P}$, augmented with two unary modal operators $\Box$ and $\overset{\leftrightarrow}{\Box}$. Furthermore, four modal operators are defined as abbreviations:

Definition 1 $- \Diamond A \equiv_{def} \neg\Box\neg A.$
  $- \overset{\leftrightarrow}{\Diamond} A \equiv_{def} \neg\overset{\leftrightarrow}{\Box}\neg A.$
  $- \overset{\leftrightarrow}{\Box} A \equiv_{def} \Box A \wedge \overset{\leftrightarrow}{\Box} A.$
  $- \overset{\leftrightarrow}{\Diamond} A \equiv_{def} \Diamond A \vee \overset{\leftrightarrow}{\Diamond} A.$

The semantics of CT4O of normality is based on Kripkean possible world structures, where a *possible world* is any subset of $\mathbf{P}$. The sentences of $\mathcal{L}_C$ are interpreted in terms of a *CT4O*-model:

Definition 2 *A CT4O-model is a pair $M = \langle W, \geq \rangle$, where W is a set of possible worlds and $\geq$ is a reflexive, transitive binary relation on W.*

The satisfiability of a sentence $A \in \mathcal{L}_C$, at a world w in a CT4O-model M is defined as:

Definition 3 *Let $M = \langle W, \geq \rangle$ a CT4O-model, the satisfability at a world w, in a CT4O-model M is defined by:*

  $- M, w \models A$ *iff* $A \in w$ *for A a atomic formula*
  $- M, w \models \neg A$ *iff* $M, w \not\models A$
  $- M, w \models A \supset B$ *iff* $M, w \not\models A$ *or* $M, w \models B.$

- $M, w \models \Box A$ iff $M, v \models A$, for each v such that $w \geq v$.
- $M, w \models \overline{\Box} A$ iff $M, v \models A$, for each v such that $w \not\geq v$.

The accessibility relation $\geq$ among possible worlds in a $CT4O$-model reflects some measure of normality on all states of affairs, and it should be interpreted as follows: for possible worlds w and v, $w \geq v$ states that v is at least as normal as w. Thus from a particular world w, following the $\geq$ relation, one sees a sequence of successively "less exceptional" worlds.

The logic provides a uniform way to deal with defaults. It uses a conditional connective $\Rightarrow$ to represent default rules (or statements of normality): $A \Rightarrow B$ is read as "If A then normally B". $A \Rightarrow B$ is defined to be true just when A is false at all accessible worlds or when there is a world in which $A \wedge B$ is true and $A \supset B$ is true at all equally or less exceptional worlds. Formally:

Definition 4 $A \Rightarrow B =_{def} \overline{\Box} (\Box\neg A \vee \Diamond(A \wedge \Box(A \supset B)))$

We introduce, also, the following abbreviation:

Definition 5 $A \not\Rightarrow B =_{def} \neg(A \Rightarrow B)$

In the CT4O logic, Modus Ponens is not valid, one can not infer B from A and $A \Rightarrow B$, but it is reasonable to conclude that normally B would hold. Formally:

Theorem 1 $\overset{CT4O}{\models} (A \wedge (A \Rightarrow B)) \Rightarrow B$

Hence, in the framework of the CT4O logic, default reasoning can be naturally modeled as the process of asking what normally follows form a set of statements, based on the validity of the weaker version of Modus Ponens.

CT4O is a system of default reasoning that can deal with the specificity of defaults and simple cases of inheritance with exceptions. For for example, from the fact that birds (normally) fly, penguins necessarily are birds, penguins do not fly, from the fact that something is a penguin, one can conclude (by default) that it normally will not fly. Formally:

$$\overset{CT4O}{\models} \begin{pmatrix} bird \Rightarrow fly \wedge \\ \Box(penguin \supset bird) \wedge \\ penguin \Rightarrow \neg fly \wedge \\ penguin \end{pmatrix} \Rightarrow \neg fly \qquad (1)$$

2.2 The CO logic

The CT4O structures reflect the minimal conditions that can be imposed on a plausibility ordering over a set of possible worlds. To obtain a logic with some further properties, more restrictions must be placed on $\geq$. The logic CO is defined when the $\geq$, besides being reflexive and transitive, is also totally connected.

The language of CO is the same of CT4O, only the definition of a CO-model changes:

Definition 6 *A CO-model is a pair $M = \langle W, \geq \rangle$, where W is a set of possible worlds, and $\geq$ is reflexive, transitive, and totally connected relation over W^1.*

The restriction imposed on $\geq$ enforces the intuitive notion that all the worlds are comparable on the scale of normality. Differently as in CT4O, the CO-models have only one path of normality. Hence, $\tilde{\Diamond} A$ is read as " A holds at some less normal world". Because there are no inaccessible worlds, the definition of $\Rightarrow$ can be reformulated as:

$$A \Rightarrow B =_{def} \tilde{\Box} \neg A \vee \tilde{\Diamond} (A \wedge B \wedge \Box(A \supset B))$$

3 Epistemic Extension of a Logic

An epistemic extension is a syntactic and semantic extension of a non-monotonic logic in such a way that the extended logic is able to deal with formulas that contain a belief operator. The extended logic represents the point of view of a particular agent (called the system) reasoning about reality and about the knowledge (or belief) of other agent. In an epistemically extended logic, the formula $p \wedge \mathcal{B}q$ should be interpreted as "the system believes p and it believes that the other agent believes q."

Let us use $\mathcal{L}^*$ to denote the epistemic extension of the non-monotonic logic $\mathcal{L}$, and the symbol $\rightsquigarrow$ to represent the way default rules are represented in both logics. [Wai93] describes some of the properties that the logic $\mathcal{L}^*$ should have, among them:

- The logic $\mathcal{L}^*$ should be a conservative extension of $\mathcal{L}$, that is $\mathcal{L}^*$ has the same deductive power as $\mathcal{L}$ when dealing with formulas without the $\mathcal{B}$ operator:

$$\alpha \overset{\mathcal{L}}{\models} \beta \quad \text{iff} \quad \alpha \overset{\mathcal{L}^*}{\models} \beta \tag{2}$$

- The logic $\mathcal{L}^*$ should also model the behavior of the $\mathcal{B}$ operator. If we assume that the modal logic KD45 is a good model for the belief operator, then

$$\text{if} \quad \overset{KD45}{\models} \alpha \quad \text{then} \quad \overset{\mathcal{L}^*}{\models} \alpha \tag{3}$$

- The system and the other agent should have the same non-monotonic reasoning abilities, or in formal notation

$$\alpha \overset{\mathcal{L}}{\models} \beta \quad \text{iff} \quad \mathcal{B}\alpha \overset{\mathcal{L}^*}{\models} \mathcal{B}\beta \tag{4}$$

- The logic $\mathcal{L}^*$ must allow for default formulas that combine the $\mathcal{B}$ operator with sub-formulas without it, and derive the "correct" conclusions from them. For example:

$$\mathcal{B}\alpha \wedge (\mathcal{B}\alpha \rightsquigarrow \beta) \overset{\mathcal{L}^*}{\models} \beta$$
$$\text{and} \tag{5}$$
$$\alpha \wedge (\alpha \rightsquigarrow \mathcal{B}\beta) \overset{\mathcal{L}^*}{\models} \mathcal{B}\beta$$

---

[1] A relation R on a set A is totally connected if for all x and y in A, xRy or yRx.

In terms of a conditional logic, $\mathcal{L}_C$, these requirements can be stated as:

$$- \overset{\mathcal{L}_C}{\models} \alpha \Rightarrow \beta \quad \text{iff} \quad \overset{\mathcal{L}_C^{\bullet}}{\models} \alpha \Rightarrow \beta$$

$$- \text{if} \quad \overset{KD45}{\models} \alpha \quad \text{then} \quad \overset{\mathcal{L}_C^{\bullet}}{\models} \alpha$$

$$- \overset{\mathcal{L}_C}{\models} \alpha \Rightarrow \beta \quad \text{iff} \quad \overset{\mathcal{L}_C^{\bullet}}{\models} \mathcal{B}\alpha \Rightarrow \mathcal{B}\beta$$

$$- \overset{\mathcal{L}_C^{\bullet}}{\models} (\mathcal{B}\alpha \wedge (\mathcal{B}\alpha \Rightarrow \beta)) \Rightarrow \beta \text{ and } \overset{\mathcal{L}_C^{\bullet}}{\models} (\alpha \wedge (\alpha \Rightarrow \mathcal{B}\beta)) \Rightarrow \mathcal{B}\beta$$

4   The Extension of CT4O

We propose an extension of the conditional logic of normality $CT4O$, which we call $CT4O^e$. The language of $CT4O^e$ ($\mathcal{L}_{C^{\bullet}}$) is that of $CT4O$ with a $\mathcal{B}$ modal operator. If A is a well formed formula (wff) of $\mathcal{L}_{C^{\bullet}}$ and it does not contain a $\mathcal{B}$ operator, then $\mathcal{B}A$ is also a wff. Thus, the language $\mathcal{L}_{C^{\bullet}}$ does not allow for the belief operator within the scope of another belief operator.

To extend the semantics, we adapt the classical Kripke structures to deal with the belief of the two agents. We use essentially the concept of possible worlds but in a somewhat different way. The possible worlds we use have two components, one to model the beliefs of the system and the other to model the possible beliefs of the system's view of the beliefs of the other agent.

We begin introducing the augmented worlds.

Definition 7 *An augmented world (A-world) is a pair $\langle w, \langle W, \geq \rangle \rangle$, where W is a set of propositional worlds, $w \in W$, and $\geq$ is a transitive, reflective relation over W.*

A-worlds are $CT4O$-models with a distinguished world. The intuition is that A-worlds are structures that allow one to interpret formulas of the type α and $\alpha \Rightarrow \beta$, where both α and β are formulas without $\mathcal{B}$.

We will now define an auxiliary relation $\geq_\Delta$ among a set of augmented worlds.

Definition 8 $\langle w_1, M_1 \rangle \geq_\Delta \langle w_2, M_2 \rangle$ *iff*

- $M_1 = M_2$ *and*
- $w_1 \geq w_2$, *where $\geq$ is the binary relation of the M_1 (and M_2).*

That is, two A-worlds can be compared under the $\geq_\Delta$ relation if their $CT4O$-models are the same and their distinguished worlds can be compared under the normality relation $\geq$ of those $CT4O$-models.

Definition 9 *A belief world (B-world) is a pair $\langle w, \mathcal{A} \rangle$, where w is a propositional world and $\mathcal{A}$ is a set of augmented worlds.*

The first component of the belief worlds allows one to interpret formulas related to the beliefs of the system, formulas of the form α, where α does not have any ocorrence of the operator $\mathcal{B}$. The second component of the belief worlds allows one to interpret formulas related to the belief of the other agent, formulas of the form $\mathcal{B}\alpha$ and $\mathcal{B}(\alpha \Rightarrow \beta)$. Thus, what still needs to be done is to define a relation of "normality" among B-worlds, so that formula that contains $\Rightarrow$ at the top level can be interpreted. We define this relation in such a way that the resulting logic has the "correct" properties.

We will define a relation among B-worlds based on a transitive, reflexive relation among possible worlds $\geq$.

Definition 10 $\langle w_1, \mathcal{A}_1 \rangle \geq_\square \langle w_2, \mathcal{A}_2 \rangle$ *iff*

- $w_1 \geq w_2$ *and*
- *for all $a \in \mathcal{A}_1$ there is $b \in \mathcal{A}_2$ such that $a \geq_\Delta b$ and for all $b \in \mathcal{A}_2$ there is $a \in \mathcal{A}_1$ such that $a \geq_\Delta b$*

We finish by defining the central concept that captures the semantics of our logic. The definition of a $CT4O^e$-model is:

Definition 11 *A $CT4O^e$-model is a pair $\langle X, \geq \rangle$, where X is a set of B-worlds, $\geq$ is a reflexive and transitive binary relation defined on the set of the first component of each B-world in X and the relation $\geq_\square$, based in the relation $\geq$ defined as in 10, is the relation of normality among the B-worlds of X.*

Furthermore we require X should not have "holes" in the following sense: if $\langle w, \{\langle w_i, M_i \rangle\}_{\{i \in I\}} \rangle \in X$ and if $\{\langle w_i', M_i \rangle\}_{\{i \in I\}} \rangle$ is a set of augmented worlds, such that for all $i \in I$, $\langle w_i, M_i \rangle \geq_\Delta \langle w_i', M_i \rangle$, then there is w_0 such that $w \geq w_0$ and $\langle w_0, \{\langle w_i', M_i \rangle\}_{\{i \in I\}} \rangle \in X$.

Satisfiability of formula α in a $CT4O^e$-model is defined as expected. Given that $M = \langle X, \geq \rangle$ is a $CT4O^e$-model, $\geq_\square$ is the relation defined on the set X, based in the relation $\geq$, x is a particular B-world of X, Π_1 and Π_2 are the first component and second component functions for pairs (conveniently extended for sets of pairs[2]), then we define satisfiability of a formula α at a B-world x of a $CT4O^e$-model as:

Definition 12
- $M, x \models \alpha$ iff $\alpha \in \Pi_1(x)$ for α an atomic formula.
- $M, x \models \neg \alpha$ iff $M, x \not\models \alpha$.
- $M, x \models \alpha \supset \beta$ iff $M, x \models \beta$ or $M, x \not\models \alpha$.
- $M, x \models \square\alpha$ iff for all y such that $x \geq_\square y$, $M, y \models \alpha$.
- $M, x \models \overline{\square} \alpha$ iff for all y such that $x \not\geq_\square y$, $M, y \models \alpha$.
- $M, x \models \mathcal{B}\alpha$ iff $\Pi_2(a), \Pi_1(a) \models \alpha$, for all $a \in \Pi_2(x)$.

Finally, validity in a model and validity are defined as usual:

Definition 13 *A wff α of $\mathcal{L}_{C^e}$ is valid on a $CT4O^e$-model $M = \langle X, \geq \rangle$ (written $M \models \alpha$) iff $M, x \models \alpha$ for each $x \in X$,*

---

[2] $\Pi_1(A) = \{x | \langle x, y \rangle \in A\}$

Definition 14 α *is* $CT4O^e$-*valid (written* $\overset{CT4O^e}{\models} \alpha$*) just when* $M \models \alpha$ *for every* $CT4O^e$-*model M.*

4.1 Results

The structure defined gives to the logic $CT4O^e$ a semantics, such that all the requirements of an epistemic extension of a logic mentioned above are satisfied. Thus we have the following results:

Theorem 2 *If* $\alpha, \beta \in \mathcal{L}_C$ *then:* $\overset{CT4O}{\models} \alpha \Rightarrow \beta$ *iff* $\overset{CT4O^e}{\models} \alpha \Rightarrow \beta.$[3]

Theorem 3 *If* $\overset{KD}{\models} \alpha$ *then* $\overset{CT4O^e}{\models} \alpha.$

Theorem 4 *If* $\alpha, \beta \in \mathcal{L}_C$ *then* $\overset{CT4O}{\models} \alpha \Rightarrow \beta$ *iff* $\overset{CT4O^e}{\models} \mathcal{B}\alpha \Rightarrow \mathcal{B}\beta.$

Theorem 5 $- \overset{CT4O^e}{\models} (\alpha \Rightarrow \mathcal{B}\beta \wedge \alpha) \Rightarrow \mathcal{B}\beta$
$- \overset{CT4O^e}{\models} (\mathcal{B}\alpha \Rightarrow \beta \wedge \mathcal{B}\alpha) \Rightarrow \beta$

The proof of these results can be found in [Mont96].

The logic just defined provide us with a framework where the knowledge of the another agent can be represented and reasoned about, and the essential properties of specificity of CT4O remain true when the system reason about the knowledge of the other agent. Thus according to theorem 4, if the system believes initially that if there are birds the other agent believes that they fly and there are birds then, by default, the system believes that the other agent believes that they fly. Formaly:

$$\overset{CT4O^e}{\models} ((bird \Rightarrow \mathcal{B} \, fly) \wedge bird) \Rightarrow \mathcal{B} \, fly$$

But the logic goes even further, taking into consideration the logic of the $\mathcal{B}$ operator itself. If to the initial assertion we add $\mathcal{B} \neg fly$ then we cannot infer by default that $\mathcal{B} \, fly$. In the same way, we have:

$$\overset{CT4O^e}{\not\models} (bird \Rightarrow \mathcal{B} \, fly \wedge bird \wedge \neg \mathcal{B} \, fly) \Rightarrow \mathcal{B} \, fly$$

Similarly, from $\mathcal{B}bird \Rightarrow \mathcal{B}fly$, $\square(\mathcal{B}penguin \supset \mathcal{B}bird)$, $\mathcal{B}penguin \Rightarrow \mathcal{B}\neg fly$, and $\mathcal{B} \, penguin$, the more specific default applys and cancels the more generic one, and one could infer that $\mathcal{B}\neg fly$. Notice that this is not similar to example 1, since in this case, the fly and $\neg fly$ are within the scope of the belief operator.

And also from the above assertions we can derive the default $\mathcal{B} \, bird \Rightarrow \neg \mathcal{B} \, penguin$, but not $\mathcal{B}(bird \Rightarrow \neg penguin)$. This last inference would be an

---

[3] In fact we can prove a stronger result: $\overset{CT4O}{\models} \alpha$ iff $\overset{CT4O^e}{\models} \alpha.$

attribution of some belief to the other agent based on the system's beliefs, which is incorrect.

An unexpected mode of inference that is allowed in $CT4O^e$ is demonstrated by the following exemple. If the system believes that: if there are birds then the other agent, normally, believes that; the other believes that the birds normally fly; and given that in the most normal states of affaires there are birds, then one can conclude by default that the other agent believes that they fly. Formaly:

$CT4O^e$
$$\models \quad \Diamond\Box bird \wedge (bird \Rightarrow \mathcal{B}\ bird) \wedge \mathcal{B}(bird \Rightarrow fly) \quad \Rightarrow \quad \mathcal{B}\ fly$$

This inference shows that $CT4O^e$ allows for some chaining across contexts: the system's defaults can be composed with the other agent's defaults.

5 The extension of CO

We can extend the logic CO, in the same way that $CT4O$ was extended. Let us remind that the difference between $CT4O$ and CO is that the normality relation in CO is totally connected.

Thus, in the definition of a A-world, $\langle w, \langle W, \geq \rangle \rangle$ we also demand $\geq$ to be totally connected. The relations $\geq_\Delta$ and B-worlds are defined in a similar way, and for the relation $\geq_\Box$ we require the base relation to be totally connected.

Definition 15 A CO^e-model is a pair $\langle X, \geq \rangle$, where X is a set of B-worlds such that $\Pi_1(X) = W$, and $\geq$ is a reflexive, transitive and totally connected binary relation defined on W, and $\geq_\Box$ is a relation totally connected on X as defined for $CT4O^e$.

Furthermore, if $\langle w, \{\langle w_i, M_i \rangle\}_{\{i \in I\}} \rangle \in X$ and if $\{\langle w_i', M_i \rangle\}_{\{i \in I\}} \rangle$ is a set of augmented worlds, such that for all $i \in I$, $\langle w_i, M_i \rangle \geq_\Delta \langle w_i', M_i \rangle$, then there is w_0 such that $w \geq w_0$ and $\langle w_0, \{\langle w_i', M_i \rangle\}_{\{i \in I\}} \rangle \in X$ and the models of the augmented worlds are CO-models..

The logic CO^e keeps all the properties of $CT4O^e$ and have some new ones. For example, from $\mathcal{B}(bird) \not\Rightarrow \mathcal{B}(penguin)$ and $\mathcal{B}(bird) \Rightarrow \mathcal{B}(fly)$ we can deduce in CO^e:

$$\mathcal{B}(bird) \wedge \mathcal{B}(\neg penguin) \Rightarrow \mathcal{B}(fly)$$

This deduction cannot be done in $CT4O^e$.

6 Conclusions

What has been accomplished? The epistemic extension of both CT4O and CO proposed in this paper extend both logics so that they can deal with formulas that contain a belief operator in such a way that all properties (and short comings) of the original logics are retained and the desired properties of epistemic extended logics (2-5) are satisfied (the property (3) is equivalent to theorem 3 given that the language does not allow for nested $\mathcal{B}$). Furthermore, we believe that the methodology used to develop the logics $CT4O^e$ and CO^e (that is, the use of augmented worlds, B-worlds, and the definition of the $\geq_\square$ relations based on the $\geq$ relation) can be used to extend some of the other semantically defined conditional logics.

But such approach has some limitations. [Bou94] proposes the logic CO^* which offers a limited solution for the problem of relevance in conditional logics. The logic is a CO logic where all propositional valuations are among the possible worlds, and the solution for the irrelevance problems depends both on the fact that the normality relation is totally connected and that all valuations are among the possible worlds. But following the methodology proposed herein it is not possible to develop an epistemic extension of the logic CO^*, since it is not possible to construct a structure where all possible B-worlds are present and where the $\geq_\square$ relation is totally connected.

Conditional logics can be seen as a core non-monotonic logic, to which some extra logic features are added to strengthen the logic. For example, [Del87] adds to a conditional theory a set of formulas that cannot be proven false in ordered to deal with the irrelevance problem. Similar extra logic extensions are proposed in [Bel90, Del94]. We believe that the two epistemically extended conditional logics developed here could be amenable for such extra-logical extension in order to strengthen them, but with some caveats: such extra-logical strengthenings must work also within the $\mathcal{B}$ operator. That may pose some further complications.

Finally, we leave a syntactic characterization of the extended logics for future work. Since both $CT4O$ and CO have sound and complete syntactic characterizations, and since the epistemic part of these extended logics can be characterized by the standard modal logic KD, we have hopes that a sound and complete descriptions of both $CT4O^e$ and CO^e can be obtained.

7 Acknowledgments

The first author was supported by Universidad Nacional de La Plata and a scholarship from CNPq, and the second author was partially supported by CNPq grant 521464/93-5.

References

[Bel90] J. Bell. The logic of nonmonotonicity. *Artificial Intelligence*, 41:365–374, 1990.

[Del87] J.P. Delgrande. A first-order conditional logic for prototypical properties. *Artificial Intelligence*, 33(1):105–130, 1987.

[Del94] J.P. Delgrande. A preference based approach to default reasoning: preliminary report. In *Proc. of AAAI'94*, pages 902-908, MIT Press, 1994.

[Bou94] C. Boutilier. Conditional logics of Normality: a modal approach. *Artificial Intelligence*, 68(1): 87–154, 1994.

[Che80] B. F. Chellas *Modal Logic An Introduction*. Cambridge University Press. 1980.

[KLM90] S. Kraus, D. Lehmann, M. Magidor. Nonmonotonic reasoning, preferential models and cumulative logics. *Artificial Intelligence*, 44(1-2):167–207, 1990.

[Lak93] G. Lakemeyer. All they know: A study in multi-agent autoepistemic reasoning. In *Proc. of the IJCAI'93*, pages 376–381, 1993.

[Lev90] H. J. Levesque. All I know: A study in autoepistemic logic. *Artificial Intelligence*, 42:263–310, 1990.

[McC80] R. Moore. Circumscription -a form of non-monotonic reasoning. *Artificial Intelligence*, 13:27–39, 1980.

[Mont96] A. M. Monteiro. Estensões epsitemicas de duas familias de logicas não monotonicas Master thesis *in portuguese*. Instituto de Computação, UNICAMP, 1996

[Moo85] R. Moore. Semantical considerations on non-monotonic logics. *Artificial Intelligence*, 25:75–94, 1985.

[Pea88] J. Pearl. *Probabilistic Reasoning in Intelligent Systems: Networks of Plausible Inference*. Morgan Kaufman, San Mateo, CA, 1988.

[Pea89] J. Pearl. *Probabilistic Semantics for Nonmonotonic Reasoning: a Survey*. In *Proc. KR'89*, pages 505-516, 1989.

[Rei80] R. Reiter. A logic for default reasoning. In *Artificial Intelligence*, 13:81-132, 1980.

[Wai93] J. Wainer. Epistemic extension of preference logics. In *Proc. of the IJCAI'93*, pages 382–387, 1993.

A Hybrid Formal Theory of Plan Recognition and Its Implementation

José Helano Matos Nogueira
Artificial Intelligence Laboratory
UFC / UECE
Fortaleza, CE - Brazil
E-mail: helano@{lia.ufc.br, fortal.uece.br}

Antonio Luz Furtado
José Jesus Perez Alcazar
DI / PUC-RJ
Rio de Janeiro , RJ - Brazil
E-mail: furtado@inf.puc-rio.br
jose@inf.puc-rio.br

Abstract

There has been great interest in the formalization and development of systems that treat plan recognition process in Artificial Intelligence. In this paper, we develop a theoretical framework, and implement a plan recognition system. Therefore, our research work can be divided in two parts: a hybrid theory, and a feasible implementation. In the theoretical part, we develop a Hybrid Formal Theory - HFT, based in the theory of Kautz and other researchers. In the feasible part, we create a tool called Plan Recognition System - PRS.

1. Introduction

One of the central parts of intelligent reasoning is the capacity to make plans and explain them. Research on planning aims at providing methods and tools to capture this sort of behavior. Planning can be divided in two directions: plan synthesis and plan recognition. In this paper we shall deal with plan recognition: it consists of finding out an explanation of the observed actions into one or more plans. However, plan recognition does not consist only in explaining observed actions. The complexity of plan recognition arises when we try to infer a reasonable plan of actions which are not explicitly observed, but actions which are implicit into the agent's knowledge. This process is not purely deductive because it must use a powerful knowledge representation model, heuristics, and a library of typical plans.

In general, existing work only deal with what is a plan recognition process without presenting ways to finalize this process. Recently, it has been detected a trend to formalizing and specifying the plan recognition problem [CSSB91]. The main result of our work is the implementation of a plan recognition system based in Kautz's formal theory, [Kaut87]. Furthermore, we include new concepts, rules, and improvements in this theory, creating a hybrid theory. Plan recognition system works with complete or incomplete information. In addition, it can deal with total or partial plans. In spite of the complexity of partial plans, the recognition system contains heuristics rules that cuts the complexity problem down.

This paper can be divided in two parts: theoretical and practical. Theoretical part will be discussed in sections 2 and 3. The hybrid formal theory is independent of any particular algorithm or implementation. It specifies the goal of computation and provides an abstract relation from the input information to the output. Section 2 will discuss the Hybrid Formal Theory - HFT. Therefore, we will show the basic definitions, language, constraints, and a model of the event hierarchy. Heuristics rules will be discussed in section 3. The practical approach was elaborated from the hybrid formal theory. Section 4 will provide an architecture for a Plan Recognition System - PRS, typical examples, and PRS's applications. Other details of the implementation as well as more examples can be found in [Nogu94, Nogu95, Pere96].

2. Hybrid Formal Theory

2.1 Basic Definitions

Some definitions are necessary to represent our hybrid formal model of plan recognition.

Definition 1 (*Event*)
An event $E_i(x)$ is a unary predicate that represents acts and plans from the **x** agent (human or machine). A ε - set is a set of events consisting of a sequence $E_0(x), E_1(x), \ldots, E_n(x)$ representing plans and actions.

$$\varepsilon = \{ E_0(x), E_1(x), \ldots, E_n(x) \}$$

Definition 2 (*Abstraction - abs*)
Let two events $E_i(x), E_j(x) \in \varepsilon$. We say that E_j *directly abstracts* E_i iff for every event E_i, we have E_j, but the inverse is not true. The transitive closure of the abstraction is valid, and the fact that E_j abstracts E_i is written **abs($E_j(x)$, $E_i(x)$)**. Therefore, E_j abstracts E_i, iff, the second-order logic axioms are valid:

(I) $\forall E_i, E_j \, [abs(E_j(x), E_i(x)) \leftrightarrow (\forall x.E_i(x) \rightarrow E_j(x))]$
(II) $\forall E_i, E_j, E_k \, [abs(E_i(x), E_j(x)) \wedge abs(E_j(x), E_k(x)) \rightarrow abs(E_i(x), E_k(x))]$

In a graphic form

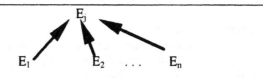

Fig. 1 - Abstractions

Definition 3 (*Specialization - spec*)
  The inverse of abstraction is specialization. Specialization can be defined:

  $$\mathbf{spec}(E_i(x), E_j(x)) \leftrightarrow \mathbf{abs}(E_j(x), E_i(x)).$$

Definition 4 (*Functional Step - f*)
  A functional step $f_i(x)$ is a unary function which maps an event to the respective component

  $$E_i(x) \xrightarrow{\;fi\;} E_j(x), \text{ where } E_i(x), E_j(x) \in \varepsilon$$

In a general form we have $[f_1(x), f_2(x), \ldots, f_n(x)] : E_i(x) \rightarrow \bigwedge_{j=1}^{n} E_j(x)$

Definition 5 (*Decomposition Axiom - A_d*)
  We define a decomposition axiom $\mathbf{A_d}$ as

  $$\forall x. E_0(x) \rightarrow E_1(f_1(x)) \wedge E_2(f_2(x)) \wedge \ldots \wedge E_n(f_n(x)) \wedge C$$

where $E_0(x), \ldots, E_n(x) \in \varepsilon$; $f_1(x), \ldots, f_n(x)$ are functional steps, and C describe the constraints on $E_0(x)$.

Definition 6 (*Direct Component - comp*)
  An event $E_0(x)$ is called **direct component** from other event E_1 iff there exists at least a functional step f_i from $E_0(x)$ to $E_1(x)$. The events $E_1(x)$ through $E_n(x)$ in the decomposition axiom (definition 5) are direct components of $E_0(x)$. The component relation is the transitive closure of the direct component, and is written **comp**$(E_0(x), E_1(x), f_i(x))$ which means that $E_0(x)$ is direct component of $E_1(x)$ from the functional step f_i. Figure 2 we can see the direct component in a graphic form.

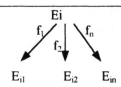

Fig 2 - Direct Components

In the graph of figure 2 we have that comp$(E_{i1}(x), E_i(x), f_1(x))$, comp$(E_{i2}(x), E_i(x), f_2(x)), \ldots,$ comp$(E_{in}(x), E_i(x), f_n(x))$

Definition 7 (*Constraint*)
  Every decomposition axiom has associated features which act as constraints on all structure of component events. A constraint C is a predicate with values of constraints V_c upon any component event E_i. All constraints must therefore be mutually consistent. Each predicate C is given from the axiom

  $$\forall x. E_i(x) \rightarrow \bigwedge_{j=1}^{n} C_j(Vc_1(x), Vc_2(x), \ldots, Vc_n(x))$$

where $Ei \in A_d$, and Vc is the predicate of valuation that represents constraints.

Definition 8 (*Compatible Events - compat*)

Two events E_j and E_i are compatible if there is an event they both abstract or are equal to. In a formal way, we have two compatible events E_j and E_k, **compat**($E_j(x)$, $E_k(x)$) if

$$\exists E_i (\forall x E_i(x) \rightarrow E_j(x) \wedge \forall x E_i(x) \rightarrow E_k(x))$$

Figure 3 below gives a graphic form to see compatible events.

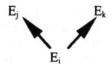

Fig 3 - Compatible events, compat($E_j(x)$,$E_k(x)$)

Definition 9 (*End Event*)

An event is called End event, written as **end(x)**, when the following formula holds:

$$end(x) \leftrightarrow \neg \exists x E_k(x)(abs(E_k(x), E_i(x))) \wedge \neg \exists x E_u(x)(comp(E_i(x), E_u(x),f(x)))$$

The End event is the fix point of our theory, and the implementation performs the following patterns of reasoning: from each agent's observation apply axioms, assumptions, and heuristics rules until an instance of End is reached. So, End event is the type of all events which are not part of some large event.

Definition 10 (*Observation*)

An agent's observation O is a pair $< E, C >$, where E is an observed event, and C contains constraints upon E; more formally, we have

$$O \equiv \exists x Ei(x) \bigwedge_{i=1}^{n} Cj(Vc_1(x), Vc_2(x), \ldots, Vc_m(x))$$

Also, we have $S_0 = \{O_1, O_2, \ldots, O_n\}$ as the set of observations from an agent.

Definition 11 (*Explanation*)

Let Γ be a knowledge base, and S_0 the set of observations from an agent; an explanation of S_0 consists of all models μ such that
(i) $\mu[\Gamma] \models \neg(\bot)$, where $\bot$ is the absurd symbol
(ii) $\mu[\Gamma] \models S_0$

Definition 12 (*Plan Recognition Problem*)

<u>Cover property</u> : A model μ is a cover model when S_0 generates (see S_0 in definition 11) an End event. Hence, a model μ is a cover model if $\mu[\Gamma] \models S_0 \wedge$ end(x) $\in \mu$

Plan recognition problem consists of finding out cover models μ from S_0.

2.3 Event Hierarchy

An *event hierarchy* is a collection of restricted-form axioms, and may be viewed as a logical encoding of a semantic network. The recognizer's knowledge is represented by a set of first-order logic statements, event hierarchy, which defines abstractions, specializations, and the functional steps between various types of events. This section defines the formal parts of an event hierarchy. An event hierarchy H is formed for a tuple $H = <H_E, H_A, H_{EB}, H_D>$[Kaut87].

Several research groups have examined the use of plan recognition in "smarts" computer systems that could answer user questions, watch what the user was doing, and make suggestions about potential pitfalls and more efficient ways of accomplishing the same tasks [ChSh94, GoLi95, KaPe88, LSP90, Nogu94, Nogu95]. So, we implemented several examples of event hierarchy in a tool we created called Plan Recognition System - PRS [Nogu94, Nogu95]. An example of event hierarchy that we implemented is illustrated in figure 4, where the wide black arrows denote abstraction or *is a* and the thin arrows denote component or *part of*. In this hierarchy there are two sorts of End events (SQL Interactive, and SQL Programmable), and five specializations (Delete, Select, Insert, From, and Where). Also, there are four component events (Column, Clause, Table, and Condition). The labels f_col, f_clause, f_table, and f_cond serve to distinguish the component arcs; they denote the functional steps (definition 4).

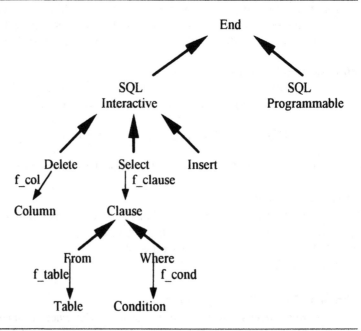

Fig. 4 - Event Hierarchy representing part of a DML language in a database SQL/ANSI

3. Heuristic Rules

The kinds of inferences performed in plan recognition do not follow from an event hierarchy alone. The abstraction hierarchy is strengthened by assuming that there are not event types outside of H_E, and that all abstraction relations between event predicates are derivable from H_A. The decomposition hierarchy is strengthened by assuming that non-End events occur only as components of other events. These rules are reasonable because the hierarchy encodes all of our knowledge of events. If the hierarchy is enlarged, the rules must be revised. Finally, we create other rule (SFA) that is used to combine information from several observations. The EXA, DJA, CUA, and MCA rules can be found in [Kaut87, Nogu94, Nogu95]. We now see SFA rule in detail .

3.1 Specific First (SFA)

The appropriated *specific first rule* (SFA) is based on both hierarchy and the specific observations that have been made. This new rule has a direct relation with MCA rule. MCA rule do not give any form to choose, among the minimal candidates plans what have greater or less priority. Hence, we create this new rule to give preferences upon minimal candidates plans. This rule state that a component event of a candidate plan more specific has preference on a component event more generic - more specific first.

The SFA rule from an event hierarchy H is built from a set of formulas that represent the minimal candidates plans, and from the specialization axiom - **spec** and component axiom - **comp**. A plan is recognized in our theory if this plan is verified with SFA rule. A SFA rule holds when

$$\text{spec}(E_i(x),E_j(x)) \wedge$$
$$\text{comp}(E_{ci}(x),E_i(x),f_u(x)) \wedge \text{comp}(E_{cj}(x),E_j(x),f_v(x)) \rightarrow (E_{ci}(x) \lhd E_{cj} \wedge E_{ci}(x) \mid E_{cj}(x))$$

where $E_i(x)$, $E_j(x) \in H_A$ and $E_{ci}(x)$, $E_{cj}(x) \in H_D$

The symbol $\lhd$ establishes the priority among events. In this case, the component event E_{ci} has preference on component event E_{cj}, indicated by $E_{ci} \lhd E_{cj}$, and the symbol $\mid$ means impediment among events. In the axiom above we have E_{ci} block the event E_{cj}, indicated by $E_{ci} \mid E_{cj}$.

4. PRS Implementation

Several works have been developed without an algorithm or an implementation of plan recognition. Therefore, we devised a hybrid theory, and extended the Kautz's plan recognition process to treat objects, some inheritances, and to give priority between events. Hence, we used this formalism to create an algorithm and a tool called *Plan Recognition System - PRS* [Nogu94, Nogu95]. The implementation performs the following pattern of reasoning: from each observation, apply heuristic rules and abstraction axioms until an instance of End event is reached. Reduce the number of alternatives by checking constraints locally. In order to combine information from two observation, equate the instance of End event inferred from each and propagate the equality, further reducing disjunctions. If all alternatives are eliminated, then conclude that the observations belong to distinct End events. Therefore, the explanation is returned by the system using all cover models of each observation.

4.1 Architecture

Users often work on several different tasks during a single session at a terminal and frequently jump back and forth between uncompleted tasks. Therefore a plan recognition system for some kind of domains must be able to handle multiple unrelated plans. The very generality of present approach is an advantage, where the focus-type heuristics used by other plan recognition systems are so not applicable. The complexity of design is in the capacity to the system to deal with various plans as well as achieve generalization, decomposition, and some introspection reasoning.

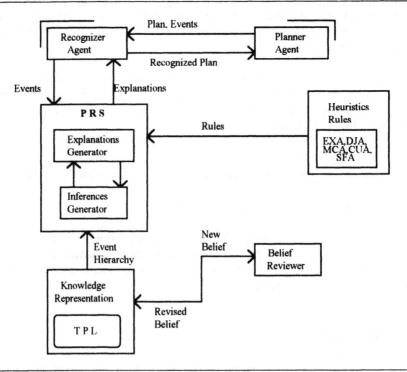

Fig. 5 - PRS architecture

As illustrated in figure 5, we present the PRS architecture. The recognizer agent (human or machine) observes a plan or a specific event, and from this observation it tries to find out the planner agent (user) intentions. This can be made only if the recognizer agent interact with the plan recognition system - PRS. The PRS has two fundamentals modules: Explanation Generator and Inference Generator. Explanations or recognized plans are obtained from the event hierarchy (knowledge model), heuristics rules, and from the Typical Plan Library - TPL. This architecture also has a belief revision module responsible for assimilation and belief review. However, the belief revision module will be implemented in the next version of the PRS.

4.2 Applications

Plan Recognition can be used in several areas of knowledge as databases [Nogu94, Nogu95], intelligent interfaces and assistants [Goli95, LSP90], operating systems [Kaut87], software reusability, and other. To show the generality of the use of plan recognition, we created in figure 6 a small part of the Tributary Law knowledge base, called TRIBUTUS. The thin component arcs signify the number of the law used, for example, art_150_fc means article 150 of Federal Constitution. We have added the type End as an abstraction of all government incomes. The basic specialization of End event are duties. We have simplified the hierarchy by making the specialization of tribute; in the actual knowledge base, tribute and monetary penalty are caused by other conditions.

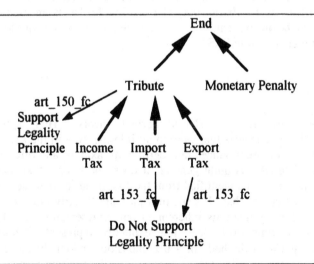

Fig. 6 - An event hierarchy with priorities to Tributary Law

At this point, let us suppose that the President of Camelot called Arthur King increase the import tax to chariots made in Caninde without specific law to do this. If the population queried:

Can Arthur King increase the import tax without law ?

Suppose that we have modeled the hierarchy in figure 5 with Kautz theory [Kaut87] or other theories based in that work, as [ChSh94, Goli95, KoPo89, Vila90]. In these theories we have that tribute support_legality_principle and do_not_support_legality_principle from art_150_fc and art_153_fc respectively; and how import_tax is a kind of tribute, they have two cover models:

μ_1 = [support_legality_principle, art_150_fc, import_tax, tribute, end] and
μ_2 = [do_not_support_legality_principle, art_153_fc, import_tax , tribute, end]

But these models are incompatible; the increase of import tax can not be true with two incompatible principles: do_not_support_legality and support_legality. This kind of inconsistency occurred because these theories do not have rule to deal with priorities, and exceptions.

In our Hybrid Formal Theory, we have just one model:

μ = [do_not_support_legality_principle, art_153_fc, import_tax, tribute, end]

This conclusion occurred because using SFA do_not_support_legality_principle is a component event of import tax that is more specific than tribute, then do_not_support_legality_principle *blocks* the component support_legality_principle. Hence, the answer from the question is *Yes*, Arthur King can increase import tax to the chariot obey the art_153_fc that is an exception to art_150_fc. Figure 6 below we can see a screen dump from this question and respective answer implemented in PRS.

5. Conclusion

In this work we created a Hybrid Formal Theory - HFT adding the necessary formalization to concepts that were in an informal way in the literature of plan recognition. Therefore, we produced new definitions, axioms, and rules for plan recognition process. The HFT is quite general. It does not assume that there is a single plan underway that can be identified from the first input, or that the sequence of observations is complete, or that all steps in a plan are linearly ordered. On the other side, there are some limitations inherent in our representations of plans. In particular, the current framework does not explicitly represents beliefs, and disjunctions cannot appear in the body of a decomposition axiom. In the practical side, we have implemented, in PROLOG, a generic Plan Recognition System - PRS. This system implements the HFT using lists of events as main data structure, where it is possible to perform inferences and generate the explanations of agent's observations. Furthermore, it was possible to deal with some kinds of problems that were not treated in the literature as the use of objects, priorities, and exceptions upon plan recognition. However, the current version of PRS has limitations: it does not treat beliefs revision and learning. These limitations shall be treated in future work.

References

[ChSh94] Charniak E. , Shimony S. E. "Cost-Based Abduction and MAP Explanation", Artificial Intelligence Journal, volume 66, number 2, 1994

[CSSB91] Cohen R. , Song F. , Spencer B. , Beek P. V. "Exploiting Temporal and Novel Information from the User in Plan Recognition", User Modeling and User-Adapted Interaction, volume 1, 1991

[GoLi95] Goodman B. A. , Litman D. "On the Interaction between Plan Recognition and Intelligent Interfaces", User Modeling and User-Adapted Interaction, volume 1, 1991

[GoCh88] Goldman R. , Charniak E. "A probabilistic ATMS for plan Recognition", AAAI-88, Workshop on Plan Recognition, 1988.

[KaPe88] Kautz H.A. , Pednault, P. D. "Planning and Plan Recognition", AT&T Technical Journal, volume 67, 1988

[Kaut87] Kautz H. A. "A Formal Theory of Plan Recognition", Morgan Kaufman, 1987.

[LSP90] Levi K. R. , Shalin, V. L. , Perschbacher D. A. "Learning Plans for an Intelligent Assistant by Observing User Behavior", International Journal of Man-Machine Studies, volume 33, 489-503, 1990

[Nogu94] Nogueira J. H. M "Analysis and Implementation of a Formal Theory of Plan Recognition", Technical Report, MCC 25/94, DI/PUC-RJ, Rio de Janeiro, Brazil, 1994

[Nogu95] Nogueira J. H. M "Plan Recognition - A Hybrid Formal Theory and Implementation of a Plan Recognizer", M.Sc. Thesis, DI/PUC-RJ, Rio de Janeiro, Brasil, 1995

[Pere96] Perez J. J. A. "Planning: a Survey", Technical Report, DI/PUC-RJ, Rio de Janeiro, Brazil, 1996

[Vilain90] Vilain M. "Getting Serious about Parsing Plans: a Grammatical Analysis of Plan Recognition", AAAI-90, Proceedings Eighth Conference National on Artificial Intelligence, MIT Press, Cambridge, Ma., 1990

Algorithms ρ for $\mathscr{L}$-standard State Graphs : Results About Termination and Admissibility

Henri Farreny

IRIT, 118 Route de Narbonne, 31 062 Toulouse cédex, France

Abstract : We formally extend various works dealing with Heuristic Search in state graphs, focusing on 1) the notion of path length, 2) the characteristics of the state graphs, 3) the procedures that control the choices of the states to be expanded, 4) the rules that govern the update operations, 5) the properties of the evaluation functions. We present new general theorems concerning the termination at a goal state, the admissibility and the sub-admissibility.

1 Introduction

This paper is a part of a global study [3, 4] that aims to compare and to extend various works dealing with *heuristically ordered search* in state graphs. Below we recall the *precise* definitions of Nilsson's A and A* [11, 12], then we report under which *exact* conditions these algorithms terminate by discovering a solution possibly optimal. In Section 2 we propose a formal extension. In Section 3 we present general theorems about the termination discovering a path to a goal state. In Section 4 we present general theorems concerning the length of the discovered path.

1.1 Algorithms A of Nilsson

The algorithm described in Fig. 1 is widely known as *algorithm A* [13]. It searchs a goal state by progressively expliciting the state graph from the start state « s ». The state graph is supposed to be *son-finite* (i.e. the number of sons of any state is finite) and *arc-valued* (i.e. a *cost* denoted c(m,n) is associated to each arc (m,n) which joins a state « m » to a state « n »). The set of the state goals is denoted by « T » (line 5) ; if a goal is discovered, the algorithm writes the reversed state list of a path from the start state to the found goal (lines 17, 18) and terminates (line 5).

The execution of the algorithm is constituted by state *extractions* (lines 4 to 6) followed by the *expansions* of the extracted states (lines 7 to 15). The algorithm uses an *evaluation function* to direct its choices. We denote « $f_x(n)$ » the later value of the evaluation function at the state « n » when the extraction « x » is about to be executed ; the index « x » is aimed to recall that the same state « n » may be successively evaluated in different ways, according to the successive extractions. The algorithm systematically extracts from « open » (lines 4 and 21-22) one of the states that own the minimal evaluation. By definition, the evaluation function must have the following form : $f_x(n) = g_x(n) + h(n)$, where « g_x » is the *standard term* while « h » is the *heuristic term*. The standard term g_x is recursively defined hereafter :

Before any extraction (x = 0), only s has appeared and let $g_0(s)$ be equal to 0.

At the time of the extraction of rank x,

for each son n of state m extracted at rank x

if n has already appeared before extraction x

then $g_x(n) = \min (g_{x-1}(n), g_{x-1}(m) + c(m,n))$ else $g_x(n) = g_{x-1}(m) + c(m,n)$

for each n, appeared before extraction x, which is not a son of m, $g_x(n) = g_{x-1}(n)$

Clearly : for any state n, $g_x(n)$ measures the length of a path[1] from s to n in the state graph and $g_x(n)$ decreases (not strictly) when x increases ; thus, when n is fixed,

---

[1] For Nilsson, the length of $\mathscr{P}$ is the *sum of the costs of its arcs*, i.e. : $\mathscr{L}$ add($\mathscr{P}$).

we may consider $g_X(n)$ as a decreasing overestimate of the minimal path length, if any, from s to n (this minimum is denoted $g^*(n)$ below). In Fig. 1, $g_{memo}(n)$ keeps track of the minimum of values $g_X(n)$ calculated until now for state n ; likewise, $f_{memo}(n)$ memorizes the minimum of values $f_X(n)$ calculated until now for n ; father(n) records the state whose expansion led to fix the later value $g_{memo}(n)$. The *heuristic term* h(n) only depends on state n at which h is applied and not of the extraction rank : we say that the heuristic term is *static* (but the standard term is *not static*). Nilsson's A algorithms (and most of the derived ones) suppose that arc costs are strictly positive and that the values of the heuristic term are positive in the wide sense.

```
1   procedure Heuristically-Ordered-Search-A-of-Nilsson
2       open ← {s} ; closed ← {} ; gmemo(s) ← 0 ; fmemo(s) ← h(s)
3       until open = {} repeat
4       │   m ← simple-extraction
5       │   if m ∈ T then edit-reverse-path stop endif
6       │   open ← open – {m} ; closed ← closed + {m}
7       │   for each n son of m repeat
8       │   │   gneo ← gmemo(m) + c(m,n)
9       │   │   if n ∈ open and gneo < gmemo(n) then update-father&gmemo&fmemo endif
10      │   │   if n ∈ closed and gneo < gmemo(n) then  update-father&gmemo&fmemo
11      │   │                                      open ← open + {n}
12      │   │                                      closed ← closed – {n} endif
13      │   │   if n ∉ closed and n ∉ open then  update-father&gmemo&fmemo
14      │   │                                 open ← open + {n} endif
15      │   endrepeat
16      endrepeat
17   procedure edit-reverse-path
18       until m = s repeat write m ; m ← father(m) endrepeat ; write "s"
19   procedure update-father&gmemo&fmemo
20       father(n) ← m ; gmemo(n) ← gneo ; fmemo(n) ← gmemo(n) + h(n)
21   procedure simple-extraction
22       return state n* of open such as fmemo(n*) = min          fmemo(q)
                                                 q ∈ open
```

Figure 1 : *Heuristically Ordered Search, algorithm A of Nilsson.*

1.2 Algorithms A* of Nilsson

The measure (according to the length function ; here : $\mathcal{L}_{add}$) of a minimal path, if any, from n to the set T of goal states, is often denoted $h^*(n)$ in the literature ; so, $h^*(s)$ is the length of a minimal path, if any, from the start state to the set of goals. For Nilsson [13] and other authors, algorithms A are designated by A* when the state graph $\mathcal{G}$ and the heuristic term h satisfy : $\forall$ n state of $\mathcal{G}$, $0 \leq h(n) \leq h^*(n)$. We say that h is a *lower-bounding* function (note : this property also depends on $\mathcal{G}$).

1.3 Termination at a Goal and Admissibility for A and A*

An algorithm is *admissible with respect to a state graph* $\mathcal{G}$ if, when applied to $\mathcal{G}$, it terminates finding a path from s to T whose length is $h^*(s)$. The admissibility of the A*'s is proved in [12, 13, 14] supposing that, at once : 1) the state graph $\mathcal{G}$ is son-finite and *goal-accessible* (i.e. it includes at least one goal state), 2) $\exists \, \delta > 0$, $\forall$ (m,n) arc of $\mathcal{G}$, $c(m,n) \geq \delta$ (this property characterizes the so-called *δ-graphs*), 3) h $\geq$ 0. Under the same conditions, any A terminates finding a path to a goal.

Hereafter, we shall mention various descendants of the A's, without recalling their definitions : particular A of Harris [6], HPA [16, 14] and extended A [15, 14] of

Pohl, B of Martelli [10], A_ϵ^* of Pearl-Kim [14], A_ϵ of Ghallab-Allard [5], C of Bagchi-Mahanti [1], BF* of Pearl-Dechter [14, 2], B' of Mero [11], IDA* of Korf [8], D of Mahanti-Ray [9], A** of Decter-Pearl [2], SDW of Köll-Kaindl [7].

2 Formalizations and Generalizations

We now propose several ways to generalize the A*'s and A's of Nilsson and many of their descendants.

2.1 Algorithms ρ — Algorithms ρ of Type 1

We call *basic algorithm ρ for Heuristically Ordered Search* the code presented in Fig. 2. Later, we shall make the algorithm more precise (to remove the non determinism of the procedures called in lines 4, 8 to 10) and we shall consider the application circumstances (what evaluation functions ? what kind of length ? what state graphs ?). The reference to the evaluation function f_X is only done in the assignment instructions of the lines 2, 8 and 13, in order to fire 1) an evaluation *now* according to n and according to the execution of the algorithm up to *now*, then 2) an assignment for the variables « $f_{memo}(s)$ », « evolution » and « $f_{memo}(n)$ ».

```
1    procedure basic-algorithm-ρ
2       open ← {s} ; closed ← { } ; f_memo(s) ← f_X(s)
3       until open = { } repeat
4          m ← extract-state-of-open-according-to-values-f_memo-for-the-states-in-open
5          if m ∈ T then edit-reverse-path ; stop endif
6          open ← open – {m} ; closed ← closed + {m}
7          for each n son of m repeat
8             evolution ← according-to-characteristics-of-n-including-f_X(n)
9             if evolution and n ∈ open then update endif
10            if evolution and n ∈ closed then  update
11                                       open ← open + {n}
12                                       closed ← closed – {n} endif
13            if n ∉ closed and n ∉ open then  father(n) ← m ; f_memo(n) ← f_X(n)
14                                       open ← open + {n} endif
15         endrepeat
16      endrepeat
17   procedure edit-reverse-path
18      until m = s repeat write m ; m ← father(m) endrepeat ; write "s"
```

Figure 2 : Heuristically Ordered Search : basic algorithm ρ
The procedures called in lines 4, 8, 9 and 10 are not yet precisely determined.

When a state n appears for the first time (line 13), the evaluation of n is assigned to $f_{memo}(n)$; so for s, in line 2. When n appears again, value $f_{memo}(n)$ may be modified by the update procedure (lines 9 and 10) not yet specified. According to the manner to make the line 4 more precise, we may define different *extraction modes* (see Para. 2.4). The lines 7 to 15 realize the expansion of the extracted state. Each extracted state that it is not a goal (test in line 5) is immediately *expanded* : *all* its sons are considered (the *partial* expansions are not allowed in this approach). The lines 7 to 15 correspond to the first appearance or eventually a new appearance of the sons of state m lately extracted of open when executing the lines 4 and 6. The execution of the line 8 assigns « true » or « false » to « evolution » according to whether it is decided or not that value $f_{memo}(n)$, or pointer father(n), must evolve ; this decision may take into account the value of the function f at n *now* , i.e. : $f_X(n)$; but we may also exploit other characteristics of the current state. According to the manner for governing the evolution of $f_{memo}(n)$ and father(n) in lines 8 to 10, we may define different *types* for algorithms ϱ. Basic algorithm ϱ includes partially determined update orders, (lines 9 and 10 in Fig. 2). We say that the ϱ is of *type 1* when the update orders comply with the following rules : at the time of the expansion of any state m and for any son n of m, 1) $f_{memo}(n)$ receives $f_x(n)$ except if the $f_{memo}(n)$ value was already smaller and 2) father(n) receives m except if $f_{memo}(n)$ is not lowered by the step 1. Evidently, A and A* are particular cases of ϱ of type 1 .

Algorithms ϱ and ϱ of type 1 do not refer to any cost of arc or path ; they may be applied to *non* arc-valued graphs. When the state graph is arc-valued, we may be interested in the length of the paths from s to T, possibly discovered ; nevertheless, if we do not know anything about the relations between the evaluation values of the states and the length of the paths from s to these states, it will be *a priori* difficult to compare the length of the found path with respect to the length of a minimal path. At the contrary, we shall further propose formulas of sub-admissibility for algorithms ϱ of type 1 which exploit particular evaluation functions. We shall also present some algorithms ϱ called of *type 2* or *type 3* whose codes explicitly refer to some costs of arcs or paths. Before, we propose a broadened definition for the *length* of paths.

2.2 Generalization of the Notion of Path Length

Commonly the length of a path is calculated as the sum of the costs of its arcs. However, Pearl [14] looks at other path lengths, especially the maximal cost of the arcs defining the path. Other authors use the minimum or the product of the arc costs. Below, we propose a general definition for the length. Let $\mathbb{V}$ be a subset of $\mathbb{R}$ which forms a monoid[2] with a two place operation Θ increasing in the wide sense (in right place and in left place). Such a monoid $(\mathbb{V},\Theta)$ is called *monoid of arc values*. Let $\mathbb{V}$ be a subset of $\mathbb{R}$. We denote $\mathbb{C}_\mathbb{V}$ the set of all the sequences of arcs that are valued in $\mathbb{V}$, completed by the empty sequence. We denote c a function which associates to each arc u in $\mathbb{C}_\mathbb{V}$ a value c(u) in $\mathbb{V}$; c is called *valuation function* on $\mathbb{V}$ of the arcs of $\mathbb{C}_\mathbb{V}$. $\mathbb{C}_\mathbb{V}$ forms a monoid with the operation of concatenation of finite arc sequences (the identity element is the empty sequence), called *concatenation monoid related to* $\mathbb{V}$. Let $(\mathbb{V},\Theta)$ be a monoid of arc values, $\mathbb{C}_\mathbb{V}$ the concatenation monoid related to $\mathbb{V}$, c the valuation function on $\mathbb{V}$ for the arcs of $\mathbb{C}_\mathbb{V}$. We call *length associated to the monoid* $(\mathbb{V},\Theta)$ *and to the function c*, the function $\mathcal{L}$ whose domain is $\mathbb{C}_\mathbb{V}$, whose range is $\mathbb{V}$ and that respects the following rules : 1) $\forall$ u arc of $\mathbb{C}_\mathbb{V}$, $\mathcal{L}(u) = c(u)$, 2) $\mathcal{L}$ (empty sequence of arcs) $= e_n$, 3) $\forall S',S'' \in \mathbb{C}_\mathbb{V}$, $\mathcal{L}(S' {_\circ} S'') = \Theta(\mathcal{L}(S'),\mathcal{L}(S''))$. Note : $\mathcal{L}$ is *the* morphism from the monoid $\mathbb{C}_\mathbb{V}$ to the monoid $\mathbb{V}$, that recovers the function c. Taking $\mathbb{V} = \mathbb{R}$ (or $\mathbb{N}$, etc.) and $\Theta = +$, we find again the classical form of path length calculated adding the arc lengths ($\mathcal{L}_{add}$). Other examples of lengths (especially with $\Theta = \times$, min, max...) are presented in [3, 4].

Now, we may generalize standard term g_x, presented in Para. 1.1, replacing the operation + by the operation Θ.

2.3 Other Types of Updates — Algorithms ϱ of Type 2 or 3

We distinguish two types of updates that depend on the generalized standard term g_x (other types could be considered). We say that an algorithm ϱ is of *type 2* if, at the time of the expansion of any state m and for any son n of m : 1) $f_{memo}(n)$ receives $f_x(n)$ except if the $f_{memo}(n)$ value was already smaller and 2) father(n) receives m except if the value of $g_{memo}(n)$ is not lowered when m is expanded. We

---

[2] $\mathbb{V}$ is closed under Θ, Θ is associative and admits an identity element in $\mathbb{V}$.

say that an algorithm ρ is of *type 3* if, at the time of the expansion of any state m and for any son n of m : 1) $f_{memo}(n)$ receives $f_x(n)$ except if the value of $g_{memo}(n)$ is not lowered when m is expanded 2) father(n) receives m except if the value of $g_{memo}(n)$ is not lowered when m is expanded. Any Nilsson's A (or A*) is simultaneously of types 1, 2 and 3, because for any state n, the staticity of the heuristic term leads $f_{memo}(n)$ and $g_{memo}(n)$ to be lowered at the same time. For the same reason, it may be easily verified that HPA's Pohl, Harris'A, Martelli's B, Pearl-Kim's A_ε^*, Ghallab-Allard's A_ε, Bagchi-Mahanti's C, Korf's IDA* and Köll-Kaindl's SDW are simultaneously of types 1, 2 and 3. Pearl's BF* algorithms are of type 1. Extended A's of Pohl, Mero's B$'$, D's of Mahanti-Ray and A**'s of Dechter-Pearl are of type 3. We did not meet any published algorithm whose type is not 1 or 3.

2.4 Extraction Modes — $\mathcal{E}$-extraction — Algorithms $\rho_\mathcal{E}$

The line 4 in Fig. 1 (Nilsson's A) orders a *simple extraction* . In order to propose a generalization of this extraction mode, we introduce the notion of *overpassed function*. Let a function $f \mid x \in D \subset \mathbb{R} \to f(x) \in \mathbb{R}$. We shall say that *f is overpassed on D* when : $\forall\, x \in D, \exists\, y \in D, f(x) \leq y$. Likewise, we shall say that *a set S_1 is overpassed by a set S_2* when : $\forall\, x \in S_1, \exists\, y \in S_2, x \leq y$. Consider a particular application of an algorithm ρ . Suppose that there exists a function $\mathcal{E}$ widely increasing and overpassed on $\mathbb{W}$, such as during this application, for any rank of extraction, $\mathcal{E}(\min_{q \in \text{open}} f_{memo}(q)) \geq \min_{q \in \text{open}} f_{memo}(q)$. Suppose that the algorithm systematically extracts a state ñ of « open » such as : $f_{memo}(ñ) \leq \mathcal{E}(f_{memo}(n^*))$ We shall say that the algorithm ρ uses $\mathcal{E}$-*extraction* and it will be then denoted by $\rho_\mathcal{E}$. We may distinguish $\rho_\mathcal{E}$ of type 1, 2 or 3. The simple extraction is a particular case of the $\mathcal{E}$-extraction (take $\mathcal{E}$ equal to the identity function $\mathcal{I}$). The following algorithms use simple extraction too : HPA's of Pohl, A's of Harris, extended A's of Pohl, BF*'s of Pearl, Mero's B$'$ algorithms, D's of Mahanti-Ray, A**'s of Dechter-Pearl and SDW's of Köll-Kaindl. The expression *best-first* (« best-first algorithm », « best-first search ») refers to such an extraction mode. Pearl-Kim's A_ε^* and Ghallab-Allard's A_ε use a form of $\mathcal{E}$-extraction, taking : $\mathcal{E} = (1 + \varepsilon)\cdot\mathcal{I}$. Martelli's B, Bagchi-Mahanti's C, Korf's IDA* use other particular forms of $\mathcal{E}$-extraction.

2.5 Algorithms $\tilde{A}$ — Algorithms $\tilde{A}_\mathcal{E}$

These algorithms are only defined when we consider state graphs that are arc-valued in a monoid $(\mathbb{V},\Theta)$; a length $\mathcal{L}$ is associated with such a monoid. An $\tilde{A}$ is a ρ whose evaluation function satisfies the constraint : $\forall$ i rank of extraction, $\forall$ n son of extract$_i$, $f_i(n) = \Theta(g_i(n),h_i(n))$ where $g_i(n)$ is the standard term at n while $h_i(n)$ is a value of $\mathbb{V}$ called *heuristic term* at n (the tilde on A reminds the *a priori* non staticity of h_x). The heuristic term at n may always be *interpreted* (well knowing or not, according to the context), as *an estimation* of the length of a minimal path, if any, from n to T. Clearly, the A's, extended A's of Pohl, B's, A_ε^*'s, A_ε's, C's, B$''$s, D's and SDW's are $\tilde{A}$'s. At first sight, the BF*'s and the A**'s are only ρ 's ; because they are defined on the *group* $(\mathbb{R}^+,+)$, f_x may be formulated as $f_x = g_x + h_x$, thus they are also $\tilde{A}$'s. Each HPA behaves as an $\tilde{A}$, because its evaluation function is *proportional* to this of an $\tilde{A}$. Each IDA* behaves as an $\tilde{A}$ *during each iteration*. We call $\tilde{A}$ of type 1, 2 or 3 the algorithms $\tilde{A}$ that are ρ 's of type 1, 2 ou 3 respectively. We call $\tilde{A}_\mathcal{E}$ (possibly of type 1, 2 or 3) the $\tilde{A}$'s that work with $\mathcal{E}$-extraction.

2.6 Worth-Considering Properties for h_x or f_x

The properties we propose below are more general than those commonly met. Still we denote $\mathbb{V}$ the domain of the arc values (a length $\mathcal{L}$ is defined on $\mathbb{V}$, the h_x

values belong to $\mathbb{V}$), $\mathbb{W}$ the range of f_X and $\mathcal{G}$ the state graph dealt with.

A heuristic term h_X is *-*locally upper-bounded when an $\tilde{A}$ is applied to $\mathcal{G}$*, if and only if : there exists a function F whose range is $\mathbb{V}$, which is defined for any state n of $\mathcal{G}$ that is evaluated and such that h* is defined at n, and which satisfies : $h_X(n) \leq F(n)$. We shall say that h_X is *-locally upper-bounded *by F*. Examples of such heuristic terms are : the h_X's that are upper-bounded (i.e. : $\exists M \in \mathbb{V}$, $\forall$ n evaluated state, $h_X(n) \leq M$), or *semi-static* (i.e. : $\forall$ n evaluated state, $h_X(n)$ is allowed to take only a finite number of distinct values), or simply *static* (i.e. : $\forall$ i and j ranks of extraction for which n is evaluated, $h_i(n) = h_j(n)$) ; or still : the h_X's that satisfy relations such as : $h_X \leq (1 + \alpha) \cdot h^* + H$, where the constants α and H are positive or zero. The A's, HPA's, B's, $A_{\mathcal{E}}^*$'s, $A_{\mathcal{E}}$'s, C's, IDA*'s and SDW's use static heuristic terms. It may be easily verified that the extended A's of Pohl use semi static h_X. It may be verified that the B''s and D's use *-locally upper-bounded h_X's. We denote $\tilde{A}^F$ any $\tilde{A}$ that exploits a *-locally upper-bounded h_X (A^F if h_X is static) ; in the particular case where h_X is lower-bounding, we denote such algorithms by $\tilde{A}^*$ (A^* if h_X is moreover static). We denote $\tilde{A}_{\mathcal{E}}^F$ an $\tilde{A}^F$ that uses $\mathcal{E}$-extraction ; if h_X is lower-bounding we denote it by $\tilde{A}_{\mathcal{E}}^*$ ($A_{\mathcal{E}}$ if h_X is moreover static). Evaluation function f_X is *-*locally upper-bounded when an algorithm ρ is applied to $\mathcal{G}$*, if and only if : there exists a function F whose range is $\mathbb{W}$, defined for any state n of $\mathcal{G}$ that is evaluated and such that h* is defined at n, satisfying : $f_X(n) \leq F(n)$. It may be verified that Dechter-Pearl's A**'s use *-locally upper-bounded f_X's. We denote ρ^F the ρ that exploits a *-locally upper-bounded f_X and $\rho_{\mathcal{E}}^F$ the ρ^F's that use $\mathcal{E}$-extraction.

Given a state n, we denote $[h_X(n)]_X$ the sequence of values taken by the heuristic term h_X for the ranks of extraction x when $h_X(n)$ is evaluated. Heuristic term h_X is *finitely decreasing when an algorithm $\tilde{A}$ is applied to $\mathcal{G}$*, if and only if : for any n state of $\mathcal{G}$ evaluated, there does not exist any infinite sub-sequence of $[h_X(n)]_X$ that is strictly decreasing. Examples of such heuristic terms are : the semi-static functions and therefore the static functions. Evaluation function f_X is *finitely decreasing when an algorithm ρ is applied to $\mathcal{G}$*, if and only if : for this application, for any n state of $\mathcal{G}$ evaluated, there does not exist any infinite sub-sequence of $[f_X(n)]_X$ that is strictly decreasing. The A's, HPA's, extended A's of Pohl', B's, $A_{\mathcal{E}}^*$'s, $A_{\mathcal{E}}$'s, C's, B' algorithms, IDA*'s, D's and SDW's use finitely decreasing h_X's and f_X's.

The heuristic term h_X is m_T-*coincident when an algorithm $\tilde{A}$ is applied to $\mathcal{G}$*, if and only if : $\exists m_T \in \mathbb{V}$, $\exists m'_T \in \mathbb{V}$, $\Theta(m_T, m'_T) \geq e_n$, $\forall t \in T$ evaluated, $h_X(t) \geq m_T$. That is clearly the case for the A's and also for the HPA's, extended A's of Pohl', B's, $A_{\mathcal{E}}^*$'s, $A_{\mathcal{E}}$'s, C's, B''s, IDA*'s, D's and SDW's, because all these algorithms use $\mathbb{V} = \mathbb{R}^+$, $\Theta = +$ ($e_n = 0$) and a heuristic term h_X positive or zero. Because BF*'s and A**'s are defined on the group $(\mathbb{V}, \Theta) = (\mathbb{R}^+, +)$ with $\mathbb{W} = \mathbb{R}^+$, the *implicit* h_X's are positive or zero, thus m_T-coincident.

2.7 A Larger Family of State Graphs

We identify now a wide family of state graphs : the $\mathcal{L}$-*standard* state graphs. It includes all the state graphs considered in the literature about the A's and also about the HPA's, extended A's of Pohl', B's, $A_{\mathcal{E}}^*$'s, $A_{\mathcal{E}}$'s, C's, BF*'s, B''s, IDA*'s, D's, A**'s and SDW's. Let $\mathcal{L}$ the used length. A state graph $\mathcal{G}$ is $\mathcal{L}$-*uncompressible* when : $\forall M \in \mathbb{V}$, $\exists k \in \mathbb{N}$, $\forall \mathcal{C}$ *elementary* path (i.e. : without repeating any state) of $\mathcal{G}$ from s, $\mathcal{N}(\mathcal{C}) > k \Rightarrow \mathcal{L}(\mathcal{C}) > M$, where $\mathcal{N}(\mathcal{C})$ denotes the number of arcs of $\mathcal{C}$. Clearly : any δ-graph is $\mathcal{L}_{add}$-uncompressible. All the above-mentioned algorithms, except the $A_{\mathcal{E}}$'s, have been analyzed (about termination or admissibility) by their authors when applied to δ-*graphs* ; the A_ε's have been analyzed when applied to less constrained but still $\mathscr{L}$ -uncompressible graphs. We shall say that a state graph is $\mathscr{L}$ -*standard* if it is son-finite, goal-accessible, $\mathscr{L}$ -uncompressible and without *absorbant* circuit (circuit whose length < e_n ; e_n : identity element of $\vee$). It may be easily verified that any $\mathscr{L}$ -standard graph owns at least one minimal path (in the sense of $\mathscr{L}$) from s to T. All the above-mentioned algorithms have been analyzed by their authors when applied to particular $\mathscr{L}$ -standard graphs.

2.8 Property of the « Homogeneous Paths »

For any algorithm ϱ , for any rank of extraction x and for any appeared state n, we call *pointer path of state n at rank x* the path from s to n determined by reversing the sequence n, father(n), father(father(n)),..., s. We denote it $P_{x,n}$. It may be easily verified that for the ϱ's of type 2 or 3 : $\forall$ x rank of extraction, $\forall$ n state already appeared, $\mathscr{L}\,(P_{x,n}) = g_x(n)$; we shall say that the property of the *homogeneous paths* is satisfied when for any x rank of extraction, for any n state already appeared and *situated on a path from s to T*, $\mathscr{L}\,(P_{x,n}) = g_x(n)$. Generally, the ϱ of type 1 do not satisfy the property of the homogeneous paths ; but the specific constraints considered by Pearl imply that his BF*'s satisfy it.

3 General Results About the Termination

The proofs of the original theorems 3.1 and 3.2 below are given in [3][3]. Remember that $\mathbb{W}$ designates the range of the evaluation function. « extract$_i$ » denotes the ith state extracted from open ; i is called *extraction rank* ; in Fig. 2, extract$_i$ is identified by « m » (lines 4 to 7). « $\underline{f}_i(n)$ » designates the value of the evaluation function f *already assigned to the state n, available when the ith extraction begins*, i.e. at the time when line 4 is interpreted ; in Fig. 2, $\underline{f}_i(n)$ is identified by : $f_{mem\varrho}(n)$. « $f_i(n)$ » designates the value of f which is *calculated for the state n when the ith extraction is realized* ; in Fig. 2, $f_i(n)$ is identified by $f_x(n)$ (line 2, 8, 13).

The application of an algorithm ϱ to a state graph $\mathbb{G}$ admits a *ceiling* if : $\exists$ M $\in$ $\mathbb{W}$, $\forall$ i rank of extraction, $\underline{f}_i(extract_i) \leq$ M. It is *circumscribed* if : $\forall$ M $\in$ $\mathbb{W}$, $\exists$ k $\in$ $\mathbb{N}$, $\forall$ i rank of extraction, $\underline{f}_i(extract_i) \leq$ M $\Rightarrow$ $\mathscr{N}^*$(s,extract$_i$) $\leq$ k, where $\mathscr{N}^*$(s,extract$_i$) is the minimum of the number of arcs of the paths from s to extract$_i$. It is *flattened* if : $\forall$ n appeared state of $\mathbb{G}$, $\exists$ i $\in$ $\mathbb{N}$, $\forall$ j rank of extraction, j > i $\Rightarrow$ $\underline{f}_j(n) \geq \underline{f}_i(n)$.

3.1 General Theorem for ϱ 's of Type 1, 2 or 3

Let an algorithm ϱ of type 1, 2 ou 3 that is applied to a $\mathscr{L}$ -standard state graph. If the algorithm is of type 1 or 2, in order that the algorithm terminates extracting a goal state, *it is necessary and sufficient* that the application 1) admits a ceiling and 2) is circumscribed and 3) is flattened ; if the algorithm is of type 3 *it is necessary and sufficient* that the application 1) admits a ceiling and 2) is circumscribed.

We shall say that a function f defined from $D \subset \mathbb{R}$ to $\mathbb{R}$ is *infra strictly increasing* on D if and only if $\forall$ x $\in$ D, $\exists$ x' $\in$ D, $\forall$ y $\in$ D, y > x' $\Rightarrow$ f(y) > f(x). Let a function f $\mid$ x $\in$ D $\subset \mathbb{R}$ $\to$ f(x) $\in$ $\mathbb{R}$. We shall say that *f is overpassing on D* when : $\forall$ x $\in$ D, $\exists$ y $\in$ D, x $\leq$ f(y).

3.2 Theorem for ϱ_ε^F's of Type 1, 2 or 3

Let an ϱ_ε^F of type 1, 2 or 3 that is applied to a $\mathscr{L}$ -standard state graph $\mathbb{G}$. Suppose that $\mathbb{W}$ is overpassed by $\vee$. Suppose that there exists φ function

---

[3] We improve here the wording of the statements of [7] *resting on the same proofs.*

overpassing and infra strictly increasing on $\mathbb{V}$. Suppose that for any n evaluated state of $\mathring{g}$: $f_x(n) \geq \varphi(g^*(n))$. If the algorithm is of type 1 or 2 and if f_x is finitely decreasing for the considered application to $\mathring{g}$, then the algorithm terminates extracting a goal state ; if the algorithm is of type 3, without other condition, then it terminates extracting a goal state.

3.3 Rediscoveries and Generalizations

The Nilsson's A are particular cases of $\rho_{\mathscr{E}}^{F}$ of type 1, 2, 3 (F is h*, $\mathscr{E}$ is the identity function $\mathscr{I}$). The reference monoid is the group $(\mathbb{R}^+,+)$ thus the reference length is $\mathscr{L}_{add}$. Nilsson consider son-finite and goal-accessible δ-graphs, that is to say particular $\mathscr{L}_{add}$-standard state graphs. The heuristic terms h are positive. Taking $\mathbb{W} = \mathbb{V} = \mathbb{R}^+$, $\varphi = \mathscr{I}$ (identity function) we may apply theorem 4.2 : any A terminates finding a path from s to T. Let us note that theorem 4.2 may be invoked in very more general contexts ; for instance, if we relax the A's, using a non static heuristic term h_x but keeping the type 3 (and also : $f_x = g_x + h_x$, $0 \leq h_x \leq h^*$, $\varphi = \mathscr{I}$), then we obtain some A's which necessarily terminate finding a path from s to T. Likewise, theorems 4.1 and 4.2 may be applied to rediscover and extend the results about the termination concerning : the HPA's, extended A's of Pohl, B's, A_ε^*'s, A_ε's, C's, BF*'s, Mero's B' algorithms, IDA*'s, D's, A**'s and SDW's.

4 General Results to Approach the Sub-admissibility

Below we present six original properties which form a set of tools to establish formulas of sub-admissibility. See [3] for proofs. Let $\mathring{g}$ a goal-accessible state graph at which an algorithm $\tilde{A}$ is applied. It is easily verified that : at the time of any extraction, on any path of $\mathring{g}$ from s to T, there exists a state belonging to « open » whose predecessors along the path belong to « closed »; this state is called : *input of the path for the considered extraction*.

4.1 General Lemma for $\tilde{A}^F$'s of Type 1, 2 or 3

Let $\mathring{g}$ a state graph at which is applied an $\tilde{A}$ of type 1, 2 or 3 whose heuristic term h_x is *-locally upper-bounded by F (thus the algorithm is an $\tilde{A}^F$). Let $\mathscr{P}$ a path from s to T such as, $\forall$ i rank of extraction, $g_{i-1}(e_i) = \mathscr{L}(\mathscr{P}_{ei})$ and h*(e_i) is defined, where e_i is the input of $\mathscr{P}$ at the time to decide the ith extraction and $\mathscr{P}_{ei}$ is the part of $\mathscr{P}$ from s to e_i. Then : $\underline{f}_i(e_i) \leq \Theta(\mathscr{L}(\mathscr{P}_{ei}),F(e_i))$, where $\underline{f}_i(e_i)$ is the evaluation value fastened to e_i at the ith extraction. This result generalizes « lemma 3.1 » of [12] (also : « result 2 » in [13] and « lemma 1 » in [14]).

4.2 Theorem for ρ's of Type 3

Let $\mathring{g}$ a state graph without absorbant circuit. Suppose that Θ is strictly increasing in the left place. Let a ρ of type 3 applied to $\mathring{g}$. Let n any state of $\mathring{g}$. Let $\mathscr{P}$ any minimal path from s to n. Denote $\mathscr{P} = n_0, ..., n_t$ where $n_0 = s$ and $n_t = n$. $\forall$ i rank of extraction, if n $\notin$ closed, let n_k (k $\in$ $\mathbb{N}$, $0 \leq k \leq t$) the input of $\mathscr{P}$ at the time to decide the ith extraction. Then : $\forall$ j $\in$ $\mathbb{N}$, $0 \leq j \leq k \Rightarrow g_{i-1}(n_j) = g^*(n_j)$. This result generalizes the « lemma 2 » of [14].

4.3 Corollary for $\tilde{A}^F$'s of Type 3

Let $\mathring{g}$ a state graph without absorbant circuit. Suppose that Θ is strictly increasing in the left place. Let $\mathscr{P}$ any minimal path from s to T. Suppose that an $\tilde{A}$ of type 3 is applied to $\mathring{g}$, whose heuristic term h_x is *-locally upper-bounded by F. Then, $\forall$ i rank d'extraction : $\underline{f}_i(e_i) \leq \Theta(g^*(e_i),F(e_i))$ where e_i is the input of $\mathscr{P}$ at the time to decide the ith extraction while $\underline{f}_i(e_i)$ is the evaluation value fastened to e_i at this precise moment. This result yet widely includes the « lemma 3.1 » of [12].

4.4 Theorem for $\tilde{A}_{\mathscr{E}}^{F}$'s of Type 3

Let $\mathscr{G}$ a goal-accessible state graph without absorbant circuit. Let an $\tilde{A}_{\mathscr{E}}$ of type 3 applied to $\mathscr{G}$, which terminates. Suppose that, when the algorithm is applied, heuristic term h_x is *-locally upper-bounded by F (thus the algorithm is an $\tilde{A}_{\mathscr{E}}^{F}$) and m_T-coincident[4]. Suppose that Θ is strictly increasing in the left place. Then, at the time of the termination, the algorithm has found a path $\mathscr{P}$ from s to T such as : $\mathscr{L}(\mathscr{P}) \leq \Theta(\mathscr{E}(\Theta(g^*(e_i),F(e_i))),m'_T)$, where e_i is the input, when is decided the ith and last extraction, of any minimal path from s to T in $\mathscr{G}$.

4.5 Theorem of Sub-Admissibility for $\tilde{A}_{\mathscr{E}}^{F}$'s of Type 3

Let $\mathscr{G}$ a $\mathscr{L}$-standard state graph at which is applied an $\tilde{A}_{\mathscr{E}}$ of type 3, whose heuristic term h_x is *-locally upper-bounded by F during the application (thus the algorithm is an $\tilde{A}_{\mathscr{E}}^{F}$), m_T-coincident[4] and lower-bounded by an element m of $\mathbb{V}$ such as $\exists\, m' \in \mathbb{V}$, $\Theta(m',m) \geq e_n$. Suppose that Θ is strictly increasing in the left place. Then, the algorithm terminates finding a path $\mathscr{P}$ from s to T such as : $\mathscr{L}(\mathscr{P}) \leq \Theta(\mathscr{E}(\Theta(g^*(e_i),F(e_i))),m'_T)$, where e_i is the input, at the time to decide the ith and last extraction, of any minimal path from s to T in $\mathscr{G}$. This result generalizes « theorem 3.1 » of [12] (also : « result 4 » in [13] and « theorem 2 » in [14]).

4.6 Theorem of the Found Path, for ρ 's of Type 1, 2 or 3

Let a ρ of type 1 (with homogeneous paths), 2 or 3, that is applied to a goal-accessible state graph and terminates at the time of the ith extraction. Suppose that there exists a function Ω whose domain is T_f (i.e. : range of $f_x(n)$ when n runs on T) such as : for any t state of T presented to the evaluation, $g_x(t) \leq \Omega(f_x(t))$. Then, at the time of the termination the algorithm has found a path $\mathscr{P}$ from s to T such as : $\mathscr{L}(\mathscr{P}) \leq \Omega(f_i(\text{extract}_i))$. This result generalizes « theorem 2* » of [14].

4.7 Rediscoveries and Generalizations

The Nilsson's A* are also particular cases of $\tilde{A}_{\mathscr{E}}^{F}$ of type 3. The state graphs considered by Nilsson are goal-accessible and do not admit absorbant circuits. The heuristic terms are m_T-coincident (take $m_T = m'_T = 0$). The operation Θ (that is to say +), is strictly increasing in the left place. Thus we may apply theorem 4.4 : *in case of termination*, $\mathscr{L}_{add}(\mathscr{P}) \leq g^*(e_i) + h^*(e_i)$, where $\mathscr{L}_{add}(\mathscr{P})$ is the length of the found path $\mathscr{P}$ from s to T while e_i is the final input of any minimal path $\mathscr{P}_0$ from s to T (note : for any $\mathscr{L}$-standard graph, there exists a minimal path from s to T). Because e_i belongs to $\mathscr{P}_0$ (minimal) : $g^*(e_i) + h^*(e_i) = \mathscr{L}_{add}(\mathscr{P}_0)$. Thus $\mathscr{L}_{add}(\mathscr{P})$ $= h^*(s)$: *in case of termination* the found path is minimal. Really, we may right away apply theorem 4.5, which moreover assures the termination (also proved applying theorem 3.2) : the admissibility of A*'s is thus rediscovered. The admissibility may be still proved when some constraints applied to the Nilsson's A* algorithms are relaxed ; indeed, providing that the updates remain of type 3, theorem 4.5 is yet applicable to monoids $(\mathbb{V},\Theta)$ other than group $(\mathbb{R}^+,+)$, to state graphs that are not necessarily δ-graphs, to heuristic terms h_x that are not necessarily static or positive. Moreover, theorem 4.5 gives some formulas of sub-admissibility for extraction modes which may be not simple and for h_x which may be not lower-bounding. If we relax Nilsson's A* towards $\tilde{A}$'s of type 1 or 2, we can establish some formulas of sub-admissibility by combining the results 3.1, 3.2 and 4.6. Likewise, theorems 4.1 to 4.6 may be applied to rediscover and extend the known results about the admissibility or sub-admissibility concerning the HPA's, extended

---

[4] Thus : $\exists\, m'_T \in \mathbb{V}$, $\Theta(m_T,m'_T) \geq e_n$.

A's of Pohl, B's, A_ϵ^*'s, A_ϵ's, C's, BF*'s, B''s, IDA*'s, D's, A**'s and SDW's.

5 Concluding remarks and perspectives

We have extended diverse works concerning the Heuristic Search in state graphs. Our formalization and the derived results allow better understanding and comparaison of various known algorithms that reveal non exploited potentialities : new path lengths, new state graphs, new evaluation functions, new updating and expansion mechanisms. This work may be developed to tackle the problems of termination, admissibility or sub-admissibility for other variants of algorithms (for instance : the so-called *restricted-memory* algorithms and *real-time* algorithms) ; or perhaps for other variants of evaluation functions, or even other variants of state graphs, beyond the hypotheses here considered. We may also try to rediscover and extend the sub-admissibility results relative to the bidirectional algorithms (see [3], chapter 8, for preliminary work). The generalizing formalization that we have only applied here to the properties of termination, admissibility and sub-admissibility may also contribute to better apprehend *other* properties knowingly ignored in this paper ; for instance : such algorithm always finds a better solution than such other, such algorithm presents such kind of complexity in time or space, etc.

References

[1]   A. Bagchi and A. Mahanti, Three approaches to heuristic search in networks, J. ACM 32 (1) (1985) 1-27.

[2]   R. Dechter and J. Pearl, The optimality of A*, in: L. Kanal and D. Kumar, eds, Search in Artificial Intelligence (Springer-Verlag, 1988) 166-199.

[3]   H. Farreny, Recherche Heuristiquement Ordonnée — Algorithmes et propriétés, (Masson, Paris, 1995).

[4]   H. Farreny, Une généralisation pour la Recherche Heuristiquement Ordonnée : les algorithmes ρ et la propriété d'arrêt avec découverte de solution, in: Proc. of RFIA 96, Rennes, France (1996) 225-234.

[5]   M. Ghallab and D. G. Allard, A_ϵ : An efficient near admissible heuristic search algorithm, in: Proc. 8th IJCAI, Karlsruhe, Germany (1983) 789-791.

[6]   L. R. Harris, The heuristic search under conditions of error, Art. Int. 5 (3) (1974) 217-234.

[7]   A. Köll L. and H. Kaindl, A new approach to dynamic weighting, in: Proc. 10th ECAI, Vienna, Austria (1992) 16-17.

[8]   R. E. Korf, Depth-first iterative-deepening : an optimal admissible tree search, Art. Int. 27 (1985) 97-109.

[9]   A. Mahanti and K. Ray, Network search algorithms with modifiable heuristics, in: L. Kanal and D. Kumar, eds, Search in Art. Int., (Springer-Verlag, 1988) 200-222.

[10] A. Martelli, On the complexity of admissible search algorithms, Art. Int. 8 (1) (1977) 1-13.

[11] L. Mero, A heuristic search algorithm with modifiable estimate, Art. Int. 23 (1) (1984) 13-27.

[12] N. J. Nilsson, Problem-solving methods in artificial intelligence, (Mc Graw-Hill, 1971).

[13] N. J. Nilsson, Principles of artificial intelligence, (Tioga, 1980).

[14] J. Pearl, Heuristics : intelligent search strategies for computer problem solving (Addison-Wesley, 1984).

[15] I. Pohl, The avoidance of (relative) catastrophe, heuristic competence, genuine dynamic weighting and computational issues in heuristic problem solving, in: Proc. 3d IJCAI, Stanford, USA (1973) 12-17.

[16] I. Pohl, Practical and theoretical considerations in heuristic search algorithms, in: E. W. Elcock and D. Michie, eds, Machine Intelligence 8 (Wiley, 1977) 55-71.

Regression by Classification

Luís Torgo

email : ltorgo@ncc.up.pt
WWW: http://www.up.pt/~ltorgo

João Gama

email : jgama@ncc.up.pt
WWW: http://www.up.pt/~jgama

LIACC - University of Porto
R. Campo Alegre, 823 - 4150 Porto - Portugal
Phone : (+351) 2 6001672   Fax : (+351) 2 6003654
WWW : http://www.up.pt/liacc/ML

Abstract
We present a methodology that enables the use of existent classification inductive learning systems on problems of regression. We achieve this goal by transforming regression problems into classification problems. This is done by transforming the range of continuous goal variable values into a set of intervals that will be used as discrete classes. We provide several methods for discretizing the goal variable values. These methods are based on the idea of performing an iterative search for the set of final discrete classes. The search algorithm is guided by a N-fold cross validation estimation of the prediction error resulting from using a set of discrete classes. We have done extensive empirical evaluation of our discretization methodologies using C4.5 and CN2 on four real world domains. The results of these experiments show the quality of our discretization methods compared to other existing methods.
Our method is independent of the used classification inductive system. The method is easily applicable to other inductive algorithms. This generality turns our method into a powerful tool that extends the applicability of a wide range of existing classification systems.

Keywords : learning, regression, classification, discretization methods.

1. Introduction

Machine learning (ML) researchers have traditionally concentrated their efforts on classification problems. However, many interesting real world domains demand for regression tools. In this paper we present and evaluate a discretization methodology that extends the applicability of existing classification systems to regression domains. With this reformulation of regression we broaden the range of ML systems that can deal with these domains.

The idea of mapping regression into classification was originally used by Weiss & Indurkhya [19, 20] with their rule-based regression system. They used the P-class algorithm[1] for class discretization as a part of their learning system. This work clearly showed that it is possible to obtain excellent predictive results by transforming regression problems into classification ones and then use a classification learning system. Our works is based on these results. We have oriented our research into the discretization phase as opposed to Weiss & Indurkhya's work. We do not supply a complete regression learning system like those authors did. We concentrated our research on two major goals related to the problem of class discretization. Firstly, to provide alternative discretization methods. Secondly, to enable the use of these methodologies with other classification systems. As to the first goal we were able to prove through extensive empirical evaluation on four real world domains that two of our proposed discretization methodologies outperformed the method used on the cited work. These experiments also revealed that the best methodology is dependent on both the regression domain as well as on the used classification system, thus providing strong evidence for our search-based discretization method. With respect to the second goal we have used our methodologies with CN2 [2] and C4.5 [15]. Our discretization system is easily interfaced to any other classification algorithm[2].

The next section gives a brief overview of the steps involved in solving regression problems by means of classification inductive algorithms. We then present our discretization methodology on section 3. The experiments we have done are described on section 4. Finally we describe some future work and present the conclusions of this paper.

2. Mapping Regression Into Classification

In regression problems we are given samples of a set of independent (predictor) variables $x_1, x_2, ..., x_n$, and the value of the respective dependent (output) variable y[3] . Our goal is to obtain a model that somehow captures the mapping $y = f(x_1, x_2, ..., x_n)$ based on the given samples. Classification differs from this setup in that the class is categorical instead of numerical.

Mapping regression into classification is a kind of pre-processing technique that enables us to use classification algorithms on regression problems. The use of these algorithms involves two main steps. First there is the creation of a data set with discrete classes. This step involves looking at the original continuous class values and dividing them into a series of intervals. Each of these intervals will be a *discrete* class. Every example whose output variable value lies within an interval will be assigned the respective discrete class. The second step consists on reversing the

---

1 This algorithm is historically known as the K-means method in statistics and pattern recognition.

2 We already have an interface to a linear discriminant although we still do not have experimental results.

3 For reasons of simplicity we shall use the term class instead of dependent variable from now on.

discretization process after the learning phase takes place. This will enable us to make numeric predictions from our learned *regression model*. Figure 1 shows a diagram of this process:

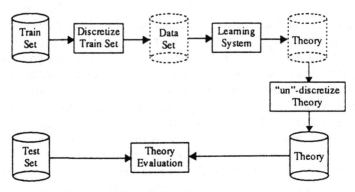

Figure 1 - Using classification algorithms on regression problems.

2.1 Methods For Splitting A Set Of Continuous Values

The key issue on a discretization process is the transformation of a set of values into a set of intervals. These intervals may then be used as discrete classes. In this section we present three methods for performing this task. All of them receive as input a set of values and the desired number of intervals.

- *Equally probable intervals (EP)*
  This strategy creates a set of N intervals with the same number of elements.

- *Equal width intervals (EW)*
  The original range of values is divided into N intervals with the same range.

- *K-means clustering (KM)*
  In this method we try to build N intervals that minimize the sum of the distances of each element of an interval to the interval's *gravity center* [4] [3]. This is basically the P-class method that is given in [20]. This method starts with the EP approximation but then tries to move the elements of each interval to contiguous intervals whenever these changes reduce the referred sum of distances.

To better illustrate these strategies we show how they group the set of values {1,3,6,7,8,9.5,10,11} assuming that we want to partition them into three intervals (N=3):
    - EP gives the intervals [1 .. 6.5],]6.5 .. 9.75] and]9.75 .. 11] with each interval containing respectively the values{1,3,6}, {7,8,9.5} and {10,11}.

---

[4] We always use the median as a centrality statistic. We prefer it to the mean to avoid outliers influence.

- Using EW we get [1 .. 4.33],]4.33 .. 7.66] and]7.66 .. 11] containing the values {1,3}, {6,7} and {8,9.5,10,11}.
- Finally KM obtains the intervals [1 ..4.5],]4.5 .. 8.75] and]8.75 .. 11] grouping the values in {1,3}, {6,7,8} and {9.5,10,11}.

The *problem* of these strategies is that they assume that we know the number of intervals that is appropriate for our problem. Our experiments show that this number is dependent not only on the domain we are dealing with, but also on the classification system that will be used after the discretization process. The methodology we present in this paper overcomes this difficulty by means of an iterative search approach.

2.2 Making predictions from the learned models

After the learning phase we obtain a theory that classifies examples into one of the chosen intervals. The next step consists on using this learned theory to predict the class value of unseen instances. Given a discrete class (an interval) we want to obtain a value that will be used as our prediction. The standard procedure is to use a measure of centrality of the interval as prediction. In our experiments we use the median of the values that originated the interval.

Evaluating the accuracy of regression models

We now address the problem of evaluating the predictive power of regression models. The standard procedure used to evaluate the accuracy of a *theory* consists on testing it on unseen data. On regression the prediction error e is given by the difference between the real value y and the predicted one $\hat{y}$. This methodology is very different from the one followed in classification problems. On these tasks errors are non-metric, i.e. a prediction is either correct or incorrect. Accuracy is thus a function of the number of errors. In regression the amplitude of errors is important.

There are several statistics that somehow try to characterize the accuracy of regression models. In our experiments we have chosed to work with two of them. One gives absolute estimates of the error (MAE) while the other provides relative estimates (MAPE) :

$$MAE = \frac{\sum_i |y_i - \hat{y}_i|}{N} \qquad MAPE = \frac{\sum_i \left|\frac{y_i - \hat{y}_i}{y_i}\right| \times 100}{N}$$

There are much more possibilities each having some advantages and some disadvantages. It is out of the scope of this paper to determine which one is more adequate to a given task.

3. Iterative Class Discretization

On section 2.1 we have shown several ways of splitting a set of values into a set of intervals. These splitting methods need to know in advance the target number of intervals (i.e. the number of discrete classes). This number is obviously dependent on the domain in state. In this section we describe an iterative search approach to solve this problem of finding the number of discrete classes to be used.

3.1 The Wrapper Approach

The goal of the class discretization process is to obtain a discrete data set that enables the classification algorithm to learn a theory that has the best possible regression accuracy. As we change the number of used classes we are changing the input to this classification system and thus varying its regression accuracy. Because of this we can easily see that the discretization process should take into account the classification system that will be used afterwards. In other terms, the used discrete classes are just a kind of parameter of the classification algorithm. The wrapper approach [8, 9] is a well known strategy which has been mainly used for feature subset selection ([8] and [10] among others) and parameter estimation [13]. Pazzani [14] also used a similar approach on feature creation which is a similar problem to ours. The use of this approach to estimate a parameter of a learning algorithm can be described by the following figure:

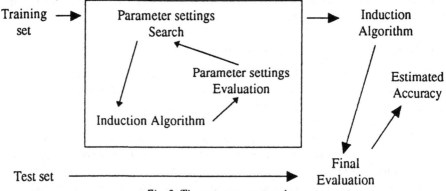

Fig. 2. The wrapper approach.

The two main components of the wrapper approach are the way how new parameter settings are generated and how they are evaluated in the context of the target learning algorithm. The basic idea is to try different parameter settings and choose the one that gives best estimated results. This best setting is the result of the wrapper process an will then be used in the learning algorithm for the real evaluation using an independent test set.

Translating this scenario to our discretization problem we basically have to find the discretization method that gives the best results. Our method tries several possible discretization settings (i.e. set of discrete classes) and chooses the one that gives the best estimated accuracy. To evaluate the candidate setups we use the well known N-fold cross validation (CV) test.

The search component of our wrapper approach consists of the process used to generate a new candidate set of classes (i.e. the search operators) and the search algorithm. We use a simple hill-climbing search algorithm coupled with a kind of lookahead mechanism to try to avoid the well-known problem of local minimum of this algorithm. The search proceeds by trying new candidate sets of classes until a certain number (the lookahead value) of consecutive worse trials occur.

We provide two alternative ways of generating a new candidate discretization setting. Both of them can be applied to the three presented splitting strategies (section 2.1). This gives six different discretization methods that can be used to create a set of discrete classes using this wrapper approach.

3.2 Generating candidate sets of discrete classes

In this section we address the problem of modifying the current discretization setting based on its estimated predictive accuracy result. The search space consists of all possible partitions of a set of continuous values. Our system has two alternative ways of exploring the search space. Both are applicable to the 3 splitting methods that were mentioned on section 2.1:

- *Varying the number of intervals (VNI)*

    This alternative consists on trying several values of the number of intervals with the current splitting strategy. We start with a number of intervals and on each iteration of the search process we increment this number by a constant value. This is the more obvious way of improving the splitting methods presented in section 2.1.

- *Selective specialization of individual classes (SIC)*

    The second alternative is a bit more complex. The basic idea is to try to improve the previously tried set of intervals (classes). We start with any given number of intervals and during the CV-evaluation we also calculate the error estimates of each individual discrete class. The next trial is built by looking at this individual error estimates. The median of these errors is calculated. All classes whose error is above the median are specialized. The specialization consists on splitting each of these classes in two other classes. We do this by applying the current splitting method to the values within that class interval. All the other classes remain the same in the next iteration.

The next section provides an illustrative example of these two search alternatives in a discretization task.

4. The Experiments

We have conducted several experiments with four real world domains.

The main goal of the experiments was to assert each discretization methodology performance when the input conditions vary. These conditions are the regression domain, the classification learning system and the regression error measure used to evaluated the learned models. Some of the characteristics of the used data sets are summarized on Table 1. These data sets were obtained from the UCI machine learning data base repository :

Data Set	N. Examples	N. Attributes
housing	506	13
servo	167	4
auto-mpg	398	7
machine	209	6

Table 1- The used data sets.

As we already referred we have used C4.5 and CN2 in our experiments. We have used as regression accuracy measures the MAE and MAPE statistics.

We *linked* our methodologies to each of these learning algorithms obtaining two new *regression learners*. We evaluate the performance of these systems with the two statistics on the chosen domains. We have obtained this evaluation by means of a 5-fold cross validation test. On each iteration of this process we have forced our discretization system to use each of the six alternative discretization methods producing six different discrete data sets that were then given to C4.5 and CN2. We have collected a set of <u>true</u> prediction errors for each of the regression models learned with the six discrete data sets. The goal of these experiments was to compare the results obtained by each discretization method under different setups on the <u>same</u> data. The 5-CV average predictive accuracy on the "auto-mpg" data set is given on Table 2 (the small numbers in italic are the standard deviations):

		VNI			KNI		
		EP	*EW*	*KM*	*EP*	*EW*	*KM*
MAE	*C4.5*	2.877	2.796	**2.783**	2.982	3.127	3.134
		±0.333	*±0.308*	*±0.299*	*±0.360*	*±0.282*	*±0.272*
	CN2	3.405	4.080	3.597	3.311	3.695	**3.053**
		±0.266	*±0.654*	*±0.641*	*±0.188*	*±0.407*	*±0.340*
MAPE	*C4.5*	12.50	12.556	12.200	12.072	**11.600**	11.996
		±1.520	*±1.980*	*±1.623*	*±2.549*	*±2.074*	*±1.195*
	CN2	15.189	15.474	15.282	14.485	14.930	**13.871**
		±1.049	*±1.631*	*±2.235*	*±0.936*	*±1.291*	*±2.069*

Table 2 - Experiments with "auto-mpg".

The best score for each setup is in bold. Due to space reasons we summarize the overall results on Table 3 where we present the winning strategies for all data sets :

Set Up	Servo	Machine	Housing	Auto-mpg
C4.5 / MAE	VNI+KM	SIC+KM	VNI+EW	VNI+KM
CN2 / MAE	SIC+EP	SIC+KM	SIC+EW	SIC+KM
C4.5 / MAPE	VNI+KM	SIC+KM	SIC+KM	SIC+EW
CN2 / MAPE	SIC+EP	SIC+EW	VNI+KM	SIC+KM

Table 3 - Summary of overall results.

Table 4 gives the rank score of each strategy. The numbers in the columns of this table represent the number of times a strategy was ranked as the Nth best strategy.

The last column gives the average ranking order for each method. The methods are presented ordered by average rank (lower values are better) :

	1st	2nd	3rd	4th	5th	6th	Avg. Rank
SIC+KM	6	2	3	1	0	4	2,24
VNI+EP	0	7	3	5	1	0	2,29
VNI+KM	4	1	3	6	2	0	2,33
SIC+EW	3	0	3	2	7	1	2,90
SIC+EP	2	3	3	5	2	3	3,10
VNI+EW	1	3	1	0	3	8	3,48

Table 4 - Rank scores of the methods.

The main conclusion to draw from our experiments is the clear dependency of the best methodology on the used set up. There is no clear winning strategy on all domains. This proves the validity of our search-based approach to class discretization.

Table 3 shows that our selective specialization strategy (SIC) is most of the times (11 out of 16) one of the components of the best discretization method. Looking at the average rank results (Table 4) SIC+KM is the best followed by VNI+EP. SIC+KM is also the method that is the best more often. The two methods using EW splitting method have bad averages, nevertheless these methods sometimes are the best so they are not useless. On the contrary VNI+EP which was the second best on average was never the best strategy in all our experiments. Another interesting observation is the regularity observed on the "machine" data set (see Table 3) contrasting with the other data sets.

5. Relations To Other Work And Future Directions

We have presented a general class discretization method and evaluated it in conjunction with two classification algorithms. It is our goal to experiment with more systems with different characteristics.

Within the ML community other work exists on the area of continuous attribute discretization. This work usually performs a kind of pre-processing by trying to maximize the mutual information between the resulting discrete attribute and the classes (for instance [4] and [11]). This is a good strategy but it is applicable only when the classes are given. Ours is a very different problem, as we are determining which classes to consider.

Within the ML field some regression learning systems exist (for instance CART [1], M5 [16] and R^2 [17]) that could be used on these domains. These systems do not transform regression into classification tasks. Weiss & Indurkhya have demonstrated [20] that this transformation can obtain good results when compared the these more "classical" methods. They have done this with their rule-based regression system that learns with discrete classes. They have tested it on several domains (including the ones we have used). The results they report show that their system clearly outperforms CART, a Nearest Neighbor algorithm and the statistical method MARS [5]. These results were a key motivation for our work. They indicate that it is possible to obtain good accuracy with classification systems on regression problems. Their system is a two step algorithm. First there is the discretization phase where they use a method that is equal to our VNI+KM method. Finally they use the resulting discrete data set with their classification system. As we did not have available their classification system we were not able to test our discretization methods together with this system. However, we have tested their discretization method with CN2 and C4.5. The experiments showed that the best method depends on both the domain as well as on the used classification system (Table 3). This fact does not enable us to definitely say that our methods are <u>always</u> better than the VNI+KM method. Nevertheless, these results reinforce our search-based approach that is able to chose the discretization method to use depending on both these factors. Table 4 also shows that on average both SIC+KM and VNI+EP are better then VNI+KM. This seems to indicate that these methodologies together with Weiss & Indurkhya's classification system could even get better overall regression accuracies when compared to the other "classical" regression methodologies.

One possible future improvement on our work is to try to use other search algorithms (like best-first [6], simulated annealing [18] or even genetic-based search algorithms [7]).

Another interesting research topic as to do with the inability of classification systems to take advantage of the implicit ordering of the obtained *discrete* classes. Because of this, an error has always the same cost. Unfortunately this is not suitable for the evaluation measures used for calculating the accuracy of regression models. A possible way to overcome this drawback is to use a cost matrix in the learning phase. This matrix would distinguish between the errors. This error cost information is important even in the classification scenario for several domains [12]. We could use the distance between the median of each interval as the error cost of *confusing* classes. We have already implemented this idea together with a linear discriminant that is able to use cost matrices. We do not include this work here as we still do not have experimental results.

6. Conclusions

The method described in this paper enables the use of classification systems in regression domains. Previous work [20] provided evidence for the validity of transforming regression into classification. This was oriented towards one learning algorithm. Our work enables the use of a similar transformation strategy with other classification systems. This extends the applicability of a wide range of existent inductive systems.

Our algorithm chooses the best discretization method among a set of available strategies. We estimate the prediction error of each candidate method and select the best among them. The resulting discrete classes are obtained by an iterative search procedure using the chosen discretization method. This iterative search is basically a wrapper process based on a N-fold CV evaluation that estimates the predictive error resulting from using a set of discrete classes. We have also introduced five novel methods for discrete class formation.

We have showed the validity of our search-based approach by means of extensive experiments on four real world domains. These experiments indicated that a search-based approach is necessary if we want to handle several domain/learning system/error measure scenarios. The results of the experiments also showed that some of our methods for class formation were among the best on most of the cases.

We have applied our methodology to two classification inductive systems (C4.5 and CN2). It is easy to use it with other learning algorithms. This generality turns our methodology into a powerful tool for handling regression using existing ML classification inductive systems.

References

[1].   Breiman,L. , Friedman,J.H., Olshen,R.A. & Stone,C.J. (1984): Classification and Regression Trees, Wadsworth Int. Group, Belmont, California, USA, 1984.

[2].   Clark, P. and Niblett, T. (1988) : The CN2 induction algorithm. In *Machine Learning*, 3, 261-283.

[3].   Dillon,W. and Goldstein,M. (1984) : *Multivariate Analysis*.. John Wiley & Sons, Inc.

[4].   Fayyad, U.M., and Irani, K.B. (1993) : Multi-interval Discretization of Continuous-valued Attributes for Classification Learning. In *Proceedings of the 13th International Joint Conference on Artificial Intelligence (IJCAI-93)*. Morgan Kaufmann Publishers.

[5].   Friedman, J. (1991) : Multivariate Adaptative Regression Splines. In *Annals of Statistics*, 19:1.

[6].   Ginsberg, M. (1993) : *Essentials of Artificial Intelligence*. Morgan Kaufmann Publishers.

[7].   Holland, J. (1992) : *Adaptation in natural and artificial systems : an introductory analysis with applications to biology, control and artificial intelligence*. MIT Press.

[8].   John,G.H., Kohavi,R. and Pfleger, K. (1994) : Irrelevant features and the subset selection problem. In *Machine Learning : proceedings of the 11th International Conference*. Morgan Kaufmann.

[9].   Kohavi, R. (1995) : Wrappers for performance enhancement and oblivious decision graphs. PhD Thesis.

[10].   Langley, P., and Sage, S. (1994) : Induction of selective bayesian classifiers. In *Proceedings of the 10th conference on Uncerrtainty in Artificial Intelligence*. Morgan Kaufmann Publishers.

[11].   Lee, C. and Shin, D. (1994) : A context-sensitive Discretization of Numeric Attributes for classification learning. In *Proceedings of the 11th European Conference on Artificial Intelligence (ECAI-94)*, Cohn, A.G. (ed.). John Wiley & Sons.

[12].   Michie,D., Spiegelhalter,D.J. & Taylor,C.C. (1994): *Machine Learning, Neural and Statistical Classification*, Ellis Horwood Series in Artificial Intelligence, 1994.

[13].   Mladenic, D. (1995) : Automated model selection. In *Mlnet workshop on Knowledge Level Modelling and Machine Learning*. Heraklion, Crete, Greece.

[14].   Pazzani, M.J. (1995) : Searching for dependencies in bayesian classifiers. In *Proceedings of the 5th international workshop on Artificial Intelligence and Statitics*. Ft. Laurderdale, FL.

[15].   Quinlan, J. R. (1993) : *C4.5 : programs for machine learning*. Morgan Kaufmann Publishers.

[16].   Quinlan, J.R. (1992): Learning with Continuos Classes. In *Proceedings of the 5th Australian Joint Conference on Artificial Intelligence*. Singapore: World Scientific, 1992.

[17].   Torgo, L. (1995) : Data Fitting with Rule-based Regression. In *Proceedings of the 2nd international workshop on Artificial Intelligence Techniques (AIT'95)*, Zizka,J. and Brazdil,P. (eds.). Brno, Czech Republic.

[18].   van Laarhoven,P. and Aarts,E. (1987) : Simulated annealing : Theory and Applications. Kluwer Academic Publishers.

[19].   Weiss, S. and Indurkhya, N. (1993) : Rule-base Regression. In *Proceedings of the 13th International Joint Conference on Artificial Intelligence*, pp. 1072-1078.

[20].   Weiss, S. and Indurkhya, N. (1995) : Rule-based Machine Learning Methods for Functional Prediction. In Journal Of Artificial Intelligence Research (JAIR), volume 3, pp.383-403.

A Generic Model of Cognitive Agent to Develop Open Systems

E. E. Scalabrin*, L. Vandenberghe, H. de Azevedo**, J-P. A. Barthès

Université de Technologie de Compiègne
CNRS URA 817 HEUDIASYC
BP 529, 60205 Compiègne Cedex, France
E-Mail: {escalab, lvanden, hazevedo, barthes}@hds.utc.fr

Abstract. The paper presents an approach to building multi-agent systems. We are interested in complex agents able to reason about their tasks, and to display a proactive behavior, when installed on a network of heterogeneous computers. We developed the concept of a generic agent (GAg), equipped with the basic communication and "mental" structure, but ignorant, i.e., not containing any application expertise, nor having any knowledge about the external world. When building an application, actual agents are cloned from the generic agent. In addition, a specific environment, OSACA (Open System for Asynchronous Cognitive Agents), simplifies the process of creating agents on a network of heterogeneous machines. The paper discusses mainly the basic structure of the generic agent. Our approach is also illustrated with a small example of an agent which helps writing a technical paper in a research laboratory. ...

1 Introduction

A new branch of artificial intelligence studies societies of agents working together to solve problems that are naturally distributed, or too large and too complex to be solved by a single program. Our research work takes place in this context. Indeed, we are interested in complex agents able to reason about their tasks, and to display a proactive behavior, when installed on a network of heterogeneous computers. However, when one wants to develop multi-agent systems in practice, a major difficulty is to write the supporting code, to test the prototypes, and to maintain the resulting system. In particular, changes in a multi-machine environment are a real pain. Thus, we focused our work onto open systems, i.e., systems containing a variable number of agents which do not have to be halted when changes occur, i.e., when some agents join the system, or leave the system. In addition, we wanted to simplify the way to build a particular agent, by offering an off-the-shelf typical agent containing all basic mechanisms, and which can be cloned to serve as a starting point for more complex modules.

The resulting environment, OSACA (Open System for Asynchronous Cognitive Agents), gives the user the ability to create, develop, and test multi-agent

* Supported by CAPES/Brazil, grant number 1307/94
** On leave from CEFET-PR, Brazil and supported by CITS/CNPq, grant number 260139/92

systems with minimal effort. Agents are implemented in the MOSS programming environment [1]. Within OSACA [16, 15], each agent is an independent process, communicating with other agents by sending messages asynchronously. OSACA is installed on $UNIX^{TM}$, including $SPARC^{TM}$ machines running $SunOS^{TM}$ and $Solaris^{TM}$. $Mac^{TM}OS$ will be supported in the next release. UDP/IP is used to carry messages between agents in a LAN environment.

The rest of the paper is organized as follows. Section 2 presents a brief overview of Multi-Agent Systems and gives examples of different architectures. Section 3 details the generic agent, GAg, presenting its model and functionalities. Section 4 introduces an application, MEMOLAB, to illustrate how to use GAg to implement an application agent. The paper ends with some concluding remarks about the generic agent approach and future work.

2 Towards Open Systems

Multi-agent systems can be classified according to their architecture (overall organization), to the degree of autonomy of each agent, to the type of protocol they use to communicate, or their complexity. A major distinction concerns reactive vs. autonomous agents. Reactive agents are very simple without any representation of their environment. They interact using stimulus-response type behavior [6]. Thus, intelligent behaviors can emerge from a population of numerous agents [3]. Cognitive agents are very complex. Each agent is specialized and can function by itself. It has a (partial) model of its environment and acts in accordance with the model. Complex agents may have intentions to guide their behavior. The various systems proposed today differ by their overall architecture, communication possibility, and complexity of the basic agent.

Blackboard systems allow several specialists (often called knowledge sources) to interact through shared data (posted on the blackboard). Normally, communication occurs only through the shared data, which leads to a form of strong coupling, and possibilities of bottlenecks [10, 8].

In *federated multi-agent systems* [9], complex agents called facilitators, organize the work among simpler agents that notify the facilitator of the tasks they are able to handle. Receiving a request, the facilitator finds a competent agent to execute the task. Some examples of such architectures are: the ABSI [17]; the SHADE matchmaker [12] used in the SHADE project [13]; and the Knowledgeable Community [14]. Facilitator architectures rationalize communication resources. However, because a facilitator operates as a bridge between agents, its failure may prevent communication between the agents.

"Democratic" multi-agent systems gather agents which all have the same status, like in the ARCHON project [4], or in our approach [16].

Agents performing collective actions [2, 19] communication is an important issue and is usually asynchronous, performed by means of various protocols. For example, the Knowledge Query and Manipulation Language (KQML) is a language using performatives that may express their beliefs, needs, and modalities of communication [7]. The Cooperation Language (CooL) allows agent communication via a set of message types, called cooperation primitives [11]. The principle of cooperation in CooL is the Contract-Net Protocol [18].

Open systems. The openness of a system is related to the way it is implemented. In most multi-agent systems, whenever a change occurs, everything must be brought to a halt, corrections must be done, code must be recompiled, and the system usually has to be reinitialized. This process is clearly inadequate for large agent systems which must continue to function when some agents have a problem, or when new agents are brought in. Systems that support dynamic reconfiguration are called Open Systems and are difficult to develop in particular on networks of heterogeneous machines. OSACA uses a democratic approach, with independent cognitive agents, having a model of their expertise, of the world, of themselves. Agents communicate asynchronously, using a variety of protocols. They run on a network of heterogeneous workstations. OSACA is an open system. Such characteristics bring many advantages: simplifying development (which can be carried out at the right place, with the right tools), making maintenance easier (which can be performed at the level of the agent without knowing anything about the others), obtaining the best performance for each agent (skills are written in the most appropriated language) and increasing lifetime (each agent can evolve separately taking in account new technologies). The next section describes the structure of a typical agent in OSACA.

3 The OSACA Generic Agent

A generic agent (GAg) is an entity possessing basic mechanisms, structures and skills, ensuring a minimal internal and external behavior, and allowing an agent to adapt itself to a new environment. Actual agents are produced by cloning the generic agent, and thus inheriting the basic structure and mechanisms. Thus, an agent can communicate with other agents, learns what the others do, and organize itself in order to cooperate towards a common goal. Our major contribution in multi-agent systems will be defining a minimal set of mechanisms for GAg, allowing an agent to become integrated smoothly into an unknown environment. GAg might also evolve in the sense that we could add some mechanisms developed in other architectures, like internal reasoning methods [10]. Obviously, our aim is not to have a universal model, but to define an agent model allowing to develop multi-agent systems quickly and economically. GAg is also intended to favor reusing already defined structures and mechanisms.

3.1 Overall Project Organization

OSACA agents must be able to function on several tasks at the same time. Indeed, it would not be economically reasonable to clone an agent each time it receives a new request, in the same way an actor is cloned in Hewitt's approach. Thus, our agents are multi-threaded. In order to organize the work of an agent, one must provide a mechanism for distinguishing among the different tasks in which the agent is involved. We introduce the notion of project, that we prefer to the more traditional notion of task.

Projects are defined as a set of tasks possibly involving a number of different agents, and intended to solve a particular problem, e.g., writing a scientific paper, finding out how to print color slides, doing a literature search, or preparing a specific research proposal. An agent does not know the projects in which it can be involved. Thus, the architecture must provide mechanisms to learn about projects and to manage them. A project can be represented as a working context with a model of behavior and as a structure allowing the agent to realize an objective in a more organized and intelligent way than with a simple skill. A project is composed of a set of skills and a set of information whose values are bound to the project. As several agents may cooperate to accomplish a goal, every agent that participates in a project constructs a specific model of a project. Depending on the project, the conditions of the usage of skills may be different.

The first aim of a project is to allow the various contexts of work to coexist, memorizing typical parameters required to execute the skills. At the same time, one can observe the message flow to store the values of typical parameters in order to accelerate the work. In some circumstances, the agent can anticipate a request and prepare an answer. A second goal is to organize the skills used in the project. When an agent participates in a project, it has already an idea of what it will do. Finally, a third goal is to focus the agent only on useful information, avoiding cognitive overload. GAg can work without any project but using them improves efficiency.

3.2   Agent Architecture

A specificity of GAg architecture is to let an agent manage projects with minimal knowledge. An agent has several functionalities attached to six components shown on Fig. 1 and discussed in the following sections: Knowledge Base, Message Routing, Communication Management, Control, Tasks Management, and Projects Management. A seventh functionality, the External-Representation Management, is distributed among all components.

3.3   Knowledge Structure

The agent's knowledge structure is based on traditional components: a self-representation to model its skills (what it can do); an external-representation to store its knowledge about the other agents; and a communication module. We add another component: a project-representation.

Self-Representation. It allows an agent to know itself and to make itself known to the others. It models three kinds of knowledge: own-skills, needed skills, personal information. (i) Own-Skills model what the agent can do. They allow the agent to determine whether it is able to execute a request from another agent. It also allows the agent to publish its skills to the community. (ii) Needed-Skills model what the agent needs from other agents. (iii) Personal-Information contains the agent's identification and functions: name, language, ontology, etc...

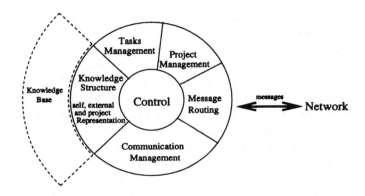

Fig. 1. Agent Architecture

External-Representation. It contains information concerning the other agents. Knowing which collaborators the agent may allows to optimize the work at different levels: to use the appropriate protocol; to address the request to the capable agent or to the most competent one; and to formulate the request in such a way that the other agent can understand it. We identify five kinds of knowledge: friend skills, request skills, short-comings, vocabulary, personal information (similar as self-representation). (i) Friend-skills store what the other agents can do. It is useful to determine quickly if another agent can satisfy a specific request. (ii) Request-Skills are stored in order to make possible and to accelerate the processing of a request. Indeed, it is interesting to store the knowledge about what the other agents could request. (iii) Short-Comings are needed for keeping information on the requests that could not be satisfied to avoid loss of time and resources. (iv) Vocabulary. The concepts manipulated by different agents may not always be exactly the same. We store the definitions of the concepts received from the other agents. In addition, we decided to time stamp the External-Representation knowledge in order to examine periodically its quality.

Project-Representation. A project is represented at two levels: project model, and project instance. (i) The project-model contains the skills (project-skills) required in the project and the associated useful information. The project-model can evolves with agent interactions. (ii) A project-instance represents a specific project based on the project-model. It can be active, suspended or finished.

3.4 Messages Routing

In OSACA, all agents networked in the same LAN can see and retrieve all the messages passing through the network. The retrieved messages are filtered and distributed by a dedicated process that places them in two waiting queues: W1 and W2. W1 contains the messages explicitly addressed to the agent (e.g. an answer) and W2 contains the messages retrieved by the agent but which were not addressed to it. The messages in W1 and W2 are processed in parallel by two different processes. Processing messages from W2 allows an agent to learn about other agents and about projects in progress.

3.5 Communication Management

Interactions among agents are structured using communication protocols, available as a protocol library. Managing several protocols allows an agent to increase the cooperation performance according to the operation to realize. Protocols can be classified in categories corresponding to the different kinds of operation. Protocols are derived from canonical Contract-Net Protocol [18], or based upon simple communications acts like request or answer.

Communication Primitives. We use a reduced number of communication primitives, to remain simple and efficient: announce, bid, request, inform, notice. Announce is a message that expresses the sender's intention to find one or more partner(s) to cooperate. Bid is a message that expresses the agent's willingness to cooperate with the sender of an Announce. Request is a message expressing the sender's intention to ask a specific agent to accomplish a service. Inform is a message intended to notify the result of an operation. This message is used as an answer to a Request. Notice is a message that express the sender's willingness to notify of any event (e.g., the acceptance or rejection of a commitment).

Communication Language. Our Inter-Agent Communication Language (IACL) has two layers: a message layer and a content layer. The message layer encodes a set of communication features that describe the parameters at the lower level of the message (e.g. sender, receiver, etc.). In addition, the message layer contains the minimal vocabulary necessary to overcome the problems concerning a common communication language between the agents. A communication language that is independent of the internal language used by the agents is the first step to making possible interactions among heterogeneous systems. The content layer is the actual content of a message, in the agent's own language representation.

Communication Protocols. An agent can use several communication protocols. In order to select a protocol, the agent considers its own needs as well as the needs of other agents. For instance, we suppose that an agent searches for another agent to perform a task such as the formatting of a list of references according to the IEEE format. The best choice is to give this task to several agents and to use the first answer. In this case, the agent decides to use B-Contract, instead of Contract-Net protocol. If it's impossible to decide, we can either try all the agent's protocols or use default protocol. We have adopted the latter solution using B-Contract as the default. B-Contract is a communication protocol derived from the original Contract-Net Protocol [18]. B-Contract specificity is a priority contract ("high" and "low"). The announcing and bidding tasks are similar to Contract-Net. However, after having evaluated the bids the manager awards a contract (with "high" priority) to the best bidder, and authorizes the other bidders to work on the contract (with "low" priority). Agents that receive a low priority contract will execute it only if they have nothing better to do. Whilst the manager waits for its answer, several events can occur, e.g. the contractor awarded a "high" priority answers before the other agents (normal situation); a contractor with a "low" priority answers before all the others (interrupt situation). In this case, the agent must reconsider its preference concerning the most appropriate contractor. A full description of events is given in [15].

We note that communication includes three different level, the common language among the agents (e.g. IACL), the discussion protocol (e.g. B-Contract, Contract-Net) and the message content (e.g. abstraction of a requested service).

3.6 Control

The control part of the agent contains the basic behaviors for cooperation with other agents. Currently, the only intention of a generic agent is to cooperate. It is possible to enrich the control by adding special mechanisms modeling other intentions. We concentrate on two behaviors: how can I say that I am competent? how can I determine which agent is competent enough to satisfy my needs?

We wrote that we store the needs expressed by the other agents. If a request corresponds to a modeled need, the own-skill is immediately found. If not, we consult the short-comings to avoid launching a heavier process to understand the request. However, if needed, the understanding process consists of asking the emitter to define the unknown concepts. Thus, the agent can determine whether or not it is competent. In both case, it learns from the process.

Candidates to send a request are found by following the links between the needed-skills and the friend-skills. This list goes to the communication manager that sends messages regarding the chosen strategies and the used protocol. The agents capable of satisfying it are memorized.

3.7 Tasks Management

The tasks are created to answer an external or internal request. Its management is carried out by a single monitor that manages a task waiting queue (Wtask) and a set of threads. The tasks have priority execution. The monitor allocates to each task a thread, waits for the operation execution, retrieves the result and passes it to the communication manager which returns the result to the requester. Free threads are allocates according to the task priority. The number of threads for a single agent is limited by δ to avoid a monitor bottleneck.

3.8 Projects Management

The project management enables the agent to learn about a project, diffusing information concerning it and evaluating the possibilities of automatically executing parts of a project. A project can be defined during the development of an agent, or as an answer to a request. In the latter case, the project model is built automatically. The agent then creates a project-instance depending on the project-model. In certain circumstances, it is possible to anticipate a request. If the skill associated to the request does not interfere with other work of the system, and if all the mandatory parameters of the skills and the associated conditions are satisfied, the skill is executed. To learn about projects, the project manager inspects all the received messages. If it identifies a new skill pertinent to the project and concerning the agent, it memorizes the skill in the project-model and enriches all the active corresponding project-instances.

3.9 External-Representation Management

We stress the fact that we only store the knowledge useful to the agent's work. Firstly, knowledge is collected during the exchanges with other agents. In a similar way, the agent has the ability to observe the message flow between other agents. It can deduce knowledge and react to it. For instance, the agent will inform another agent of its skills if it identifies a need of this other agent that it can satisfy. Secondly, in a more voluntary way, the agent sends a message to the other agents during its creation. The goal is to inform the others of its existence and to describe its skills in order to be known as quickly as possible. Such possibilities are implemented as skills of the agent, and thus are independent of the communication protocol.

4 Example

MEMOLAB and Ghostwriting. To illustrate how to implement an agent in the OSACA environment we will use an application developed in our group, MEMO-LAB [5]. The overall application is an experimental project intended to minimize the loss of collective knowledge in a research group. The idea in MEMOLAB is to offer a set of services that are helpful in daily work. When technically possible, some services encapsulate software tools directly related to the group's production activities. Other services are intended to improve efficiency by representing the laboratory's activities (notebooks, a group dictionary, etc.). All services are implemented as autonomous agents. Each user interacts with the system through his proxy agent. Thus, even after departure the proxy will be able to answer questions concerning its owner (goals, personal remarks, etc.).

Thereafter, we present how to proceed to define an OSACA agent. As example, we introduce Redac, an agent able to help with the writing of documents.

Implementation. An agent can request other agents to help it. The programmer does not know, when coding the skill, which agents will be present in the network during execution. To keep the coding process independent of the other agents, the programmer uses the standard "I/O" format supported by GAg. For instance, we consider a short scenario: a programmer codes a new skill to Redac, called Select-Reference, which adds to the user's selected-reference-list a new element. Working directly with bibliographic references is a job for a bibliographic agent. Thus, the programmer has only to indicate the information required inside the code of Redac's Select-Reference skill:

```
(send *com* '=Ask :content '(SELECT-REFERENCE))
```

To perform it, Redac uses its needed-skill to obtain the possible collaborators.

Implementing the knowledge base. This involves defining the concepts, relations, methods and services that Redac must possess. It can be coded in any language accessible by Redac through an API. The programmer then has a set of skills that characterize the services proposed by Redac.

Defining Redac as a minimal agent. One uses the m-defagent macro:

```
(m-defagent :name "REDAC" :author "HILTON" :var Redac
            :doc "Agent able to help on writing a technical document")
```

Modeling Redac's skills. We present the model of a Redac skill that formats a list of bibliographic references in agreement with a given format, Format-List:

```
(m-defskill :name "Format-List" :target "Format" :symbol 'SK1
            :parameters '((:parameter "list-name" :status "obligatory")
                          (:parameter "format-name" :status "obligatory")))
```

The target attribute refers to the method that embodies the skill.

Declaring the projects. The programmer defines the projects that Redac will manage. We present one of Redac's projects:

```
(m-defproject :name "Writing-Article")
```

Declaring the Project Skills. After defining the project, the programmer defines which skills belong to it. He/she can adapt those skills to the project context with optional attributes: influence, conditions and continuation.

```
(m-defprojectskill :project-name "Writing-Article"
                   :name "Select-Reference")
```

```
(m-defprojectskill :project-name "Writing-Article"
        :continuation "Check-List" :name "List-Formatting")
```

The Formatting-Reference skill, in this project, starts a Check-List procedure as soon as List-Formatting is performed.

Activating the Agent. The knowledge base, the agent's definition, the skill models, the projects and the project-skills are written by the programmer in a text file in this example called redac-agent.lisp. To activate Redac the programmer has only to execute the activate command:

```
(ActivateAgent :name "REDAC" :file "redac-agent.lisp" :host "kaa")
```

Once activated, Redac is accessible only by messages.

5   Conclusions and Future works

The Generic Agent (GAg) of the OSACA environment provides basic structures to represent the skills, needs and projects of an agent, as well as the skills of its acquaintances. It also supports request interpreting mechanisms. Having a protocol library allows GAg to improve the cooperation performance according to the kind of requested operation. In addition, using the B-Contract Protocol gives agents the possibility of dynamic task allocation with different priority levels. GAg is a solution for a fast and economic development of specialized agents created in a simpler manner by adding the necessary skills.

We have presented a first version of the generic agent. Our research work currently concerns the following topics: (i) allowing our agents to communicate with agents using only KQML; (ii) developing mechanisms using ontologies to understand concepts exchanged between agents; (iii) defining criteria to evaluate the response to a request.

References

1. Barthès J-P., (1994), Developing Integrated Object Environment for Building Large Knowledge Based Systems, Int. J. Human-Computer Studies, vol 41, pp. 33-58.
2. Bond H., Gasser L. (1988), What is DAI ?, Reading in DAI, Morgan Kaufman Publishers.
3. Brooks R. A., (1991), Intelligence without representation, AI, vol 47, pp. 139-159.
4. Cockburn D., Jennings N. R., (1995), ARCHON: A Distributed Artificial Intelligence System for Industrial Applications, in O'Hara G.M.P., Jennings N.R., ed., Foundations of DAI, Wiley.
5. de Azevedo H., Scalabrin E. E., Barthès J-P. A., (1995), Capitalisation des Connaissances d'un Groupe de Recherche à l'Aide d'une Population d'Agents Cognitifs, 3mes Journées Francophones IAD and SMA, St Baldoph, pp. 193-205.
6. Ferber J., Drogoul A., (1992), Using Reactive Multi-Agent Systems in Simulation and Problem Solving, in Avouris N.M., Gasser L., eds., Distributed Artificial Intelligence: Theory and Praxis, Kluwer Academic Publishers, pp. 53-80.
7. Finin T., Weber J., Wiederhold G., Genesereth M., Fritzson F., McKay D., McGuire J., Pelavin P., Shapiro S., (1993), Specification of the KQML Agent-Communication Language, Technical Report EIT TR 92-04, Enterprise Integration Technologies, Palo Alto, CA, Updated in July.
8. Gasser L., Braganza C., Herman N., (1987), MACE: a Flexible Testbed for Distributed AI Research, in Huhns M.N., eds., Distributed Artificial Intelligence, Vol. 1, Pitman Publishing, London, pp. 119-152.
9. Genesereth M. R., Ketchpel S. P., (1994), Software Agents, Communications of the ACM, vol 37(7), July, pp. 48-53.
10. Hayes-Roth B., (1995), An Architecture for Adaptative Intelligent Systems, Artificial Intelligence, vol 72, pp. 329-365.
11. Kolb M., (1995), CooL Specification, Technical Report, SIEMENS AG.
12. Kuokka D., Harada L., (1995), Matchmaking for information agents, Proceedings of the Joint Conference on Artificial Intelligence.
13. McGuire J., Kuokka D., Weber L., Tenenbaum J., Gruber T., Olsen G, (1993), SHADE: Technology for knowledge-based Collaborative Engineering, Concurrent Engineering Research and Application, vol 1(3).
14. Nishida T., Takeda H., (1993), Towards the knowledgeable community, Proceedings of the International Conference on Building and Sharing of Very Large-Scale Knowledge Bases, Japan Information Processing Development Center, Tokyo.
15. Scalabrin E. E., Barthès J-P. A., (1996), OSACA 1.0 : A Primer, Technical Report, Memo UTC/GI/DI/N 121, January.
16. Scalabrin, E. E., Barthès, J-P. A., (1993), OSACA: une architecture ouverte d'agents cognitifs indépendants, PRC-IA, Montpellier.
17. Singh N., (1994), A Common Lisp API and Facilitator for ABSI, Report Logic-93-4, Logic Group, Computer Science Departement, Stanford University, March.
18. Smith R. G., (1980), The Contract Net Protocol: High-Level Communication and Control in a Distributed Problem Solver, IEEE Trans. on Computers, C29(12), pp. 1104-1113.
19. Wooldridge M. J., Jennings N. R., (1994), Agent Theories, Architectures, and Languages: A Survey, Workshop on Agent Theories, Architectures and Languages, ECAI'94, Amsterdam.

Coordination Among Individually-Motivated Agents: An Evolutionary Approach

Ana L. C. Bazzan[1]

Forschungszentrum Informatik - University of Karlsruhe
Haid-und-Neu-str. 10-14,   76131 - Karlsruhe, Germany
e-mail: bazan@fzi.de

Abstract. Approaches which tackle coordination in multi-agent systems have mostly taken communication for granted. In societies of individually-motivated agents where the communication costs are prohibitive, there should be other mechanisms to allow them to coordinate when interacting. In this paper game theory is used as a mathematical tool for modelling the interactions among agents and as a mechanism for coordination with less communication. However we want to loose the assumption that agents are always rational. In the approach discussed here, agents learn how to coordinate by playing repeatedly with neighbors. The dynamics of the interaction is modelled by means of genetic operators. In this way, the behavior of agents as well as the equilibrium of the system can adapt to major external perturbations. If the interaction lasts long enough, then agents can asymptotically learn new coordination points.

1 Introduction

One of the central research topics in multi-agent systems is how to coordinate individually-motivated agents. This kind of agents usually have their own intentions, plans and knowledge, and are willing to solve their own local goals. If the global goal of the system is to solve a given problem, then a coordination mechanism is necessary to settle the conflicts which may arise either due to the need of allocating limited resources, or due to agents having opposite intentions. Former coordination mechanisms were mostly based on communication, as for instance the contract net protocol introduced by Smith and Davis (1981) in which a severe shortcoming is indeed the communication bottleneck.

The goal of our research is to develop an approach which minimizes, and possibly eliminates the need of communication when coordinating the agents' actions. Such approach would them suit domains like, for instance traffic signals control, where the communication cost is high and a communication-based coordination is very slow.

By bringing independent and individually-motivated agents to coordinate, it is desirable that they reach a state which is not only stable, thus worth being learned, but also as favorable as possible for every participant. Some researches which have been carried out in this direction have an economic flavor due to the use of either tools of classical game theory (e.g. Rosenschein and Zlotkin, 1994) or computational markets

---

[1] the author is supported by Conselho Nacional de Pesquisa Cientifica e Tecnológica - CNPq - Brasil.

(Wellman, 1992). We shall restrict ourselves to the game-theoretical approach. Indeed game theory provides tools for modelling the interaction among agents as well as their deductive process. Such tools lead them to anticipate the opponent's action and select the best answer to it. Conflicts are embedded in the utility function and solved implicitly as agents select the equilibrium points of the game.

We introduce this analysis to the problem of coordinating individually-motivated agents acting in the domain of traffic signal control, aiming at synchronazing signals positioned at neighboring intersections on a road. Agents are involved in a long run interaction in order to select signal plans which allow them to coordinate towards a specific strategy thus permitting the traffic on the whole road to flow in a better way. The main motivation for this approach is that it has the benefit of coping with interactions in which agents are fully individually-motivated and need only to know their own payoffs and not those of the opponents, thus modelling coordination with low or no communication requirements. Another positive characteristic is that a complex n-player game can be modelled as several 2-player games.

In the next section a brief overview on solution concepts from both classical and evolutionary game theory will be given regarding the situations where rationality fails. Learning how to play an equilibrium is the main topic of section 3 and in section 4 we discuss our implementation of the evolutionary approach in the traffic signal control scenario as well as the results of our simulations. We then conclude with section 5.

2 Solution concepts from the game theory: where rationality fails

The classical game-theoretic modelling assumes that the players are rational, i.e. they all make decisions in pursuit of their objectives, namely the maximization of the expected payoff in a utility scale. A solution for a given game is the best way of playing it for every player, even in antagonistic interactions among agents having individual, possible conflicting goals. By solving the game through *introspection*, agents can predict the equilibrium point of an interaction. This has been the motivation for the use of game-theoretical techniques as a mechanism of coordination.

In classical game theory this introspective or deductive process is possible because it is assumed that players are rational and have common knowledge to some extend. These are of course strong assumptions since players are not always fully rational in their actions. Bounded-rational players do experiment because they prefer to sacrifice the immediate gain in order to learn more about the rules of the interaction they are involved in.

Another problem with the game-theoretical approach is that the equilibrium point may not be unique. However uniqueness is crucial for the majority of multi-agent interactions. Agents which rely on this modelling to negotiate with other agents may not be able to act if they are not sure of which action other agents will choose. Therefore a mechanism is required which rules out some equilibria, eventually leading to a unique equilibrium point.

Apart from introspection, an alternative explanation as to how players choose their actions is to assume that they are able to *extrapolate* from what they have observed in past interactions, provided they have been involved in similar games. In this way the equilibrium point can be learned, which seems more plausible. Therefore players do not need to know how their actions influence their opponents' actions and vice-versa. Eventually, they learn that opponents do not play certain strategies. As each one learns its opponents' preferences, the system asymptotically converges to a state represented by a set of evolutionary stable strategies (ESS), which are equilibrium points.

This approach was first discussed by Maynard Smith and Price (1973) regarding evolution of populations of animals genetically programmed to play different strategies. As the more successful have higher fitness and as natural selection favors those which are fittest, after some generations the population reaches an ESS and cannot be invaded by a mutant strategy. In their work they were concerned only with the stability of equilibria against one-shot perturbations.

After this work the interest in such evolutionary techniques have also motivated studies in areas like economics and political science, where the main concerns have been the behavior of systems on the long run (by means of playing repeatedly), and the learning component.

An important milestone regarding evolution as a metaphor for learning is the study concerning the repeated Prisoners' Dilemma (RPD) which appeared in Axelrod (1984). Nowak and May (1992) also tackled the RPD problem and first explored the pattern which appears in a two-dimensional $n_x n$ square lattice. In each site of the grid a player plays the RPD only with the immediate neighbors. Their memorilessness and pure deterministic approach was later criticized in Huberman and Glance (1993) which have run asynchronous updating of strategies claiming that in this case the coexistence of cooperators and defectors were not possible anymore. Lindgren and Nordahl (1994) on their turn, achieved patterns of coexistence using cellular automata to update strategies in the sites of the grid, a way to avoid the synchronization issue.

Not only the Prisoners' Dilemma game has been analysed under the evolutionary approach. Kandori et al. (1993) were concerned with the coordination game (like that of fig. 2), where there exist more than one strict Nash equilibrium. Which one to select has been the concern of many researches in both classical and evolutionary game theory. However, in the evolutionary approach a player does not need to know anything but his own payoffs, one for each pair of strategies, thus requiring no information about opponents' payoff matrices. Therefore they do not rely on players' rationality.

3 Learning a coordination point

Evolution as a metaphor for learning in societies of bounded-rational players has been the subject of several studies like those cited in section 2. General assumptions has been a set of random matching in a population large enough, and myopic or bounded behavior of agents. Myopia means that an action which was learned as being effective remains effective in the future. The myopic behavior can be explained by the fact that agents may have high costs during the learning process. Another assumption which is often made is inertia, justified by the cost of changing strategy. Some shortcomings arising from all the above assumptions are:

i) bounded rational players ignore that opponents are also engaged in similar learning processes, therefore ignoring that what is being learned keeps changing. Inconsistencies may occur and players may not learn or may converge to false beliefs.
ii) players may not perform experimentation.

Different approaches have been described to tackle these shortcomings which account for distinct degrees of bounded rationality and informational requirements:

1) all players know their payoff matrix, which specifies the payoffs for *every combination of action* taken by the opponents. Also they have initial subjective beliefs about opponents' strategies and are informed of all previous actions taken. This solution is discussed in Kalai and Lehrer (1993).
2) a small portion of players are informed about the distribution of strategies in the population. As the rest, the uninformed, do not change their strategy, those informed can react by playing their best response, given that distribution (Fudenberg and Kreps, 1989).
3) players are not able to calculate a best response (like above) and just use other players' best strategy as entry for some kind of automaton which gives them the best strategy as output. In this category lies most of the research related to economical aspects and also that of Nowak and May (1992).
4) players neither observe the distribution of strategies in the population nor are able to calculate best responses. However interaction are repeated and players have enough time to observe the behavior of their opponents. Besides, there is a rate of experimentation due to mutant players. These players select a strategy at random, are informed about the payoff and attempt to learn the necessary reaction to the opponents' strategies in the infinitely repeated game.

It is clear that communication requirement decreases from approach 1 to 4. As one of the goals of bringing the evolutionary approach to the signal traffic control scenario is the minimization of communication, we were motivated by the last approach. Our emphasis is towards learning among bounded-rational agents in dynamic systems, where learning means experimentation and adaptation as in reinforcement learning. We assume that agents do not know anything regarding the game and learn about it from their past observations. In game theory, this topic is explored in Kalai and Lehrer (1993), who assume that players start with subjective beliefs about individual strategies used by each opponent. Since this involves initial communication, we want to loose this assumption. In similar a work Sastry et al. (1994) consider a game of incomplete and imperfect information in which players do not even need to know that opponents exist. After some periods of interaction, players update their probability distribution concerning each of the strategies, based solely on the current action and the payoff received. As players have no information concerning others, they learn in a decentralized fashion.

There is a criticism that this kind of "passive learning" can lead to steady states which are not equilibria. Need of active learning, i. e. with experimentation, was emphasized in Fudenberg and Levine (1993) who claim that even if the players play the same game many times, they may continue to hold incorrect beliefs about the opponents' preferences unless they perform enough experimentation. In our approach, this is done through genetic operators. For instance, strings are used to code the strategies chosen in the past, i.e. during the time interval between two learning processes. The stochastic events which may happen in the network affecting the strategies that agents are choosing, are modelled by mutations.

We propose a coordination mechanism aiming at allowing agents to learn from past interactions, instead of relying on pure introspection. Such mechanism is based on an experimental learning process. Even if agents possess only little local knowledge, which they get from sensing their near environment, they are able to perform experimentation and, according also to the experimentation performed elsewhere in the neighborhood, they receive a reinforcement in their payment function. This feedback can be either communicated to each agent by the neighbors or by a controller of the network, or can be exclusively locally detected. We have not yet implemented the former case, where we will be able to study the effect of communication in the learning process. Up to now we have been concerned with the case where there is no communication, hence agents are involved in a pure self-organization process where they receive a reinforcement due to their actions performed in the near past and this value is obtained from their local sensors only.

During the learning process, a fitness for each set of strategies played is computed and it influences the next generation of strategies which will be used by the agents to perform the experimentation. Depending on the frequency of the stochastic events, the new generations of strategies is fitter and by choosing them agents are able to coordinate towards the global goal.

4 Traffic Signal Coordination: an evolutionary approach

4.1 Traffic Signal Scenario

We have simulated a scenario represented by a network K consisting of a set of agents $A = \{A_1,...,A_n\}$ assigned to intersections. The goal in the traffic signal coordination is to bring as many neighbors as possible to use the same strategy (signal plan) since these are designed to allow vehicles to flow through the intersections in the main directions, namely eastward (E) or westward (W), without stopping at red lights. A coordination towards E or W is desired, depending on which one shows the higher flow of vehicles. In this sense, a neighborhood for A_i is defined as N_i and is composed of the agents immediately related to agent A_i, which are located along the E and W direction only, since in our scenario, the heavy traffic flows typically in these direction and the side streets in the N-S direction play a minor role for the control of the network. Each agent has a set of strategies $S = \{S_W, S_E\}$ to choose among before actually running the signal plan.

Fig. 1 shows such a network. The traffic signals aligned along those directions should coordinate towards one of them in order to deal with the flow of vehicles. The fact that agents give priority to one direction only means that this direction is allotted more green time, but of course the other three directions also receive green, and the general constraints posed by safety rules like minimum green time for each lane, minimum and maximum cycle time, etc. were respected when designing the signal plans.

Besides, each intersection has local information coming from detectors on the main lanes which deliver data about the traffic state on these lanes. Having this information, an agent A_i is able to decide which strategy to use. If currently signal plan S_W is running, hence giving priority to direction W, but direction E is demanding more time than W, the agent has to shift to signal plan S_E. This change certainly modifies traffic states at the neighborhood to some extend, thus eventually leading the immediate neighbors to also change to S_E. As this decision depends on certain thresholds, it might happen that neighbors do not change strategy. In this case it is desired that A_i returns to S_W by learning that it is better off when coordinating with neighbors.

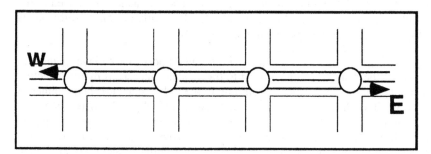

Fig. 1. Network of Traffic Intersections

As to what concerns the use of evolutionary techniques in the traffic signal coordination scenario, our research differs on a few points from those cited in the previous sections. First, in the traffic scenario the state of the network lasts hardly more than a few hours. After a major change happens, agents should re-coordinate and reach an equilibrium in short time. Of course it depends on how the thresholds that demand a change in traffic signal plans are set. Generally speaking the equilibrium, once reached, will last until a major change involving several neighbors happens.

Once an agent perceives a local change in its traffic state and changes strategy, it does not have reasons for believing that the neighbors will continue doing what they have done so far, because they all will get different payoffs from those they got in the past. In this way, it behaves like a new agent with no further knowledge apart from the local one and have to readapt to the new situation. Depending on the number of agents in this condition and of course whether they interact among themselves (are in the same neighborhood), the equilibrium point will eventually change. In general, for one agent to coordinate towards the opposite strategy it is necessary that it be surrounded by neighbors already running this strategy most of the time. And of course, once an agent has learned to play a strategy with high probability, the only way for it to experiment new strategies is through a change in the traffic patterns in its neighborhood. If such a change does not happen, agents will have no chance to coordinate with neighbors.

The second particularity in the traffic scenario is a consequence of its relatively unstable nature: it is desirable that agents do not need to communicate each change to the neighbors because this is not cost-effective. We thus depart from the standard assumptions made in classical game theory by not requiring that the agents have full knowledge of each others' strategies and that they have known prior distributions on any parameters of the game.

Third, the general assumption that the dynamics of the game is perturbed by stochastic shocks is already an intrinsic characteristic of the traffic domain, where the flow of vehicles entering and leaving the network in a given direction is stochastic. Therefore we do not employ any extra model for such shocks.

Finally, another important difference is that in the traffic scenario, it makes no sense for each agent to interact with the entire population. The interaction is reduced to the neighborhood N_i. It is worth noting that in a small population an equilibrium is reached faster but can still be upset by low mutation rates.

At each period, agents interact separately with the neighbors in a 2-player game and can play one of the strategies as an answer to traffic states measured by the detectors at the main lanes of the intersection. According to the traffic state, it is better either to play S_W or S_E. In each case, the choice results in a payoff which also depends on the strategy chosen by the neighbor. Due to the lack of communication among agents, the general traffic pattern remains unknown to them. If the trend is that traffic flows predominantly in the direction W, for instance, agents running strategy S_W are better paid than those running strategy S_E.

In game theory this is modelled by a move of Nature, which determines how agents are paid. In the example discussed below, agents are paid according to the values shown in the matrix M_W of fig. 2. That means that two neighbor agents running S_W get each a payoff of 2. If they are running S_E, they get each a payoff of 1. And finally, if they run opposite strategies they get zero. In case the flow of vehicles is in direction E, agents are paid according to the values shown in the matrix M_E of fig. 2.

These so-called pure coordination games have been extensively studied. There exist two equilibria in pure strategies: $G_W = (S_W, S_W)$ and $G_E = (S_E, S_E)$, one pareto-dominating the other. A third equilibrium in mixed strategies is reached when $1/3$ of the population plays the pareto-dominant equilibrium and $2/3$ plays the other equilibrium.

4.2 Model

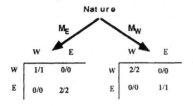

Fig. 2. Payoff Matrices for both moves of Nature

In order to model the events which happen in a real traffic network, a tool was developed in which the strategies chosen by the agents within time can be simulated. Such choices reflect the stochastic nature of the events, which are independent and decentralized, that means they happen at individual agent level. Events happen at discrete periods of time. At the beginning of the interaction, the traffic flow pattern is defined by a move of the Nature, which determines the payment for each agent. This information is not explicitly communicated to them, but they are able to deduce it by reading the detectors values. Then based on this local knowledge only, each agent has to decide which strategy to play at each period of time. The choices are recorded in a string. Depending on the strategies played in the neighborhood, each agent gets a payoff which is summed up regarding each strategy played.

At each period, there is a probability p_l for each agent to learn how good the set of strategies played in the near past. The more fit a string of strategies, the more the agent considers it as a good response to the behavior of the neighbors. Therefore, the agent runs it proportionally more often, until it detects a major change in the traffic situation at the intersection, i.e. a change which requires the shift of signal plan to give preference to the traffic in the opposite direction. Until such change is detected, the agent is better off if running the set of strategies which proved to be the best in the past. By doing this, agents may reach a coordination of traffic signals which is the global goal.

Besides the learning probability, at each stage agents have also a small probability of mutating. Mutation is important since it is a way to model the changes in traffic situations which occur at a local level. Without mutation the dynamics of the system and its final outcome would depend on the initial distribution of the strategies among agents. By allowing agents to react to local changes, the equilibrium may shift because one equilibrium point can upset the other if a sufficient number of agents suffers mutations. The higher the mutation rate, the more unstable the system. However there is another parameter which affects stability: the population size. For sufficiently large populations, an equilibrium can only upset another after an extremely long time. As populations here are small, this is not likely to happen.

Two kinds of mutation may happen. The first, with probability p_m, intends to model failures in the system causing one or more agents to lose the information already learned. The second kind of mutation happens with probability p_s and represents a traffic state change at the intersection, which is detected through the sensors. This demands a change in strategy regardless of what has already been learned.

A mutant strategy can either invade the neighborhood if it causes a modification in neighbors' traffic states or die out. In this last case, it dies also on the site where the mutation first happened, because after n periods the agent which has suffered the mutation learns to coordinate again and abandons its mutant strategy. This shows how the global goal of a neighborhood, namely coordination, upsets a local goal.

4.3 Results

Several scenarios have been simulated, varying the learning and mutation parameters and letting agents choose their strategies. Among the population, interactions between two neighbors can be of three types: they either select WW, EE or miscoordinated strategies (EW or WE). The number of times each type of interaction appears in the population is summed up in order to verify the pattern of each during time. Ideally, either WW or EE (depending on the matrix Nature has chosen) continually increases, while the other two types nearly disappears (apart from mutations). The time needed to reach this pattern of coordination is used as a measure of how fast the whole population coordinates.

Simulations show that the most important parameter is the learning frequency, which is determined by the learning probability p_l. If learning periods occur frequently, the neighborhood is quickly led to the equilibrium in mixed strategy, when 2/3 of the agents play one equilibrium and 1/3 plays the other. This is of course undesirable. Once agents have reach an equilibrium the only way to depart from it is through a mutation. However both kinds of mutation discussed above have small probability and the upsetting of this undesired equilibrium may take long.

On the other hand, if the learning frequency is low, it takes too long for agents to reach an equilibrium. In our scenario, it is desirable that agents react to a change and learn how to coordinate in a new situation within few cycles of the signal plan, i.e. within minutes. Simulations were carried out in order to calibrate the system regarding p_l. For the calibration, we have assumed that the goal of the agents (though unknown to them) was to coordinate towards the direction W. Therefore, Nature pays agents according to M_W and all pairs of agents are expected to reach the equilibrium $G_W = \{S_W, S_W\}$. This is exactly the situation of a morning or an evening peak when the heavy traffic flows preferentially in one direction. In general p_m is not large enough to affect the dynamics of the system. The probability of local change p_s, has varied from one in 100 (unstable scenario) to one in 300 (very stable scenario).

Simulations were repeated at least 50 times in each condition. In the very stable situation (p_s suffers one change of state in 300), and for p_l = 0.33 (one chance in 3 of learning) the time needed to coordinate is 10 cycles. In the less stable scenario (with p_s set to one in 100), the time needed to learn increases to 18 cycles.

Decreasing the learning frequency has a stronger effect on the time required to coordinate. In the stable situation it takes up to 198 cycles for a coordination to be reached, for the case where the learning frequency is one in 20. In less stable situations they have not even coordinated during the simulation horizon (200 cycles). Therefore, p_l has to be kept above 0.2 for any p_s if the coordination is to be achieved fast.

5 Conclusion

Although game theory has played an increasing role as a mathematical tool and language in multi-agent systems, its assumption concerning rationality is widely recognized as too strong. Another important criticism is that the classical game theory do not attempt to profit from the fact that agents can learn a deal by playing repeatedly. In the evolutionary game theory, rationality is replaced by natural selection and utility payoff by fitness. Therefore evolution has increasingly been seen as a metaphor for learning the equilibrium.

Concerning the state-of-the-art in multi-agents systems, these can profit from such an evolutionary approach as a mechanism of coordination which minimizes the need of communication once agents need not to know the goals of the neighborhood; they can play and learn it. For example in the scenario discussed here, agents perceive only their local goals which is not necessarily the major goal in the neighborhood.

The approach discussed here proved to be suitable for the traffic signal control scenario in which it is important that agents communicate as little as possible when coordinating towards a desired state. However once such equilibrium is reached, agents should not be stuck on it if Nature has changed their traffic states. On the contrary they should adapt to a new equilibrium. This is done by means of mutations introduced at an individual agent level. If on the one side this introduces instability in the system, on the other hand it is the opportunity for agents to re-coordinate. Moreover this instability also happens in the real traffic scenario when major changes in traffic states take place and the system, either centralized or decentralized, has to cope with it.

As for the extensions of the approach to other cases not covered here, we see no difficulty in extending the modelling to more complex situations where agents have a bigger set of strategies. However time needed to learn the coordination is likely to increase. Another issue that we want to investigate is the effect of communication in the learning process. In such situation, the reinforcement received from neighbors is likely to change the future actions of an agent to some extend. Agents have to find out which reinforcement were more truthful, which have contributed better, and so on.

References

Axelrod, R. (1984). *The Evolution of Cooperation*. Basic Books, New York.

Fudenberg, D. and D. Kreps (1989). A Theory of Learning, Experimentation and Equilibrium in Games. Stanford University. Cited in Kalai and Lehrer, 1993.

Fudenberg, D. and D. Levine(1993). Steady State Learning and Nash Equilibrium. *Econometrica*, **61**: 547-573.

Huberman, B.A. and N. S. Glance (1993). Evolutionary games and computer simulations. *Proc. Natl. Acad. Sci.*, **90**: 7716-7718.

Kalai, E. and E. Lehrer (1993). Rational Learning leads to Nash Equilibrium. *Econometrica*, **61**: 1019-1045.

Kandori, M., G.G. Mailath and R. Rob. Learning, mutation and long run equilibria in games. *Econometrica*, **61**: 29-56.

Lindgren, K. and M.G. Norhahl (1994). Evolutionary dynamics of spatial games. *Physica D*, **75**: 292-309.

Maynard Smith, J. and G. R. Price (1973). The logic of animal conflict. *Nature*, **246**: 15-18.

Nowak, M.A. and R.M. May (1992). Evolutionary games and spatial chaos. *Nature*, **359**: 826-829.

Rosenschein, J.S. and G. Zlotkin (1994). *Rules of Encounter*. The MIT Press, Cambridge (MA)-London.

Sastry, P.S., V.V. Phansalkar and M.A.L. Thathachar (1994). Decentralized Learning of Nash Equilibria in Multi-Person Stochastic Games with Incomplete Information. *IEEE Trans. on Systems, Man and Cybernetics*, **24**: 769-777.

Smith, R.G. and R. Davis (1981). Frameworks for cooperation in distributed problem solving. *IEEE Trans. on Systems, Man and Cybernetics*, **11**, 61-70.

Wellman, M. P. (1992). A general equilibrium approach to distributed transportation planning. In *Proc. of the tenth National Conf. on Artificial Intelligence*, San Jose, California.

Adaptive Hierarchical Censored Production Rule-Based System : A Genetic Algorithm Approach

K.K.Bharadwaj [*]
DCCE / IBILCE / UNESP, S.J.Rio Preto, SP, BRAZIL
E-mail : drkkb@nimitz.dcce.ibilce.unesp.br
and

Nabil M.Hewahi
Director, Computer Centre, Ministery of Housing
Biet Hanoun, Gaza Strip, ISRAEL

and
Maria Augusta Brandao
DCCE / IBILCE/UNESP, S.J.Rio Preto, SP, BRAZIL

Abstract

An adaptive system called GBHCPR (Genetic Based Hierarchical Censored Production Rule) system based on Hierarchical Censored Production Rule (HCPR) system is presented that relies on development of some ties between Genetic Based Machine Learning (GBML) and symbolic machine learning. Several genetic operators are suggested that include advanced genetic operators, namely, Fusion and Fission. An appropriate credit apportionment scheme is developed that supports both forwardand backward chaining of reasoning process. A scheme for credit revision during the operationsof the genetic operators Fusion and Fission is also presented. A prototype implementation is included and experimental results are presented to demonstrate the performance of the proposed system.

Keywords : Genetic Algorithm, Machine Learning, Hierarchical Censored Production Rules

1. Introduction

John Holland[10] introduced a method of studying natural adaptive system and designing artificial adaptive systems based on Darwinian natural selection and Mendelian genetics. This method eliminates weak elements by favoring retention of optimal and near optimal individuals (survival of the fittest), and recombines features of good individuals to perhaps make better individuals. Genetic algorithms(GAs) use this method to search the representation space of artificial adaptive systems, that represent a problem's search space as sequences(strings) of symbols chosen from somealphabet(usually a binary alphabet).The algorithm performs optimization by manipulating a finite population of chromosomes. In each of a number of cycles called generations, the GA creates a set of new chromosomes by crossover, inversion, and mutation, which correlate to processes in natural reproduction.

Like any other adaptive system, genetic based adaptive rule-based systems [4], [6], [13] have the ability to adapt, or learn, in response to their environment. and their

---

[*] On leave from the School of Computer and Systems Sciences, Jawaharlal Nehru University, New Delhi, INDIA-110067. The research of the first author is supported by the Brazilian foundation CNPq under Grant No. 301597/95-2.

ability to generate new rules helps the system to solve a large class of problems. Filtering capacity is also one of the advantages of genetic based adaptive systems in which such systems have low sensitivity to noise and incomplete information. However, since the representation of rules is a very low level one, designing the system messages, and observing its behaviour is quite difficult. On the other hand application of genetic algorithm to higher level rule languages[1], [5], [7], makes it easier to incorporate existing knowledge, to explain the knowledge learned through experience, and to combine several forms of learning in a single system.

The first attempt to use the standard rule structure (<*IF* condition *THEN* action>) in GBML was presented by stackhouse and Zeiglar [13]. The system combines a simplified symbolic production system with tailored genetic-like operators in the learning of a robot navigation problem.

As an extension of standard Production Rule, Michalski and Winston [12] proposed the Censored Production Rule (CPR) of the form (<*IF* Condition *THEN* Action *UNLESS* Censor>) as an underlying representational and computational mechanism to enable logic based systems to exhibit variable precision in which certainty varies while specificity stays constant. To address the various problems and shortcomings with CPRs system , Bharadwaj and Jain[2] have introduced a concept of Hierarchical Censored Production Rule (HCPR). A HCPR is a CPR augmented with specificity and generality information which can be made to exhibit variable precision in the reasoning such that both certainty of belief in a conclusion and its specificity may be controlled by the reasoning process. Such a system has numerous applications in situation where decision must be taken in real time and with uncertain information [2].

In this paper, we present an adaptive system called GBHCPR (Genetic Based Hierarchical Censored Production Rule system).The system that relies on development of some ties between GBML and symbolic machine learning. We suggest genetic operators for the HCPRs system and also develop an appropriate credit assignment scheme.

2. The GBHCPR System

The GBHCPR system is based on the HCPRs system presented by Bharadwaj and Jain[2]. Following [2], the general form of HCPR is :

> (< Action *IF* Condition
>   *UNLESS* Censor
>   *GENERALITY* General-information
>   *SPECIFICITY* Specific-information >)

A few related HCPRs are given below and it is shown how they are linked in a HCPR-tree structure, as depicted in Fig. 1.(This represents a rule-base to find answers to queries of the type " What is X doing?" when supplied with relevant input data) :

{*level* 0}
Is_in_city(X,Y) *IF* [Lives_in_city(X,Y)]
               UNLESS [Is_on_tour(X)]
               GENERALITY [ ]
               SPECIFICITY [Is_at_home(X) , Is_outside_home(X)]

{*level* 1}
Is_at_home(X) *IF* [Time(night)]
               UNLESS [Is_doing_overtime(X) , Works_in_night_shift(X)]
               GENERALITY [Is_in_city(X,Y)]
               SPECIFICITY [ ]

Is_outside_home(X) *IF* [Time(day)]
               UNLESS [Is_ill(X) , Watching_TV(X) , Bad_weather]
               GENERALITY [Is_in_city(X,Y)]
               SPECIFICITY [Is_working_outdoor(X),
                                    Is_entertaining_outdoor(X)]

{*level* 2}
Is_working_outdoor(X) *IF* [Day(working)]
               UNLESS [National_holiday, Is_unemployed(X)]+
               GENERALITY [Is_outside_home(X)]
               SPECIFICITY [ ]

Is_entertaining_outdoor(X) *IF* [Day(Sunday)]
               UNLESS [Met_an_accident(X)]
               GENERALITY [Is_outside_home(X)]
               SPECIFICITY [ ]

X is_in_city Y

X is_at_home   **X is_out_side_home**

X is_working_outdoor   **X is_entertaining_outdoor**

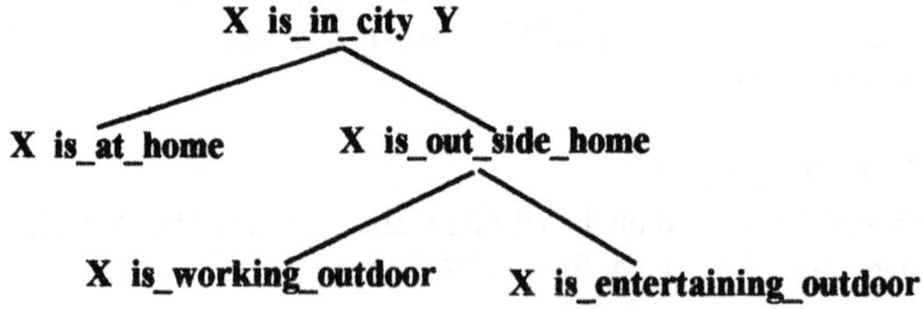

Fig.1. A HCPR-tree for life queries.

Here (Fig.1.), any HCPR is a more specific case of its parent. Thus, the root HCPR represents the most general concept. Once this is verified, we can descend to its children for more specific information, depending on our requirement and resources available. If any HCPR we reach is blocked, either due to one of the preconditions being false or one of the censor conditions being true, there is no need for any further search of its children. The hierarchical structure of the HCPR tree has played a very crucial role in the development of the proposed system, especially in the development of various genetic operators. GBHCPR system slightly resembles some of the recent work on genetic programming, because the modified operators work on tree structure[11]. However, the tree structure of HCPR-trees under the GBHCPR system is unique.

2.1. The Basic Cycle
The basic cycle of GBHCPR is divided into two phases. The algorithms corresponding to the two phases are given below.

Phase-I
Input : Master HCPR-tree set
The master set is the initial ad hoc knowledge base which may not be able to solve all the problems but must contain enough conditions, actions, specificity and generality to allow state transitions necessary for an acceptable solutions to all the problems in P. However HCPR-trees may not necessarily be optimal, reasonable or even properly structured.
Output :Two working HCPR-tree sets for each problem
Phase-I (Fig.2 (a).) is divided into two stages, where in the first stage, two transit sets TRS-I and TRS-II are generated thereby two ad hoc HCPR-tree sets WS-I and WS-II are constructed for each problem , and during the second stage these two ad hoc sets undergo evolutionary process thereby improving their ability to solve more problems if possible. The competition between the two working sets, WS-I and WS-II, expedite the learning process.

Phase- II
Input : Working sets WS-I and WS-II for each problem set and the master HCPR-tree set.

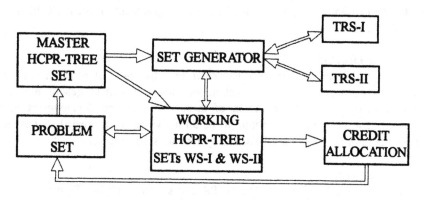

(a)

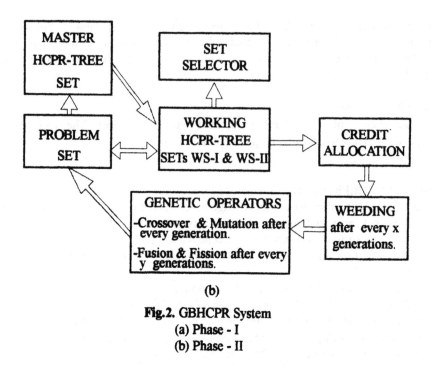

Fig.2. GBHCPR System
(a) Phase - I
(b) Phase - II

Output : One Mature Set (MS) for each problem.
Mature set is the set which is able to solve all the problems in the problem set or it is the better set of the two working sets in terms of the number of problems it can solve.

The GBHCPR system operates in a loop during this phase (Fig.2.(b).)steps are repeated until either all problems are solved or maximum number of generations is reached. GBHCPR system at the end chooses better of the two working sets WS-I and WS-II (the one having higher credit) as the final genetically learned HCPR-tree set, called the Mature Set (MS).

2.2. Genetic Opretors

Development of genetic operators has been an active area of research and since genetic operators are one of the most important component of genetic algorithms, further investigation and application of these operators and development of new advanced genetic operators continue to be an active research area[6]. A number of genetic operators suitable for GBHCPRs system are suggested below:

A. *Set Crossover*

This is performed by selecting one HCPR-tree set from TRS-I (TRansit Set I) and another from TRS-II (TRansit Set II) (TRS-I and TRS-II are sets containing HCPR-trees sets and explained latter in the algorithm), which are then cut and crossed.

B. *Inversion*
The inversion operator applied to a set of HCPR-trees first specifies two HCPR-trees indicating the beginning and the end of the sequence of HCPR-trees to be inverted and then inverts the chosen sequence of HCPR-trees resulting in a new form (ordering) of HCPR-tree set.

C. *AND Algorithm for Independent HCPRs*
The AND algorithm combines two independent HCPRs chosen at random into a new higher order HCPR.

D. *Scaling Algorithm for a Linear System*
In a linear system[15], the condition C repeated N times should produce the sequence of N identical actions A. Hence the HCPR

[A] *IF* [C]   [N*A] *IF* [N*C]
    UNLESS [k]   generates   *UNLESS* [k]
    GENERALITY [G]   *GENERALITY* [G]
    SPECIFICITY [X1,X2,X3]   *SPECIFICITY* [X!,X2,X3]

E. *HCPRs Crossover*
The crossover suggested in [15] for standard rule structure can be extended to HCPR system as explained below. Given two HCPRs

[A11] *IF* [p1,p2]   [B12] *IF* [p9,p5,p3]
    UNLESS [k1]   and   *UNLESS* [k2]
    GENERALITY [A1]   *GENERALITY* [B1]
    SPECIFICITY [A111,A112]   *SPECIFICITY* [B121]

the application of crossover would generate the following new HCPRs (by swapping the condition parts in the above HCPRs) :

[A11] *IF* [p9,p5,p3]   [B12] *IF* [p1,p2]
    UNLESS [k1]   and   *UNLESS* [k2]
    GENERALITY [A1]   *GENERELITY* [B1]
    SPECIFICITY [A111,A112   *SPECIFICITY* [B121]

F. *Mutation*
  Two types of mutation operators are proposed for the GBHCPR system.
(a) HCPR mutation
(b) HCPR-tree mutation
Based on intragenic mutation[6],[9], HCPR mutation is suggested that would remove redundant or unrelated conditions from the HCPR depending on some mutation probability value. Following example illustrates the usefulness of this operator :

Let us consider the HCPR
    John is at home *IF* [It is sunday, It is raining , John has a car]
                UNLESS [John is sleeping , John is doing overtime]
                GENERALITY [ ]
                SPECIFICITY [ ]

in which [John has a car] is a redundant condition and [John is sleeping] is unrelated censor condition. Application of HCPR mutation operator may produce a better rule :

John is at home *IF* [It is sunday, It is raining]
> *UNLESS* [John is doing overtime]
> *GENERALITY* [ ]
> *SPECIFICITY* [ ]

Under HCPR-tree mutation, the children of two siblings chosen at random from a HCPR-tree are exchanged

G. *Fusion*

Fusion as a genetic operator is a combination of two HCPR-trees to generate one or more new HCPR-trees:

Fusion (HCPR$_i$, HCPR$_j$) $\rightarrow$ HCPR$_k$

such that cr(HCPR$_k$) = cr(HCPR$_i$) + cr(HCPR$_j$), where HCPR$_i$ and HCPR$_j$ are the parents, and HCPR$_k$ is the offspring. cr(HCPR$_i$) is the credit of the ith HCPR-tree.

Here the two HCPR-trees HCPR$_i$ and HCPR$_j$ are related satisfying the condition,

Ri $\cap$ Rj $\neq \phi$, where Ri and Rj are the sets representing condition (properties) parts of the HCPRs corresponding to the root nodes in HCPR$_i$ and HCPRj respectively.

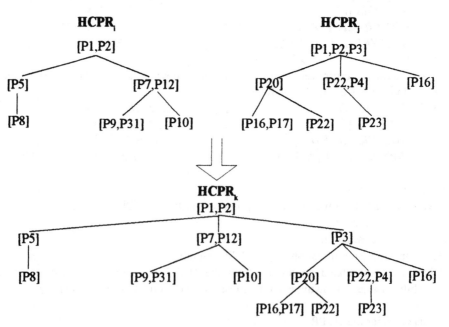

Fig.3. Illustration of Fusion operation between HCPR$_i$ and HCPR$_j$ generating HCPR$_k$ (case a).

Under this condition the following two cases would arise :

case a. $R_i \subseteq R_j$ or $R_j \subseteq R_i$

case b. $R_i \not\subset R_j$ and $R_j \not\subset R_i$

The Fusion operator can be considered as a heuristic crossover because it is similar to the crossover genetic operator in the sense that a newly generated HCPR-tree gets its characteristics from both the parents which are chosen at random. Clearly the offspring $HCPR_k$ bears a structural relationship to both the parents $HCPR_i$ and $HCPR_j$. Fig.3. illustrates Fusion operation (Case a). During the Fusion operation, how to randomly generate sub HCPR-trees and perform credit revision are the two main issues. (see [8])

H. *Fission*

Fission is a process which is applied in general after Fusion to restructure a HCPR-tree. Fission operator causes a change in a HCPR-tree 's structure creating a new HCPR-tree and can be regarded as genetic mutation operator. The general form of Fission operator can be given as

$$\textit{Fission}(HCPR_i) \rightarrow (HCPR^*_i) \text{ , where } cr(HCPR^*_i) = cr(HCPR_i).$$

During Fission operation the $HCPR_i$ tree chosen for restructuring is removed while the resultant $HCPR^*_i$ tree is retained. The credit revision during Fission involves almost the same technique as that of credit revision during Fusion[see [8]).

2.3 Credit apportionment scheme

The credit apportionment scheme developed is a genetic reward scheme based on Stackhouse and Zeiglar[13] and Westerdale[14]. The rational behind the proposed formulae for credit apportionment is the assumption that, the measure of performance of the HCPR-tree set depends on the utilization of HCPRs and HCPR-trees included in the set. The proposed scheme divides the payoff to all HCPRs participating in the solution path according to their importance and complexity. The credit of a HCPR-tree is the accumulated credit of its constituent HCPRs and the credit of a HCPR-tree set is the accumulated credit of its trees (see[8]).

3. Implementation and Experimental Results

GBHCPR system is implemented in muLISP 87 using *Frame* structure to represent HCPR-trees. A master set (ad hoc knowledge base) was fabricated consisting of 74 HCPRs forming 19 HCPR-trees. Three experiments are conducted to show the performance of the proposed system in which nineteen problems are to be solved. The first experiment is conducted using a master set (ad hoc knowledge base) initially capable of solving only five problems. Two more experiments were conducted using better structured initial master sets (initially capable of solving ten and fifteen problems) to test the effect of initial knowledge structure on the system's behaviour. A comparision between the average performance of the system for the three cases is shown in Fig.4.

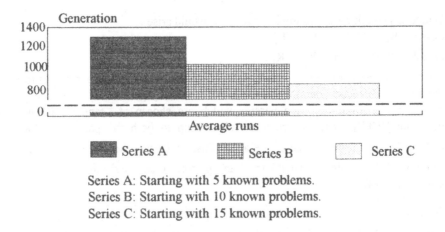

Series A: Starting with 5 known problems.
Series B: Starting with 10 known problems.
Series C: Starting with 15 known problems.

Fig.4. Average of three diferent runs under Equipment selection.

4. Conclusion

An adaptive system based on Hierarchical Censored Production Rules (HCPRs) system has been presented that relies on development of some ties between a combined approach of Genetic-Based Machine Learning and symbolic machine learning. Several genetic operators are suggested that suit the proposed system including advanced genetic operators, namely, Fusion and Fission. An appropriate credit apportionment scheme is developed that takes care of forward as well as backward chaining of reasoning process.

It is shown how the structure of the initial knowledge base affects the performance of the system and the results confirm that better is the structure of the initial knowledge base, a fewer number of generations are required. However, as expected, the problems corresponding to the upper level nodes are learned faster as compared to the more specific problems corresponding to the lower level nodes in HCPR-trees

It may be seen that the inherent parallelism [3] in the hierarchical structure of HCPRs is used to adapt the proposed scheme for Parallel Distributed processing to improve its efficiency and accuracy.Another significant area of further research would be to explore possibility of handling other problem domains using the GBHCPR system.

5. References

[1] J.Bala, K.De Jong, and P.Pachowicz, "Using genetic algorithms to improve the performance of classification rules produced by symbolic inductive methods," in Z.W.Ras and M.Zemankova (Eds.), Methodol., for Intelligent Systems, 6th Inter. Symposuim, Charlotte, N.C., USA, pp 286-295, 1991.

[2] K.K.Bharadwaj and N.K.Jain, "Hierarchical Censored Production Rules (HCPRs) System," Data and Knowledge Engineering, vol.8, (North Holland), pp 19-34, 1992.

[3] K.K.Bharadwaj and Renu Varshneya " Parallelization of Hierarchical Censored Production Rules (HCPRs) System" Information and Software Technology, Butterworth- Heinemann(UK), vol.27,No.8,pp453-460,1995.

[4] K.A.De Jong, "Genetic-algorithms based learning," in Y.Kodraloff and R.S.Michalski (Eds.), Mchine Learning: An Artificial Intelligence Approach, vol.3, Morgan Kaufmann Publishers, Los Altos, CA, pp 611-637,1990.

[5] S.Forrest, "A study of parallelism in the classifier system and its applications to classification in KL-ONE semantic networks," Ph.D. dissertation, Ann arbor, University of Michigan, 1985.

[6] D.E.Goldberg, "Genetic-based machine learning: whence it came,where it's going," in M.S.Elzas, T.I.Oren, and B.P.Zeiglar, Eds. Model. and Simul. Methodol.,knowledge systems paradigms,Elsevier Science Publishers B.V. (North Holland), 1989.

[7] J.Grefestette, "A system for learning control strategies with genetic algorithms," 3rd Inter. Conf. on Genetic Algorithms, Fairfax, VA.Morgan Kaufmann Publishers, pp 183-190, 1989.

[8] N.M.Hewahi ,Genetic Algorithm approach for Adaptive Hierarchical Censored Production Rule-Based System, Ph.D dissertation, School of Computer and Systems Sciences, Jawaharlal Nehru University, New Delhi, India, 1994.

[9] J.H.Holland, "Escaping brittleness: The possibilities of general-purpose learning algorithms applied to parallel rule-based systems," in R.S.Michalski, J.G.Carbonell, and T.M.Mitchell, Eds. Machine Learning: An Artificial Intelligence Approach, 1986.

[10] J.H.Holland, "Adaptation in natural and artificial systems," Ann Arbor: The University of Michigan press, 1975.

[11] J.R.Koza, "Genetic programming on programming of computers by means of natural selection", MIT, 1992.

[12] R.S.Michalski and P.H.Winston, " Variable Precision Logic,"Artificial Intelligene, vol.29, pp 121-145, North Holland, 1986.

[13] C.P.Stackhouse and B.P.Zeiglar, "Learning plateaus in adaptive Rule-Based system," in M.S.Elzas, T.I.Oren, and B.P.Zeiglar, Eds. Model. and Simul. Methodol., Knowledge Systems' paradigms, Elsevier Science Publishers B.V.(North Holland), pp 359-379, 1989.

[14] T.H.Westerdale, "A reward scheme for production systems with overlapping conflict sets," IEEE Trans. on Sys., Man,and Cyber., vol. SMC-16, no.3, pp 369-383, May/June 1986.

Finding Optimal Representations
Using
the Crossover Correlation Coefficient

Piet Spiessens and Bernard Manderick[1]

Computer Science Department, Vrije Universiteit Brussel, Pleinlaan 2, B–1050 Brussel. Email: bernard@arti.vub.ac.be

Abstract. In order to apply genetic algorithms (GAs) successfully to a given problem one has to find a good representation for potential solutions to that problem. Roughly speaking a good representation is one where building blocks for the problem's solution are relatively insensitive to crossover disruption, i.e., the building blocks have short defining lengths. However, such a representation is difficult to find if heuristic or background knowledge about the problem is lacking.

In this paper, it is shown how the GA itself can be used to first search for a good representation for a given problem and subsequently solves that problem using the found representation. The main question we have to address is how a representation can be evaluated without solving the problem first. The hypothesis put forward is that a good representation is one for which crossover shows a high correlation between the fitnesses of parents and their offspring.

1 Introduction

One major decision to be taken when using the GA concerns the representation problem: How do we encode potential solutions to a problem as bitstrings. In this paper, we consider only bitstring representations. The way the coded information is distributed over the genotype is very important for the performance of the GA. According to the schema theorem, defining bits of a building block should be put together on the genotype in order to minimize crossover disruption – see Section 2 for details.

Knowing in advance the building blocks requires prior knowledge about the problem to be solved and the lack of this knowledge is exactly what makes a problem hard. The power of the GA is that it considers problems as a black box. Coding potential solutions and assigning fitnesses to them are the only requirements for its application. No other knowledge about the problem is needed.

So, we face a dilemma here. In order to apply the GA successfully we need a good representation but to find one we need prior knowledge about the problem at hand. Either this knowledge is available and then heuristic or knowledge-based techniques are probably better. Or we lack this knowledge and run the risk that we encode interacting pieces of information far apart on the genotype and this might prevent the GA from finding high quality solutions.

Two approaches to tackle the representation problem are possible. A first one is to extend the GA so that it can search for a good representation at the same time that it is searching for good solutions. In order to do so, new genetic operators and new encoding schemes are required. The first attempts in this direction already date back to 1972, but we had to wait until the introduction of messy GAs to see success along this line [4].

A second approach is to search first for a good representation and once it is found to use it to optimize the problem at hand. The main question to be addressed here is: How can a representation be evaluated without solving the problem first. The hypothesis put forward in this paper is based on fitness landscape analysis [7] and states that a good representation is one for which crossover shows a high correlation between the fitnesses of parents and their offspring.

The rest of the paper is organized as follows. First, we explain the representation problem using a 30-bit deceptive problem. In Section 3, we argue that the correlation coefficient ρ_x of the crossover operator can be used to evaluate different representations. Third, we discuss the performance of the approach introduced in Section 3 on two test problems and conclude. For more experiments we refer to [10].

2 The Representation Problem

First, we introduce the 30-bit deceptive problem and then we discuss and illustrate the importance of the genetic representation for the performance of the GA using this problem.

The representation problem we try to solve is the following: given a bitstring representation for a problem, find an reordering of the genes scuh that crossover disruption is minimal. Such a representation will be called an *optimal representation*. The representation we start with is called the *standard representation* and each reordering can be represented by a permutation of the genes as they appear in the standard order. We will also use the word ordering instead of representation.

The 30-bit deceptive problem is used as a bench mark in our experiments since it is very hard and even impossible to solve if the optimal representation is not known in advance. Moreover, messy GAs could find this optimal representation [4].

2.1 A 30-bit deceptive problem

Deceptive problems are constructed in such a way that they mislead the GA. The simpliest fully deceptive problem [4] is defined for bitstrings of length 3. The function values for each string are displayed in Table 1.

Genotype	Fitness	Genotype	Fitness
000	28	100	14
001	26	101	0
010	22	110	0
011	0	111	30

Table 1. The 3-bit problem with deceptive ordering

From Table 1 it can be verified immediately that besides the global optimum 111 there is one local optimum 000. Moreover, according to the schema theorem [5, 3] the search will be biased towards the local optimum 000.

Ten of these 3-bit problems can be combined into a 30-bit problem. The corresponding fitness function is obtained by summing the fitness values of the 10 subproblems, and has $2^{1}0$ local optima.

Whether the 30-bit problem can be optimized by the GA depends on the ordering of the genes [4]. If the 3-bit subproblems are simply concatenated, i.e., the ordering is

$$1\ 2\ 3\ 4\ 5\ 6\ldots 28\ 29\ 30$$

where the genes $3(i - 1) + 1$, $3(i - 1) + 2$ and $3(i - 1) + 3$ correspond with the bits of the ith 3-bit subproblem, $i = 1, \ldots 10$. In other words, co-adapted genes are near each other (the linkage is tight) and it is possible to solve the problem because we have a good ordering.

On the other hand, if the linkage is loose, i.e., the ordering of genes is

$$1\ 4\ 7\ldots 2\ 5\ 8\ldots 3\ 6\ 9\ldots 24\ 27\ 30$$

then no GA can solve the problem.

For a random ordering of genes, some of the 3-bit subproblems can be optimized by a GA (on average 25 %), but the global solution will not be found.

2.2 Representations and GA-performance

As already noted in [4], building blocks are the key to understand the relation between GA-performance and the representation used.

The *Schema Theorem* [5, 3] provides the following lower bound on the growth of the expected number of members $m(H, t)$ of the schema H:

$$m(H, t + 1) \geq m(H, t)\frac{f_t(H)}{\hat{f}_t}\left(1 - p_X \cdot \frac{\delta(H)}{l - 1} - p_\mu \cdot o(H)\right)$$

where $m(H, t)$ and $m(H, t + 1)$ are the number of instances of the schema H at time t and $t + 1$, $f_t(H)$ is the average fitness of the members of H in the population at time t, $\hat{f}_t$ is the average fitness of the whole population at time t, l is the genotype length, p_X is the crossover probability, p_μ is the mutation probability, $\delta(H)$ is the defining length of the schema H, and $o(H)$ is the order of H.

This theorem indicates that members of short, low-order schemata with above average fitness, the so-called *building blocks*, experience exponential growth in the population.

Moreover, it also makes clear that schemata with long defining lengths are more susceptible to disruption by the crossover operator than short schemata. This observation implies that a problem can be solved more efficiently by the GA *if its representation is chosen such that above-average schemata have short defining lengths*. Put in biological terms, we can say that co-adapted genes must be near each other, or that the linkage must be sufficiently tight.

Crossover disruption can be minimized by choosing a representation where the linkage is sufficiently tight. In general however, it is very difficult to provide this representation a priori because not enough is known about the problem, i.e., the problem is considered as a black box. In many cases, having no information about which genes are co-adapted is precisely what makes the problem hard.

Another problem associated with representations is schemata deceptiveness. This problem stems from the premise that building blocks (the short, low-order schemata with above-average fitness) will combine to form ever longer above-average schemata that will eventually contain the bit strings with optimal fitness, i.e. the *building block hypothesis*). Representations that do not satisfy this requirement are called deceptive. In such a case the GA is led to the wrong parts of the search space and never converges to the global optima.

As with crossover disruption, it is virtually impossible to provide the GA a priori with a representation that is not deceptive. Again, the only possibility seems to search for such a representation.

The above observations explain why the GA is very successful on the deceptive problem of Section 2.1 when the tight ordering is used, much less successful for a random ordering, and fails for the loose ordering.

3 Optimizing Representations using ρ_χ

In this section, we use fitness landscape analysis [7] and argue that for optimal orderings the correlation coefficient ρ_χ of the (two-point) crossover operator χ is high since such orderings also minimize crossover disruption. This argument allows us to first search for an optimal ordering for a given problem and then use that ordering to solve that problem.

To make the above argument plausible, we first define the crossover correlation coefficient ρ_χ. In the next subsections, we explain how we represent orderings, how we evaluate them using ρ_χ, and how we search for optimal orderings.

3.1 The Crossover Correlation Coefficient ρ_χ

Suppose that we have a series of pairs of parents $(p_{i_1}, p_{i_2}, i = 1, \cdots, N$, and that we apply to each pair two-point crossover to generate the corresponding offspring c_i. Suppose also that F_{p_i} is the mean fitness of the ith parent pair and that F_{c_i} is the fitness of their offspring. This way, we obtain a series of mean parent fitnesses F_{p_i} and a series of offspring fitnesses $F_{c_i}, i = 1, \cdots, N$. The correlation coefficient ρ_χ of the two-point crossover is defined as the correlation coefficient between these two series – see [7] for more details.

This ρ_χ makes it possible to evaluate different orderings. On the one hand, if the ordering is optimal then co-adapted genes of two parent genotypes remain intact in the offspring, since the chance of crossover disruption is very small. Consequently, the average fitnesses of the parents and their offspring will be highly correlated, i.e. ρ_χ will be high. On the other hand, if gene linkage is not tight, co-adapted genes are separated from each other, and ρ_χ will be low.

In other words, the crossover correlation coefficient ρ_χ makes it possible to predict the amount of crossover disruption for a particular ordering: crossover disruption is minimized and ρ_χ is maximized for optimal representations.

The advantage of using the correlation coefficient ρ_χ is that the search does not need to be conducted at the same time good solutions are sought. This will be explained in Section 3.4.

3.2 Representation of Orderings

Since there are no two simultaneous searches, one for the optimal representation and one for the optimum of the problem, we do not need the extended genotype representation as used for example in messy GAs [4]. We do not need the value of genes, only their position. We will therefore code a representation as a permutation P in integer-string form. If G_1 is a genotype in the standard representation provided by the user (gene one in first position, gene two in the second position, and so on), P is the permutation encoding the new representation, then $G_2 = P.G_1$ gives the genotype in the new representation.

For example, if G_1 is the genotype

$$1\ 0\ 1\ 1\ 0$$

and the permutation matrix P is

$$\begin{pmatrix} 0\ 0\ 1\ 0\ 0 \\ 1\ 0\ 0\ 0\ 0 \\ 0\ 0\ 0\ 1\ 0 \\ 0\ 0\ 0\ 0\ 1 \\ 0\ 1\ 0\ 0\ 0 \end{pmatrix}$$

which we can code as the integer string

$$3\ 1\ 4\ 5\ 2$$

then G_2 is given by $P.G_1$ which is equal to

$$1\ 1\ 1\ 0\ 0$$

3.3 Evaluation of Orderings

In order to calculate the crossover correlation coefficient ρ_χ for a particular representation, a random sample of pairs of parents is needed and for each pair we have to generate crossover points in order to apply two-point crossover.

We decided to do this only once, and use it to evaluate all representations. This has two advantages. First, we avoid having noisy fitnesses for orderings. If different orderings have different ρ_χ then this has to be related to the ordering itself since all other things remain equal. If we were to take new samples for every ordering, a comparison between two ordering would be less accurate. Second, the computation time reduces significantly. The fitnesses of the parents need to be computed only once. A disadvantage is that the search might be biased towards this sample.

The calculation of the ρ_χ for a particular ordering proceeds as follows. Suppose that the ordering is represented by the permutation matrix P.

- Using P, the fixed sample of pairs of parents is converted from the standard ordering to the ordering that is being evaluated.
- The two-point crossover operator is applied to all parent pairs. Also the crossover points are chosen only once. Furthermore, the crossover points are not chosen uniformly. Instead, the distance between the two points is chosen from a binomial distribution with mean $l/2$, where l is the genotype length. This way, we get a maximal amount of crossover disruption information from the sample of parent pairs.
- After the crossover operation we have the offspring in the new ordering. Before the fitnesses of the offspring can be computed, they have to be transformed back to the standard ordering. This means that we first have to compute the inverse of the permutation matrix P which is same as its transposition, i.e. $P^{-1} = P^T$
  If G is a genotype in the new ordering, $P^{-1}.G$ gives the genotype in the standard ordering.
- The fitnesses of the offspring are computed.
- Finally, the fitnesses of the parents and their offspring are used to calculate the crossover correlation coefficient ρ_χ of the new ordering.

It is clear that the larger the sample, the more accurate the ρ_χ will be. If the sample size is small, not enough different allele combinations of co-adapted genes will be present, and the ρ_χ could be misleading. In our experiments, we have not experimented with the sample size. We have taken a fixed, but fairly large sample size: 2×1024 parents.

In Figure 1, we summarize the evaluation of an ordering.

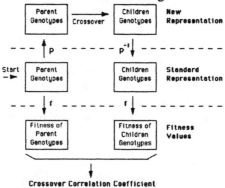

Fig. 1. The evaluation of a ordering

3.4   Search for Optimal orderings

Since any ordering can be represented as a permutation of the genes in the standard ordering, we can use the ordering GA to search for the optimal ordering. The ordering GA uses permutations as representations instead of bitstrings. Many mutation and crossover operators from which we have to choose exist for this GA.

It is clear that the adjacency-based (or edge) crossover [13] is ideally suited for this task. If an ordering has a high fitness it is because co-adapted genes are near each other. The relative order of these genes, or their absolute position, is only of secondary importance.

From experiments with the Traveling Salesman Problem, we have concluded that there is nothing to be gained by using an additional mutation operator when adjacency-based crossover is used. Apparently, it introduces enough diversity into the population [10]. Hence, we didn't use mutation.

In the experiments described in the next Section, we use a fine-grained parallel ordering GA [8, 11, 12] with the following parameters: the selection strategy is tournament selection, the neighborhood size $s = 4$, the crossover rate $\chi = 1.0$, and the population size $N = 1,024$. These parameter values are recommended in [10].

The genotypes represent possible orderings and the fitness of a genotype is the crossover correlation coefficient ρ_χ for this ordering. As mentioned above, the only genetic operator used is adjacency-based crossover.

4 Experimental Results

In this section, we summarize experiments done with two test problems: the deceptive function described in Section 2.1 and a graph bipartition problem. The deceptive function was chosen to demonstrate the power of our approach, and the bipartition problem to illustrate how constraints can be handled. Experiments with De Jong's test suite [2] and other problems are reported in [10].

4.1 The Deceptive Function

The first test problem is described in Section 2.1. To test the relation between the correlation coefficient ρ_χ and crossover disruption we calculated the ρ_χ for the tight, loose and random orderings. The results, which are averaged over 20 samples of 2×1024 parent genotypes, are shown in Table 2 (we used the same random ordering as in [4]).

Ordering	ρ_χ	$\delta(H)$
tight	0.905	2
loose	0.277	20
random	0.485	15.5

Table 2. The crossover correlation coefficients ρ_χ for the tight, loose and random orderings and their relation with the defining length δ of the best building blocks.

Clearly, there is a relation between the ρ_χ and the ordering of the genes. This is a strong indication that the approach taken here is feasible and that the ρ_χ can indeed be used as a fitness measure in a genetic search for optimal orderings.

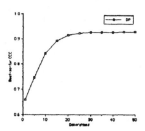

Fig. 2. Result on Goldberg's 30-bit deceptive problem (DG).

The result of a typical run for the 30-bit deceptive function is shown in Figure 2.

Figure 2 shows that $\rho_\chi = 0.65$ in the beginning of the search (approximately the ρ_χ for a random ordering), and quickly raises to 0.93. At this point, around generation 30, the optimal ordering is found.

This is a significant result because without prior knowledge of the optimal ordering , no GA can ever solve this problem – Section 2.1. So far, only messy GAs have been able to solve the same problem [4].

4.2 A Graph Bipartition Problem

We have included the graph bipartition problem below for two reasons. First, we know in advance the optimal ordering. So, we can check the results that we have obtained. Second, it poses problems for the approach presented here. The reason for this is that it is a constrained problem and therefore the ρ_χ is not a good predictor for crossover disruption. We succeeded after a minor change in calculating ρ_χ.

The graph bipartition problem is a multilevel 64-node problem. The task is to divide the graph into two equal subgraphs such that the number of edges connecting nodes belonging to different subgraphs is minimized. The genotype length $l = 64$, i.e. one bit for each node: a 0 (or 1) means that the corresponding node belongs to the first (or second) subgraph. Consequently, only bitstrings with an equal number of 0s and 1s represent legal solutions. In order to assign a fitness to all bitstrings, the following fitness function is used for a genotype g

$$cutsize(g) + 0.1(Z(g) - O(g))^2$$

where $Z(g)$ is the number of 0s, and $O(g)$ is the number of 1s in the genotype g.

The above problem is called $RT4$ in a test suite defined in [10]. Figure 3 shows this test problem. The minimal partitioning is of course obtained with a cut between the two cubes. Figure 4 shows the positions of the genes for the left cube. The gene positions for the right cube are obtained by adding 32 to the gene positions of the left cube. It is clear that this is the optimal ordering for this problem. So, it is no surprise that its ρ_χ is very high: 0.89. Using the optimal ordering, the minimal cutsize is encoded as 32 zeros followed by 32 ones (the complement of this genotype is of course also optimal).

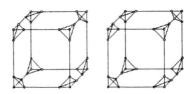

Fig. 3. Test problem RT4

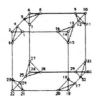

Fig. 4. The representation of RT4 (left cube only)

First, we were unable to find the optimal representation for this problem. This failure can be explained by looking at the fitness function of $RT4$ – see Equation 4.2.

The search for an optimal partitioning of the graph proceeds in two stages. In the first stage, the search focuses on getting genotypes with an equal number of 0s and 1s, i.e. legal genotypes. This is due to the second term which causes the fitness to drop quadratically as the imbalance between the 0s and 1s grows. In the second stage, the search focuses on reducing the cutsize.

Because of these two stages, the random genotypes that constitute the sample to calculate ρ_χ are rated mainly in terms of their imbalance between 0s and 1s. The problem is that these fitnesses contain little or no linkage information. Hence, the ρ_χ do not point to the optimal ordering and the search fails.

There are two ways to solve this problem. First, the sample genotypes can be chosen so that they all have an equal number of 0s and 1s. Secondly, the fitness function can be altered so that it only counts the cutsize. These two modifications will have approximately the same effect. Here, we chose to alter the fitness function, which gives us the new problem $RT4\prime$. Figure 5 demonstrates that with this modification, the optimal ordering is found.

5   Conclusion

In this paper, we have discussed how the correlation coefficient of crossover can be used to optimize problem representations. We have shown that this technique is capable of

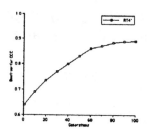

Fig. 5. Result on test problem *RT4*

finding the optimal ordering of a difficult deceptive problem. Without prior knowledge of the optimal ordering, the standard GA can not solve this problem. We have further demonstrated the generality of our approach by testing it on a graph bipartition problem and showing how constraints can be handled.

References

1. Belew, R. K. & Booker, L. B. (Eds.) (1991). *Proceedings of the Fourth International Conference on Genetic Algorithms*. Morgan Kaufmann, San Mateo, CA.
2. K. A. De Jong. *An Analysis of the Behavior of a Class of Genetic Adaptive Systems*. PhD thesis, University of Michigan, 1975.
3. Goldberg, D. E. (1989). *Genetic Algorithms in Search, Optimization, and Machine Learning*. Addison Wesley, Reading, MA.
4. Goldberg, D. E. (1989). Messy Genetic Algorithms: Analysis and First Results. *Complex Systems*, 3(5), 1989.
5. J. H. Holland. *Adaptation in Natural and Artificial Systems*. The University of Michigan Press, Ann Arbor, 1975.
6. G. E. Liepins and M. D. Vose. Representational issues in genetic optimization. *Journal of Experimental and Theoretical Artificial Intelligence*, 2(2), 1990.
7. Manderick, B., de Weger, M., & Spiessens, P. (1991). The genetic algorithm and the structure of the fitness landscape. In [1].
8. Manderick, B. & Spiessens, P. (1989). Fine-grained parallel genetic algorithms. In [9].
9. J. D. Schaffer, editor. *Proceedings of the Third International Conference on Genetic Algorithms (ICGA-89)*. Morgan Kaufmann, San Mateo, 1989.
10. Piet Spiessens. *Fine-Grained Parallel Genetic Algorithms: Analysis and Applications*. PhD thesis, Free University of Brussels, AI Laboratory, 1994.
11. Spiessens, P. & Manderick, B. (1990). A genetic algorithm for massively parallel computers. In *Proceedings of the International Conference on Parallel Processing in Neural Systems and Computers (ICNC-90)*.
12. Spiessens, P. & Manderick, B. (1991). A massively parallel genetic algorithm: Implementation and first analysis. In [1].
13. D. Whitley, T. Starkweather, and D. Fuquay. Scheduling problems and traveling salesmen: The genetic edge recombination operator. In [9].

An Evolutionary Algorithm for Resource-Constrained Project Scheduling and Multiple Execution Modes

Oscar Ciro López, Dr.[1]
Ricardo M. Barcia, Ph.D[1]
Osama Eyada, Ph.D[2]
Fernando O. Gauthier, Dr.[1]

[1] Universidade Federal de Santa Catarina
Programa de Pós-Graduação em Engenharia de Produção
Cx.P. 476. Tel: (048) 231-9596/ FAX: (048) 234-1255
CEP 88040-900 - Florianópolis - SC
e_mail: oscar@eps.ufsc.br

[2] Department of Industrial and System Engineering
Virginia Polytechnic Institute and State University
Blacksburg, Virginia 24061-0118 - USA

Abstract

This paper is concerned with the problem of resource-constrained project scheduling under multiple performing modes. A heuristic solution based on Genetic Algorithms is proposed. Furthermore, the resource leveling concept is incorporated into the procedure as a form of guidance in the search of a solution that yields not only the shortest duration, but a leveled solution as well. A comparison with more traditional approaches is provided using benchmarks available in the literature. The results show the efficiency of the proposed algorithm.

Keywords: Project Scheduling, Resource Allocation, Genetic Algorithms

1 Introduction

The scheduling problem arises inevitably whenever is necessary to make a daily routine for any planned work and is concerned with the allocation of resources over time to perform a series of tasks.

One of the main issues in project scheduling occurs when there are limited resources to be distributed among the project activities. Because resources available are not always sufficient to satisfy the demands of concurrent activities, priorities have to be established. Typically, priorities are defined in terms of sequencing decisions for each project task. The objective is to make sequencing decisions so as to minimize the increase in project duration, subject to resource and precedence constraints. This problem is referred to as *resource-constrained project scheduling*.

The definition of the problem, a survey of the research works for resource-constrained scheduling problem and an introduction to Genetic Algorithms, will be discussed in the next section. Section three will discuss the specific implementation of this heuristic for the problem under consideration. Section four will be devoted to the discussion of the computational results, together with the conclusion drawn from the results. The final section will contain a summary and conclusions.

2 Literature Review

2.1 Project Scheduling

According to Bennington and McGinnis (1973) and Talbot (1982), one can assume without loss of generality that the general project scheduling problem can be represented by an acyclic (activity-on-node) graph $G = (N,P)$ where N, the set of nodes, correspond to the *activities* and P, the set of arcs, correspond to the *precedence relations*. Associated with each activity $i \in N$ ($i = 1,..,n$), is a set of possible *durations* d_i and the corresponding amount requirements r_{ij} of *resource* of type j ($j = 1,...,m$). The availability of resource j in period t can be written as $a_j(t)$. Each duration-resource combination is called a *mode*.

A feasible solution to the problem is one which will satisfy, first, the limitations on the resources, and secondly, the technological restriction on the order in which the tasks can be performed (Mohanthy and Siddiq, 1989).

Thus, the general multi-mode resource-constrained project scheduling problem consists of determining the start time of a set of interrelated activities in such a way that resource restrictions are satisfied while optimizing some managerial objective. Each activity can be performed in one of several modes, and each mode is characterized by a known duration and given resource requirements (Boctor, 1990).

Unfortunately, most practical problem varieties in the resource-constrained scheduling problem are representative of the NP-hard class of combinatorial problems (Lenstra and Rinnooy Kan 1978, Blazewicz et al. 1983, Boctor 1990). Given that computational time grows exponentially with problem size, generating optimal solutions even for modest real-word projects remains computationally impractical. Alternative solutions using complete enumeration techniques have been proposed. However, these approaches have been successful only for small size projects (Davis and Patterson 1975, Patterson 1984, Moder *et al.* 1983).

In order to overcome the limitations of optimality-based procedures heuristic-based procedures have been extensively developed. Such heuristic-based approaches for real-world resource-constrained project scheduling are today the most efficient way in obtaining consistently "good" solutions in a reasonable computing time (Davis and Patterson 1975, Moder *et al.*, 1983, Boctor 1990).

In addition, for most projects, there are fixed dates for beginning and ending the project. The resource leveling problem arise when sufficient total resource are available, but it is desirable or necessary to reduce the amount of variability in the pattern of resource usage over the project duration (Moder *et al.* 1983).

The problem addressed in this work was first introduced by Elmaghraby (1977). Slowinski (1981) presented the case of different activity performing modes for different resource categories (renewable, nonrenewable, and doubly constraints). This approach used multiple optimality criteria for a preemptive scheduling version of the resource allocation problem based on a multiobjective linear programming.

Talbot (1982), introduces methods for formulating and solving a general class of nonpreemptive resource-constrained project scheduling problem in which the duration is a function of resources committed to it. Deckro and Herbert (1989), developed optimal models for two specific case by extending traditional project scheduling models to the resource constrained project crashing case. Patterson *et al.* (1990), reported a computational experience to solve the multiple activity mode version of the resource-constrained project scheduling problem for both minimizing project duration time and maximizing project net present value objectives.

Drexel and Gruenewald (1993) present a stochastic scheduling method for formulating and solving the general class of nonpreemptive project scheduling problems with general resource availabilities and requirements as well as multi-mode time resource tradeoff.

2.2 Genetic Algorithms

From an Operations Research perspective, the concept of Genetic Algorithms (GA) can be understood as the intelligent exploitation of a random search. Initially developed by Holland (1975), GA have been applied to variety of problems ranging from game-playing to network design. In GA, each candidate solution (a point in the search space) is encoded in a *chromosome*. Each chromosome has an associated *fitness value*, which links it to the *objective function* of the problem. The chromosomes are grouped in a set called *population*.

The Genetic Algorithm search procedure works by combining the chromosomes through domain-independent *genetic operators*. The chromosomes are selected based on their fitness values (the better the fitness value, the higher its the chance of being chosen). The combination process generates a new population. This reproductive plan is repeated as many times as is desired. Since the reproduction is based on the fitness value, eventually the new population can improve the current solution. Once the objective function value reaches a desired accuracy, i.e. no significant change from one generation to another, the process is finished.

3 Genetic Algorithms For Project Scheduling

None of the models previously described consider the limited resource allocation problem and the resource leveling problem at the same time in a unique approach. The main reason for this is that all procedures for each one of these problem are developed under antagonic assumptions, such as limited and no limited resource availability. Furthermore, while extending the total scheduling is acceptable in limited-resource scenario, it is not acceptable for resource leveling.

In addition, none of the current solutions addresses resource usage efficiency as an element affecting the solution quality. Many of available scheduling procedures attempt to produce feasible solutions by systematically generating the solution space, evaluating objective function, and choosing the best. However, it is possible to obtain different schedule solutions with the same objective function value (for instance the same project duration) but with a different resource utilization profile.

A Genetic Algorithm based model is proposed to overcome the limitations of current approaches. Through this approach, it is possible to solve the resource-constrained scheduling problem taking into account alternative ways for completing the project activities while reducing variability in the pattern of resource usage.

The general flowchart of the proposed algorithm is presented in Figure 1. Within this algorithm the initial population is generated at random by using a proper procedure. The process continues evaluating each solution of this initial population in relation to the value of its objective function. In the next step the reproduction, crossover an mutation operators are performed in order to generate futures populations. At this time, resources fluctuations are introduced in the procedure in order to obtain a solution (when the stop criterion is achieved), not only with the shortest duration, but with the lower fluctuation rate as well (López, 1995).

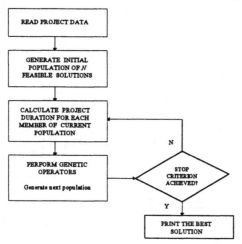

Fig. 1. The Proposed Genetic Algorithms Heuristic

3.1 Solution Coding

To use GA in the context of project scheduling, it is necessary to represent a feasible schedule in a proper structure. The proposed GA paradigm represents chromosomes (a legal feasible schedule) as an ordered list in which each activity occupies one unique position such that no activity appears in the list before any of its predecessors. Figure 2 depicts the chromosome encoding.

Start	Activity 1	Activity 2	....	Activity n	End

Fig. 2. Single-Mode Representation

The scheduling of each activity on the chromosome is carried out in the order defined by the list. It should be noted that the choice of activity from the list does not determine the actual scheduling of the activity. In fact, only a resource allocation priority is established for that activity. The scheduling is done by assigning to each activity the earliest date when there are sufficient resources for its execution.

In order to deal with the multi-mode case, the procedure has to be modified to allow for different execution modes for each activity. In this sense, a feasible solution can be represented by an ordered list of activities where each activity composed by a sublist. The sublist contains all the possible modes of execution for a particular activity. The unique mode to be assigned to the activity is chosen from the sublist. Figure 3 shows the chromosome representation for the multi-mode case.

Initial activity				Activity i					Final activity			
0_1	1_2	...	0_m	0_1	...	1_{m-1}	0_m		1_1	0_2	...	0_m

Fig. 3. Multi-Mode Representation

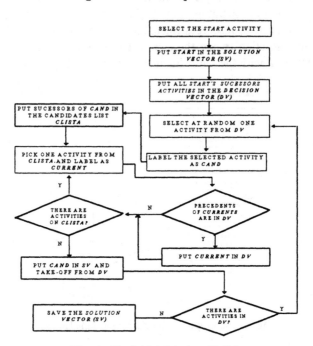

Fig. 4. The Initial Solutions Builder

To determine a scheduling, first an execution mode is randomly selected and marked with number 1. Then the earliest date when there are sufficient resources to execute the activity, according to the mode considered, is assigned to it. Figure 4 shows the procedure procedure used to generate at random the initial population of individuals (solutions). The procedure is based on adaptation of the method suggested by R.A. Jones (1984).

3.2 Design Details

In traditional Genetic Algorithms implementations, the fitness function represents a measure of the quality of a solution in relation to the objective function. In the present work, due to the minimization problem, schedules with higher durations have lower fitness values. Consequently the probability of selecting these solutions for next generations is low. The fitness function used in the model was:

$$y = \begin{cases} C_{max} - x, x < C_{max} \\ 0, x \geq C_{max} \end{cases} \qquad (1)$$

where, x represents the duration of each feasible schedule in the current population. C_{max} corresponds to the higher project duration value observed in the current population.

However, during the GA implementation phase, a phenomenon that was observed is that as the algorithm proceeds, the population converges to a set of very similar chromosomes among which it is hard to discriminate if current fitness function is used. Since, GA use a controlled probability to generate new solution from parent solutions, *Weighted Resource Utilization Factor* (WRUR) model is proposed as a discriminating procedure that increase or reduce the probability of accepting a given solution. This factor, based on resource leveling concepts, is defined as:

$$WRUF_k = \Sigma w_i f_i, \quad WRUF_k \in [0,1], \quad k = 1,2,...,m \tag{2}$$

Where:

w_i = weight that measure the importance of resource of type i, $\Sigma w_i = 1$;

k = element (solution) of current population;

f_i, = resource leveling function for resource of type i, f_i, $\in [0,1]$;

$f_i = \dfrac{1}{1+V(X)}$, where $V(X)$ represents the resource variance.

Also, the proposed procedure mitigates the problem of dominance of outstanding chromosomes at early stages. The original fitness function was modified to include the WRUF as follows:

$$y = \begin{cases} (C_{max} - x) - (1 - WRUF), x < C_{max} \\ 0, x \geq C_{max} \end{cases} \tag{3}$$

Thus, according to the proposed model, the resource-constrained project scheduling problem can be viewed as a particular case of the more general project scheduling and leveling with limit resources problem (by doing WRUF = 1 in 3).

By incorporating the leveling concepts, a scheduling method was developed, which has the capacity to converge to a set of similar solutions in terms of objective function value. In addition, reducing the fluctuation of resource usage over project duration.

The remaining procedures of the model implementation are fairly standard. Traditional values for crossover rate, mutation rate and population size were used. The crossover operator implemented was the *Cycle Crossover - CX*. However, it should be noted that applying usual CX operator does not work due to precedence constraints. Therefore, it has been modified to generate feasible solutions using the mutation operator. The mutation operator was used as a mechanism that allows to reestablish precedence relationships.

4 Computational Experimentation And Analysis Results

To illustrate the use and to evaluate the performance of the proposed paradigm a set of originally 25 single-mode problems adopted from the construction project scheduling literature were used. Nine test problems from this set were used and solved by Li and Willis (1992) while the 16 other projects were used by Badiru (1988). The test constrcution projects range in size from 7 to 80 activities. The number of resource types varies from 2 to 10. The structure of the test projects vary from 5,78 to 69,82, measured using the quantitative criterion of the complexity proposed by Badiru (1988). The characteristics of the network examples are summarized in Table 1.

Yet, to evaluate the performance of the heuristic when used to solve muti-mode version, the original single execution mode problems were modified as follows: 1) M $(1 \leq M \leq 3)$ additional modes for each activity were randomly generated; 2) the duration and resource requirements for the new modes were generated in such a way that original resource limits were not modified and, 3) the duration and resource requirements of the first mode which is always the shortest one corresponding to the original mode;

The performance of the proposed model is compared to heuristic solutions reported by Badiru (1988) and Li and Willy (1992) for these problems. In addition, nine available optimal solutions are utilized for comparison with solutions obtained by the proposed model and other models. In the multi-mode case, the main evaluation criterion is the percentage increase of project duration above the shortest duration found using the shortest duration mode.

The results are shown in Tables 2 and 3. From Table 2, it can be seen that the proposed algorithm, for the single-mode version, outperforms the other models. The model produced the smallest percentage increase over the critical path length for the whole set of examples. The average percentages increase obtained by the proposed paradigm are 46% and 34% while the other heuristics produced an average percentage increase that varies from 56% to 72% and 42% to 56%, for the first and the second set of problem respectively.

Table 3 shows that, for the single-mode case, the percentage increase over the CPM duration (calculated by using unconstrained resources) is always smaller than that given by the best heuristic. It is also shown that the proposed model produces a percentage increase, for the multi-mode case, most of the time smaller than that for the single-mode version.

The results indicate that, for the examples by which optimal solution are available, the genetic algorithm based model also match these solutions. These findings demonstrate the good performance of the proposed algorithm to solve construction resource-constrained scheduling problem.

5 Summary And Conclusions

A GA-based model for solving multiple resource constrained construction scheduling problem has been presented. The model can handle both the single-mode case as well as the multi-mode version of this problem. Further the algorithm incorporate resource leveling concepts which allow the handle the minimization of project duration while reducing the fluctuation of resource usage over project time.

This model considers the traditional resource-constrained project scheduling as a particular case of a more general time-resource-constrained project scheduling. Twenty-five network examples were used to test the performance of the algorithm. The results indicate that the model outperforms the results reported in the literature.

Finally, It was found that the multi-mode version of the proposed heuristic produced an average percentage increase over the CPM project duration of 36% while the average percentage increase, produced by other models, range from 46% for the best benchmark heuristic to 42% for the single-mode version of the GA based model. These results indicate the relevance of considering multiple execution modes rather than the traditional single execution mode. It is reasonable to conclude that using multiple execution mode gives more flexibility to the resource-constrained allocation process.

Table 1. Characteristics Of The Examples Used

Project No.	Num. of Activities	Complexity[1]	Max. num. of resource types	Average no. of modes for each activiy[2]	Optimal duration	CPM duration
1	24	30.91	3	2.41	-	71
2	21	12.15	4	2.14	-	74
3	15	17.27	4	2.33	-	238
4	12	7.33	2	1.75	-	23
5	16	8.98	3	2.18	-	125
6	40	24.20	5	2.87	-	46
7	55	18.13	4	1.87	-	26
8	73	69.82	10	1.54		75
9	27	24.12	3	2.63	-	37
10	80	37.24	2	1.43	-	85
11	51	35.87	2	1.69	-	93
12	7	13.77	4	2.00	-	9
13	7	5.85	3	1.71	-	8
14	43	14.61	4	1.95		48
15	13	10.65	4	1.46	-	18
16	7	8.10	2	1.62	-	11
17	9	13.08	3	2.77	23	16
18	12	13.65	3	1.57	17	16
19	13	9.62	3	1.14	39	36
20	13	7.29	4	1.26	13	8
21	16	17.42	2	1.68	88	80
22	16	10.8	6	1.47	45	28
23	27	19.39	3	1.77	35	33
24	30	12.07	6	1.63	35	33
25	27	24.12	3	2.77	64	31

[1] Badiru's measure (1988)   [2] Multi-mode case

Table 2. Percentage Increase Of Project Duration Above Critical Path Length

No	ACT IM	ACT RES	TIM RES	GEN RES 1	GEN RES 2	RO T	MT S	ML TS	ML CT	SP D	LP D	HN IS	CA F	GA
1	69	89	76	79	69	77	80	69	82	79	83	79	77	58
2	20	19	19	19	19	23	20	20	20	23	19	19	19	7
3	53	73	53	73	53	61	75	53	53	61	73	53	61	54
4	35	39	43	39	35	39	35	35	43	43	52	39	35	30
5	40	38	50	50	50	50	38	40	40	50	50	40	38	38
6	65	67	67	67	63	74	72	65	63	83	80	76	70	54
7	58	92	77	96	77	42	46	58	46	50	88	46	42	38
8	93	124	125	135	104	85	145	93	100	97	127	113	96	79
9	116	132	119	132	119	89	132	116	95	103	132	132	89	81
10	35	39	35	34	35	33	51	35	32	34	59	42	34	31
11	82	87	80	90	82	69	96	82	76	67	112	84	69	70
12	89	89	89	89	89	89	89	89	89	89	89	89	89	89
13	13	50	13	50	13	50	13	13	13	50	13	50	13	13
14	88	94	92	94	81	88	96	88	85	94	88	102	88	75
15	33	22	33	33	33	33	33	33	33	33	33	33	22	11
16	36	55	55	55	55	55	18	36	36	18	55	36	55	9
	58	69	64	71	61	60	65	58	57	61	72	65	56	46

Badiru's Study (1988)

Table 2. Continuation...

No	Optim.[1]	Technol. Ranking	EST	EFT	LST	LFT	Total Float	ACTIM	ACTRES	Li & Willis	GA
17	44	50	50	56	56	50	50	50	44	50	44
18	6	31	50	19	44	31	63	44	13	38	6
19	8	31	22	25	8	11	8	8	19	8	8
20	63	88	88	100	75	63	75	75	100	63	63
21	10	40	40	35	15	25	25	15	15	15	10
22	61	79	64	79	64	64	89	64	64	64	61
23	6	24	21	42	9	18	42	9	18	15	6
24	6	27	18	9	18	9	9	18	6	9	6
25	106	126	126	139	135	119	139	135	135	116	106
	34	55	53	56	47	43	56	47	46	42	34

[1] As reported.   Using Li and Willis's Study (1992)

Where:

ACTIM = Activity-Time	MLCT = Minimum Late Completion Time,
ACTRES = Activity-Resource	SPD = Shortest PERT Duration,
TIMRES = Time-Resource	LPD = Longest PERT Duration,
GENRES = w ACTIM = (1-w) ACTRES,	HNIS = Highest Number of Immediate Sucessors,
ROT = Resource Over Time,	CAF = Composite Allocation Factor
MTS = Minimum Total Slack,	GA = Proposed GA Paradigm
MLST= Minimum Late Start Time,	Total Float = Ascendant total Float
EST = Ascendant Earliest Start Times	ACTIM = Descendent Activity-Time
EFT = Ascendant Earliest Finish Times	ACTRES = Descendent Activity-Resources
LST = Ascendant Latest Start Times	LI and WILLIS = Backward Scheduling
LFT = Ascendant Latest Finish Times	

Table 3. Summary Of Percentage increase over the CPM project duration

Probl. No.	Best Heuristic[1]	Proposed GA model: Single Mode version	Proposed GA model: Muti-Mode version
1	69	58	51
2	19	7	4
3	53	54	30
4	35	30	22
5	38	38	6
6	63	54	63
7	42	38	62
8	85	79	88
9	89	81	78
10	32	31	21
11	67	70	51
12	89	89	22
13	13	13	13
14	81	75	83
15	22	11	6
16	18	9	9
17	44	44	44
18	13	6	6
19	8	8	3
20	63	63	75
21	15	10	0
22	64	61	36
23	9	6	21
24	6	6	12
25	116	106	97
Average	46	42	36

[1] Based on the studies of Badiru (1988) and Li e Willis (1992).

6 References

BADIRU, A.B. Toward The Standardization Of Performance Measures For Project Scheduling Heuristics. *IEEE Trans. On Eng. Mng..* v. 35, n. 2, p. 80-89. 1988.

BENNINGTON, G.E. e McGININIS, L.F. A Critique Of Project Planning With Resource Constrain, In: *Symp. on the theory of sched. and its appl.* Lectures Notes in economic and mathematical systems. Springer-Verlag. p. 1-38. 1973.

BLAZEWICZ, J., LENSTRA, J.K. e RINNOOY KAN, A.G.H. Scheduling Subject To Resource Constraints: Classification And Complexity. *Discrete Applied Mathematics.* v. 5, p. 11-24. 1983.

BOCTOR, F.F. Some Efficient Multi-Heuristic Procedures For Resource-Constrained Project Scheduling. *Europ. Jour. of Op. Res..* v. 49, p. 3-13. 1990.

DAVIS, E.W. e PATTERSON, J.H. A Comparison Of Heuristic And Optimum Solutions In Resource-Constrained Project Scheduling. *Management Science.* v. 21, n. 8, p. 944-955. 1975.

DECKRO, R.F and HEBERT, J.E. Resource Constrained Project Crashing. *OMEGA..* v. 17, n. 1, p. 69-79. 1989.

DREXEL, A. e GRUENEWALD, J. Nonpreemptive Multi-Mode Resource-Constrained Project Scheduling. *IIE Transaction*, v. 25, n. 5, p. 74-81. 1993.

ELMAGHRABY, S.E. *Activity Networks: Project Planning and Control by Network Models.* Wile, New York. 1977.

HOLLAND, J.H. *Adaptation In Natural And Artificial Systems.* University Of Michigan Press, Ann Arbor. 1975.

JONES, R.A. Resource Scheduling: A Monte Carlo Approach to CPM. *Proceeding of CIB W-65.* p. 422-427. 1984.

LENSTRA, J.K. e RINNOOY KAN, A.H.G. Complexity Of Scheduling Under Precedence Constraints, *Operations Research.* v. 26, n. 1, p. 22-35. 1978

LI, K.Y., e WILLIS, R.J. An Iterative Scheduling Technique For Resource-Constrained Project Scheduling. *Europ. Jour. Op. Res.* v. 56, p. 370-379. 1992.

LÓPEZ, O.C., *Um Algoritmo Evolutivo Para A Programação De Projetos Multi-Modos Com Nivelamento De Recursos Limitados.* Tese de Dout.. UFSC, 1995.

MODER, J.J., PHILLIPS, C.R. e DAVIS, *E.W. Project Management With CPM, PERT And Precedence Diagramming.* 3rd ed., Reinhold, New York. 1983.

MOHANTHY, R.P. e SIDDIQ, M.K. Multiple Projects Multiple Resources-Constrained Scheduling. *Int. Jour. Prod. Res.* v.27, n.2, p.261-280. 1989.

PATTERSON, J.H. Comparison Of Exact Approaches For Solving The Multiple Constrained Resource Project Scheduling Problem. *Mng. Science.* v.30, n. 7, p. 854-867. 1984.

PATTERSON, J.H., TALBOT, F.B., SLOWINSKI, R. e WEGLARZ, J. Computational Experience With A Backtracking Algorithm For Solving A General Class Of Precedence And Resource-Constrained Scheduling Problems. *Europ. Jour. Op. Res.* v. 49. p. 68-79. 1990.

SLOWINSKI, R. Multiobjective Network Scheduling With Efficient Use Of Renewable And Nonrenewable Resources. *Eur. J. Op.Res.* v.7, p.265-273. 1981.

TALBOT, F.B. Resource-Constrained Project Scheduling With Time-Resource Tradeoffs: The Nonpreemptive Case. *Mng. Sc.* v.28, n.10, p. 1197-1210. 1982.

Evaluating the Robustness and Scalability of Revision-Based Natural Language Generation

Jacques Robin

jr@di.ufpe.br
http://www.di.ufpe.br/~jr
Departamento de Informática, Universidade Federal do Pernambuco
Recife, Brazil

Abstract. This paper presents the first quantitative, corpus-based evaluation of the same-domain robustness and scalability of a new revision-based language generation model, in comparison to the traditional single pass pipeline model. Robustness is defined as the proportion of sentences, in a given corpus test sample that can be generated using only knowledge structures abstracted from another sample. Scalability is defined as the proportion of knowledge structures, among those needed to generate *all* sentences from a given corpus test sample, of those already acquired from another sample. Results show that the incremental revision model is far more robust and significantly more scalable than the single pass model.

1 Introduction

The project STREAK focuses on the specific issues involved in generating short, newswire style, natural language texts that *summarize* vast amounts of input tabular data in their historical context. A series of previous publications presented complementary aspects of this project: motivating corpus analysis in [8], new revision-based text generation model in [5], system implementation and rule base for the sports domain in [6] and empirical evaluation of the *portability* to another domain (the stock market) of the rule base in [7].

The present paper completes this series by describing a second, empirical, corpus-based evaluation, this time quantifying the *same-domain robustness and scalability* of the new revision-based language generation model, as compared to the traditional single pass model. This is the first time that different language generation models are quantitatively and empirically compared. The goal of this paper is twofold: (1) quantifying the robustness and scalability gains stemming from the compositionality of revision, and (2) providing a general, semi-automatic methodology for evaluating the robustness and scalability of language generation models, on the basis of the semantic and syntactic knowledge structures that they rely on. The results reveal a 41% gain in robustness (from 38% to 79%), and a 16% gain (from 47% down to 33%) in inertia to scalability, when switching from the traditional single pass pipeline generation model to the more compositional and flexible incremental revision model.

2 An overview of STREAK

The project STREAK was initially motivated by analyzing a corpus of newswire summaries written by professional sportwriters[1]. This analysis revealed four characteristics of summaries that challenge the capabilities of previous report generators: (1) concise linguistic forms, (2) complex sentences, (3) optional and background facts opportunistically slipped as modifiers of obligatory facts, and (4) high paraphrasing power. Previous report generators [3] [1] were architectured as a single pass pipeline with two main components: (1) a content planner selecting the facts to express *independently of how to express them*, and (2) a linguistic realizer *subsequently* choosing the words and syntactic form for each selected fact. By greatly increasing the number of content planning and linguistic realization options that the generator must consider, as well as the mutual constraints among them, the four characteristics above make generating summaries using such a single pass pipeline impractical.

The example run given in Fig. 1 illustrates how STREAK overcomes these difficulties. It first generates a simple draft sentence that contains only the obligatory facts to include in any game report (location, date, game result and key player statistic). It then applies a series of revision rules[2], each one *opportunistically* adding a new fact[3] that either: (1) complements an already included fact (*e.g.*, revision of sentence 2 into 3), or (2) justifies its relevance by providing its historical background (*e.g.*, revision of sentence 1 into 2).

STREAK stops revising when the summary sentence reaches linguistic complexity limits empirically observed in the corpus (*e.g.*, 50 word long or parse tree of depth 10).

3 Acquiring Knowledge Structures from Corpus Data

The rules driving the revision process in STREAK were acquired by reverse engineering[4] about 300 corpus sentences. First, these sentences were classified in terms of: (1) the combination of domain concepts they expressed, and (2) the thematic role and syntactic category used to express each of these concepts.

The resulting classes, called *realization patterns*, abstract the mapping from semantic to syntactic structure by factoring out lexical material and syntactic details. Two examples of realization patterns are given in Fig. 2. For generators (such as ANA [3]) which use both simple and complex *stored* realization patterns to map concept *combinations* onto *whole* phrases in *a single* pass, this level of analysis is sufficient. In contrast, for a generator like STREAK which *dynamically derives* complex phrases from basic ones through incremental revisions (each revision introducing a new individual concept), a finer level of analysis is needed.

---

[1] This 800,000 word corpus covers a whole NBA (National Basketball Association) season.

[2] In Fig. 1, the rule used is indicated above each revised sentence.

[3] Highlighted in bold in Fig. 1.

[4] *i.e.*, analyzing how they could be incrementally generated through gradual revisions.

1. **Initial draft (basic sentence pattern):**
   "Dallas, TX – Charles Barkley *scored* 42 points Sunday as the Phoenix Suns defeated the Dallas Mavericks 123 97."
2. **Adjunctization of Created into Instrument:**
   "Dallas, TX – Charles Barkley **tied a season high with** 42 points Sunday as the Phoenix Suns defeated the Dallas Mavericks 123 97."
3. **Coordinative Conjoin of Clause:**
   "Dallas, TX – Charles Barkley tied a season high with 42 points **and Danny Ainge** added 21 Sunday as the Phoenix Suns defeated the Dallas Mavericks 123-97."
4. **Absorb of Clause in Clause as Result with Agent Control:**
   "Dallas, TX – Charles Barkley tied a season high with 42 points and **Danny Ainge came off the bench** to add 21 Sunday as the Phoenix Suns defeated the Dallas Mavericks 123-97."
5. **Nominalization with Ordinal Adjoin:**
   "Dallas, TX – Charles Barkley tied a season high with 42 points and Danny Ainge came off the bench to add 21 Sunday as the Phoenix Suns **handed** the Dallas Mavericks **their 13th straight home** defeat 123 97."
6. **Adjoin of Classifier to NP:**
   "Dallas, TX – Charles Barkley tied a season high with 42 points and Danny Ainge came off the bench to add 21 Sunday as the Phoenix Suns handed the Dallas Mavericks their **league worst** 13th straight home defeat 123 97."

Fig. 1. Complex sentence generation through incremental revisions in STREAK.

Realization patterns were thus grouped into *surface decrement pairs* consisting of: (1) a more complex pattern (called the *target* pattern), and (2) a simpler pattern (called the *source* pattern) that is structurally the closest to the target pattern, among patterns with one less concept[5].

The structural transformations from source to target pattern in each surface decrement pair were then hierarchically classified, resulting in a revision rule hierarchy. For example, the surface decrement pair $< R_b^2, R_b^1 >$ shown in Fig. 2 is one of the pairs from which the revision rule **Adjunctization of Range into Instrument** was abstracted. This rule involves displacing the **Range** argument of the source clause as an **Instrument** adjunct, to accommodate the new verb and object expressing the added fact. In the hierarchy, this revision rule is a specialization of the general **Adjunctization** rule, and a sibling of the rule **Adjunctization of Created into Instrument** used to revise sentence 1 into 2, in STREAK's run shown in Fig. 1 (where the **Created** argument role "42 points" of the verb "to score" in 1 becomes the **Instrument** adjunct "with 42 points" in 2).

---

[5] *i.e.*, the source pattern expresses the same concept combination than the target pattern minus one concept.

R_b^2: **target** realization pattern of the revision rule
Adjunctization of Range into Instrument.

winner	aspect	type		streak	length			score	game-result	loser
agent	action	affected/located			location	instrument				
proper	verb	NP			PP	PP				
		det	classifier	noun		prep			NP	
							det	number	noun	PP
Utah	extended	its	win	streak	to 6 games	with	a	99-84	triumph	over Denver
Boston	stretching	its	winning	spree	to 9 outings	with	a	118-94	rout	of Utah

R_b^1: surface decrement of pattern R_b^2 above and **source** pattern of the revision rule
Adjunctization of Range into Instrument.

winner			score	game-result	loser
agent	action	range			
proper	support-verb	NP			
		det	number	noun	PP
Chicago	claimed	a	128-94	victory	over New Jersey
Orlando	recorded	a	101-95	triumph	against New York

Fig. 2. A surface decrement pair of realization patterns.

4 Evaluation Methodology

Goal and Basic Principles. The object of the evaluation is the *general revision-based model* of language generation, rather than its particular implementation in the system STREAK. It thus does not directly evaluate STREAK's outputs. It rather evaluates the special knowledge structures required by its underlying revision-based model.

The particular properties of this generation model that are evaluated are: (1) *same-domain robustness* – the percentage of other text samples from the same domain that can be generated without acquiring new knowledge – and (2) *same-domain scalability* – the percentage of new knowledge needed to fully cover these other samples.

Evaluation is performed in two rounds on the basis of *corpus data*. In the first round, the 'training' (or 'acquisition') sample consists of 190 sentences from the original corpus covering the 1991-1992 NBA season and from which STREAK's knowledge structures were acquired through reverse engineering. The test sample consists of 130 sentences from the following 1992-1993 NBA season[6]. For the second round, the acquisition sample consists of the union of the acquisition and the test samples of the first round, while the test sample consists of 240 sentences from the next 1993-1994 season.

---

[6] The same semantic and discursive restrictions were used to select representative sample sentences from each corpus.

The evaluation procedure is *comparative*, contrasting the respective percentages obtained for:

- The basic concept clusters[7], basic realization patterns, and *revision rules* required by STREAK's revision-based model.
- The basic *and complex* concept clusters, and the basic *and complex* realization patterns required by the single pass pipeline model of previous report generators.

Evaluation Parameters. Four parameter pairs were defined: the *realization robustness* and *realization scalability* parameter pair evaluates the generation process as a whole, while three finer-grained, mutually orthogonal parameter pairs identify the bottlenecks within this process. Each of these three parameter pairs focuses on a different generation sub-task. The *conceptual* robustness and *conceptual* scalability parameters evaluate the *content selection* task (*i.e.*, deciding what to say). The *clustering* robustness and *clustering* scalability parameters evaluate the *content organization* task (*i.e.*, deciding when to say what). The *paraphrasing* robustness and *paraphrasing* scalability parameters evaluate the *linguistic realization* task (*i.e.*, deciding how to say it).

Except for the conceptual parameters, which are the same for both models, the definitions of the other parameters for each model involve different knowledge structure sets and different subsets in the test corpus partition. This partition is shown in Fig. 3, and the robustness parameter definitions based on it are shown in Fig. 4. The scalability parameters are defined in Fig. 5. Note that the higher their value, *the less* scalable is the generation model. They thus actually measure *inertia* to scalability.

Partially Automating the Evaluation. The software tool CREP [2] was developed to partially automate reverse engineering of corpus sentences. The basic idea behind CREP is to approximate a realization pattern by a regular expression whose terminals are words or parts-of-speech tags (POS-tags). CREP will then automatically retrieve the test corpus sentences matching those expressions.

Because a realization pattern abstracts away from lexical items to capture the mapping from concepts to syntactic structure, approximating such a pattern by a regular expression of words and POS-tags involves encoding each concept of the pattern by the disjunction of its alternative lexicalizations (*e.g.*, the nouns "victory" or "triumph" for the **game-result** concept of R_b^1 in Fig. 2). In a given domain, there are therefore two sources of inaccuracy for such an approximation: (1) lexical ambiguity resulting in false positives by over-generalization, and (2) incomplete vocabulary resulting in false negatives by over-specialization. Thus, although automated corpus search using CREP expressions considerably speeds-up corpus analysis, manual intervention remains necessary.

---

[7] A concept cluster is a combination of concepts that are recurrently grouped inside specific syntactic constituents across corpus sentences (*e.g.*, <**game-result** , **winning streak extension**> are very often clustered together in the second clause of basketball summary lead sentences).

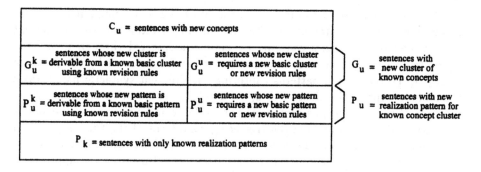

Fig. 3. Test corpus partition for robustness evaluation.

	Conceptual	Clustering	Paraphrasing	Realization
Single Pass Pipeline	$\dfrac{|P_k|+|P_u|+|G_u|}{|P_k|+|P_u|+|G_u|+|C_u|}$	$\dfrac{|P_k|+|P_u|}{|P_k|+|P_u|+|G_u|}$	$\dfrac{|P_k|}{|P_k|+|P_u|}$	$\dfrac{|P_k|}{|P_k|+|P_u|+|G_u|+|C_u|}$
Incremental Revision	$\dfrac{|P_k|+|P_u|+|G_u|}{|P_k|+|P_u|+|G_u|+|C_u|}$	$\dfrac{|P_k|+|P_u|+|G_u^k|}{|P_k|+|P_u|+|G_u|}$	$\dfrac{|P_k|+|P_u^k|}{|P_k|+|P_u|}$	$\dfrac{|P_k|+|P_u^k|+|G_u^k|}{|P_k|+|P_u|+|G_u|+|C_u|}$

Fig. 4. Robustness parameter definitions.

Conceptual, both models $= \dfrac{|\text{new concepts}|}{|\text{all concepts}|}$

Clustering, one pass $= \dfrac{|\text{new clusters of known concepts}|}{|\text{all clusters of known concepts}|}$

Clustering, revision $= \dfrac{|\text{new revision rules}|}{|\text{all revision rules}|+|\text{all basic clusters}|}$

Paraphrasing, one pass $= \dfrac{|\text{new realization patterns for known concept clusters}|}{|\text{all realization patterns for known concept clusters}|}$

Paraphrasing, revision $= \dfrac{|\text{new basic realization patterns}|+|\text{new revision rules}|}{|\text{all basic realization patterns}|+|\text{all revision rules}|}$

Realization, one pass $= \dfrac{|\text{new concepts}|+|\text{new clusters}|+|\text{new realization patterns}|}{|\text{all concepts}|+|\text{all clusters}|+|\text{all realization patterns}|}$

Realization, revision $= \dfrac{|\text{new concepts}|+|\text{new basic clusters}|+|\text{new basic patterns}|+|\text{new revision rules}|}{|\text{all concepts}|+|\text{all basic clusters}|+|\text{all basic patterns}|+|\text{all revision rules}|}$

Fig. 5. Scalability parameter definitions.

While the presence of an individual concept or of a realization pattern in corpus sentences can be directly detected by running a CREP expression, concept clusters and revision rules can only be *indirectly* detected through their associated realization patterns. A concept cluster can be detected by the presence of *any* of the realization patterns capturing the different syntactic paraphrases available to express the cluster. Usage of a revision rule can be detected by the presence of two test corpus sentences: one sentence following one of the *source* realization patterns matching the triggering conditions of the rule (*e.g.*, R_b^1 in Fig. 2 for the rule **Adjunctization of Range into Instrument**), and another sentence following the *target* realization pattern resulting from the application of the rule to this source pattern (*e.g.*, R_b^2 in Fig. 2 for the rule **Adjunctization of Range into Instrument**).

For each evaluation round and each type of knowledge structure, the semi-automatic partition of the test corpus consists of the following steps:

1. For each knowledge structure known from the acquisition corpus, write a set of CREP expressions to detect its usage in a text corpus.
2. Validate the resulting expressions by refining them until they yield perfect matches on the acquisition corpus.
3. Run them on the test corpus, to split it into: (1) a match file F_y of all sentences retrieved by any of these expressions and (2) the complement no-match file F_n.
4. Since a few false-positives and false-negatives may occur even on expressions pre-validated on the acquisition corpus, manually post-edit F_y into P_k and F_n into $P_u \bigcup G_u \bigcup C_u$.
5. Extend the classification of individual concepts, concept clusters, realization patterns and revision rules, to partition F_n into P_u^k, P_u^u, G_u^k, G_u^u and C_u.

5 Evaluation Results

The evaluation results are summarized in Fig. 6. For each evaluated property, the first two rows give the variation and average of the parameters over the two evaluation rounds. The third row estimates the probability that the average gain of the revision model over the single pass model is a random artifact of corpus sampling. It was computed using either Fisher's exact test or Pearson's χ^2 test.

The dramatic jump for overall robustness (from a problematic 38.2% with the single pass model to a remarkable 79.2% with the incremental revision model) stems from the fact that while typically 3/5 of a new corpus sample will feature new complex semantic or syntactic structures, about 2/3 of them are derivable from known basic structures using known revision rules. This allows the revision model to remove both the clustering and the paraphrasing bottlenecks of the single pass model. For each robustness parameter, the result of the Fisher or χ^2 tests indicates that the impressive gains of the revision model are statistically significant.

Though less spectacular than the corresponding gain in robustness, the overall scalability gain of the revision model is still sizeable: from 47.2% down to

	Conceptual	Clustering		Paraphrasing		Realization	
		one-pass	revision	one-pass	revision	one-pass	revision
Robustness Variation	+4.0%	−7.3%	+1.9%	−11.1%	−4.7%	−10.0%	+0.9%
Robustness Average	**95.5%**	71.8%	**96.4%**	55.5%	**85.1%**	38.2%	**79.2%**
Robustness Probability	N/A	.0001		.0004		10^{-6}	
Scalability Variation	-9.4%	+11.2%	-16.0%	+14.4%	-4.5%	+14.7%	−2.8%
Scalability Average	**9.5%**	42.7%	**17.0%**	60.5%	**41.7%**	47.2%	**32.6%**
Scalability Probability	N/A	.0515		.0063		.0057	

Fig. 6. Evaluation results.

32.6%[8]. The gains for all three finer-grained scalability parameters are statistically significant. With the single pass model, both sentence organization and linguistic realization are scalability bottlenecks. The revision model essentially removes the first one.

In practical applications, coverage and knowledge acquisition are traded-off. The figures for paraphrasing robustness and scalability empirically confirm the law of diminishing returns that makes near exhaustive linguistic coverage cost-ineffective: even with the more scalable revision model, reaching 100% coverage of the new alternative linguistic forms for each sentence plan from an already excellent 85.1% comes at the cost of encoding 41.7% additional linguistic forms.

6 Related Work

Apart from STREAK, only three generation projects feature an empirical and quantitative evaluation: ANA [3], KNIGHT [4] and IMAGENE [9].

ANA generates newswire style summaries of the daily fluctuations of stock market indexes. For evaluation, Kukich measures both the conceptual and linguistic (lexical and syntactic) coverages of ANA, by comparing the number of concepts and realization patterns identified during a corpus analysis, with those actually implemented in the system.

KNIGHT generates natural language concept definitions from a large biological knowledge base. For evaluation, Lester performs a Turing test in which a panel of human judges rates 120 sample definitions (60 computer-generated and 60 human-written) by assigning grades (from A to F) for semantic and stylistic accuracies.

IMAGENE generates instructions on how to operate household devices. The implementation focuses on a very limited aspect of text generation: choosing between alternative realizations of the purpose relation in a given context. IMAGENE's contextual preference rules were abstracted by analyzing an acquisition

---

[8] Recall that, since scalability parameters really measure *inertia* to scalability, the lower their value, the more scalable the model; therefore a negative delta means improvement.

	Evaluated Properties	Basis	Procedure
ANA	conceptual and linguistic implementation coverage	corpus	manual
KNIGHT	semantic and stylistic implementation accuracy	judges	manual
IMAGENE	stylistic rules' accuracy and robustness	corpus	manual
STREAK	**revision model robustness and scalability** revision rules' portability	corpus	semi-automatic

Fig. 7. Empirical evaluations in language generation.

corpus of about 300 purpose clauses from cordless telephone manuals. For evaluation, Van der Linden compares the purpose realizations picked by IMAGENE to the one in the corresponding corpus text, first on the acquisition corpus, and then on a test corpus of about 300 other purpose clauses from manuals for other devices than cordless telephones (ranging from clock radios to automobiles).

The differences on both goals and methodology between the evaluations carried out in the projects ANA, KNIGHT, IMAGENE and STREAK are summarized in Fig. 7.

In terms of methodology, the main originality of the evaluations performed in the STREAK project is the use of CREP to partially automate reverse engineering of corpus sentences. In terms of goals, while Kukich and Lester evaluate the coverage or accuracy of a particular *implementation*, I instead focus on three properties inherent to the use of the revision-based generation *model* underlying STREAK: *robustness* and *scalability* in the present paper, and *portability* in [7]. Van der Linden does a little bit of both by first measuring the stylistic accuracy of his system for a very restricted sub-domain, and then measuring how it degrades for a more general domain.

In itself, measuring the accuracy and coverage of a particular implementation in the sub-domain for which it was designed brings little insights about what generation approach should be adopted in future work. Indeed, even a system using mere canned text can be very accurate and attain substantial coverage if enough hand-coding effort is put into it. However, all this effort will have to be entirely duplicated each time the system is scaled up or ported to a new domain. Measuring how much of this effort duplication can be avoided when relying on revision-based generation was the very object of the three evaluations carried in the STREAK project.

Perhaps evaluation in language generation has remained a rarity until now on the premise that it requires formally judging what constitutes 'good prose', a task for which humans draw upon many vague and intuitive notions. This paper suggests that instead, evaluation can be based on measuring how well the knowledge structures of a generator match those from a corpus of model texts written by professional experts. Before final evaluation, corpus analysis also allows every step in the development of a generator (from identifying the challenging issues of the application domain, to designing the system's architecture and acquiring the knowledge structures) to be based on empirical data.

Acknowledgements

The research presented in this paper is currently supported by CNPq under post-doctoral research grant 150130-95.3. It started out while I was at Columbia University working with Prof. Kathy McKeown and supported by grants from ONR, ARPA, NSF and New York State CAT.

References

1. L. Bourbeau, D. Carcagno, E. Goldberg, R. Kittredge, and A. Polguère. Bilingual generation of weather forecasts in an operations environment. In *Proceedings of the 13th International Conference on Computational Linguistics*, Helsinki University, Finland, 1990. COLING.
2. D. Duford. Crep: a regular expression-matching textual corpus tool. Technical Report CUCS-005-93, Columbia University, 1993.
3. K. Kukich. *Knowledge-based report generation: a knowledge engineering approach to natural language report generation*. PhD thesis, University of Pittsburgh, 1983.
4. J.C. Lester. *Generating natural language explanations from large-scale knowledge bases*. PhD thesis, Computer Science Department, Universtity of Texas at Austin, New York, NY, 1994.
5. J. Robin. A revision-based generation architecture for reporting facts in their historical context. In H. Horacek and M. Zock, editors, *New Concepts in Natural Language Generation: Planning, Realization and Systems*. Frances Pinter, London and New York, 1993.
6. J. Robin. Automatic generation and revision of natural language summaries providing historical background. In *Proceedings of the 11th Brazilian Symposium on Artificial Intelligence*, Fortaleza, CE, October 1994.
7. J. Robin. Evaluating the portability of revision rules for incremental summary generation. In *Proceedings of the 34th Annual Meeting of the Association for Computational Linguistics*, Santa Cruz, California, 1996. ACL.
8. J. Robin and K. McKeown. Corpus analysis for revision-based generation of complex sentences. In *Proceedings of the 11th National Conference on Artificial Intelligence*, pages 365–372. AAAI, 1993.
9. K. Van der Linden and J.H. Martin. Expressing rhetorical relations in instructional texts: a case study of the purpose relation. *Computational Linguistics*, 21(1):29–58, 1995.

Semi-Automatic Anaphora Resolution in Portable Natural Language Interfaces

Flávia A. Barros*

Departamento de Informática, Universidade Federal de Pernambuco
Cx. Postal 7851, Cidade Universitária, Recife (PE), Brazil
fab@di.ufpe.br - http://www.di.ufpe.br/~fab

Abstract. This paper describes the pronominal anaphora resolution module of SQUIRREL system, a portable natural language front end to databases originally conceived to treat single sentences. The incorporation of the *Discourse Module* aimed to provide continuous consultations, however preserving the system's overall portability.

Candidate antecedents, selected from the *user's queries* and *database answers*, are organised into a *context* stack for subsequent inter-sentential reference. The *context* is segmented in accordance to changes of topic in the current dialogue between user and interface.

When an anaphor is found in the query, suitable candidates are selected from the *context* on the basis of syntactic features, as well as domain information from the system's Data Model. When no more reliable automatic selection is possible, competing candidates are presented to the user, who chooses the referent for the anaphor.

1 Introduction

An analysis of the evolution of Natural Language Front Ends (NLFEs) to Databases (DB) in the last three decades reveals a trade off between system's portability and the offered coverage of discourse phenomena (*e.g.*, anaphora and ellipsis). That is, the more portable the system is, the less discourse facilities it offers.

Early systems, research motivated, were mainly developed for a single application. The treatment of discourse phenomena, as well, was very dependent on the system's implementation and domain (*e.g.*, LUNAR [14], LADDER [12]). The subsequent generation of interfaces emphasized portability as a requirement for commercial viability (*e.g.*, INTELLECT [10], TEAM [9]). The use of world models was reduced or eliminated, since they compromise the system's portability. As a consequence, the coverage of discourse phenomena was constrained.

This paper presents a mechanism for pronominal anaphora resolution which was developed without recourse to world models, for the sake of portability, and still offers a reliable dialogue-like mode of NL database consultation. A *Discourse Module* was incorporated into SQUIRREL system [5], a portable natural

---

* The work reported here was developed while the author was pursuing her Ph.D. at Essex University (UK), under the supervision of Anne DeRoeck.

language front end to relational databases which was originally conceived with a single-query consultation mode. The system is implemented in C-Prolog.

The module covers all singular and plural occurrences of pronouns in the subject, object and possessive forms. Simple uses of the deictic adverb *there* are treated. The system accepts more than one anaphor in the same query.

The main contributions of the work presented here are: (1) the application of theoretical work on discourse structuring to the environment of a relational DB querying system; (2) no use of world models, to safeguard portability (the *Discourse Module* does not need to be customised); (3) a transparent and reliable mode of operation, where the user holds the control of the final decision for the pronoun binding; (4) the underlying design of the *Discourse Module* can be used as a guideline within modular NLFEs with similar structure to SQUIRREL.

Early results of this research are reported in [2], whereas the work's full description can be found in [1].

The rest of this paper starts with an overview of SQUIRREL system, followed by the description of the *Discourse Module*, with some implementation details. Next, we find a brief discussion of related work and conclusions.

2 SQUIRREL System

SQUIRREL system consists of two independent components: the *Front End* and the *Back End* (*cf.* Fig. 1). Strict separation between these two components guarantees modularity and portability to the systems as a whole.

The *Front End* translates the input sentence in English into syntactic and semantic representations, later mapped into First Order Logic (FOL). These three representations are independent of the domain of application or database structure. Syntactic analysis is based on a lexicon and a context-free grammar with features [6], whereas semantic rules are written in Property Theory [13].

The *Back End* first translates the FOL representation into a Domain Relational Calculus expression (DRC) [4], based on the Extended Data Model (which provides mappings between FOL and DRC expressions). It then maps the DRC representation into Tuple Relational Calculus [4], which is finally mapped into SQL [4] with the help of the DB data model. All these representations are domain-dependent.

In order to safeguard portability, the lexicon does not contain proper nouns, which are treated as placeholders to be fully interpreted when reaching the database. The system does not carry world models. Customisation only affects the lexicon and the Extended Data Model.

SQUIRREL does not contain explicit disambiguation strategies. At each level of analysis (syntax, semantics, and domain), all possible representations are generated and released for further processing. In the *Back End*, only the appropriate representations survive the type checking (based on the Data Model constraints), and the database consultation. However, for legitimate ambiguous queries, more than one successful DB answer can be obtained. In this case, all answers are presented to the user, who must choose the desired one.

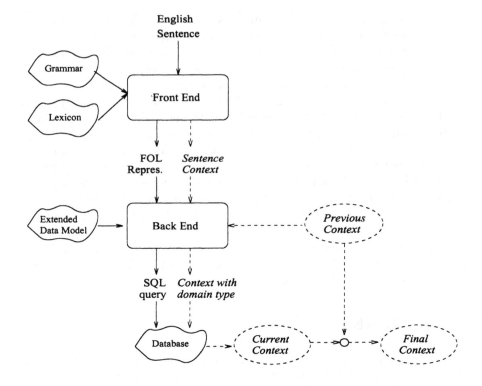

Fig. 1. SQUIRREL with the *Discourse Module*.

3   The Discourse Module

Following SQUIRREL's design principles, the anaphora resolution strategy presented here was developed without recourse to world models (to safeguard portability) and, more importantly, without fully automatic disambiguation strategies (for reliability). The user holds the control of the overall consultation process.

The *Discourse Module* centres around the *context list*, a collection of candidate antecedents which are made available for subsequent inter-sentential reference. The *context list* grows as a stack, *i.e.*, candidates selected from each query and its DB answer are stored on top of the candidates from the previous queries as the consultation unfolds. All candidates are represented in the same format.

The *context list* grows dynamically and is passed from query to query. Nevertheless, this structure does not grow indefinitely during a consultation. The stack is segmented in accordance to changes of topic in the dialogue between user and interface. The maximum number of segments held by the context is currently set to three, to allow for a return to a previous topic after a shift (Sect. 3.2).

When an anaphor is found in a query, suitable candidates are selected from the *context list* on the basis of syntactic and domain information. When no more reliable automatic selection is possible, competing candidates are presented to the user, who must choose the desired one, or reject all bindings offered by the system – in which case, candidates from previous segments with appropriate features are made available to the user (Sect. 3.3).

With these guidelines, the *Discourse Module* provides a domain-independent semi-automatic anaphora resolution process, which aims not to completely resolve an anaphoric reference at all cost, but to present the user with alternatives selected on the basis of reliable system information.

All singular and plural occurrences of pronominal anaphora are covered by the module, in subject, object and possessive forms. Simple uses of the deictic adverb *there* are also treated, allowing reference to locations (*e.g.*, address, department, etc.). The system handles more than one anaphor in the same query, treating each one at a time.

The remaining of this section is organised as follows: (1) *context list* formation; (2) structuring and update of the *context list*; and (3) resolution and binding phases.

3.1 Context Formation

The *context list* is currently composed on the basis of noun phrase heads, as this module was developed to deal with pronominal anaphora.

Two levels of the *context list* formation can be identified: the construction of the *current context*, for each query and its answer; and the building of the consultation's overall context, the actual *context list*.

Construction of the Current Context. The *current context* is obtained by the combination of the *sentence context* (with candidates selected from the current query), with the candidates derived from the DB answer (*cf.* Fig. 1).

The formation of the *sentence context* is controlled by *context rules* embedded in the system's grammar, where each syntactic rule has its associated semantic and context rules. Words in the lexicon have associated syntactic, semantic and context values already set, whereas proper nouns have their features constructed during the parsing process (since they do not appear in the lexicon). These 'word' contexts are combined according to the context rule associated with the current syntactic rule, resulting in the *sentence context*.

Further information is added to each candidate in the *sentence context* as the query is being processed: the *domain type* of the candidate, obtained from the data model in the *Back End*; and the *gender* of proper names (if any), retrieved after the query reaches the database.

The indication of which items in database answers are to be added to the *context list* is subject to customisation, as this may vary from one application to another. The Extended Data Model informs the tables' attributes from where to select candidates, which are later formatted and associated with syntactic, semantic and domain information (based on the characteristics of the database domain from which they are retrieved). In the case where the data derives from domains associated with proper nouns, gender is retrieved immediately.

Format of the Context. Each entry in the *context list* is represented in the format of a list of lists of two elements. These entries are primarily distinguished by the 'number' feature – singular or plural (see example 1 below).

Singular candidates, lexical plurals (*e.g.*, employees) and nouns which denote groups (*e.g.*, the police, the committee) will have one entry in the *current context*. Structural plurals (originating through coordination – *e.g.*, John and Mary) give rise to one plural entry with all of the nouns gathered as a collection and, in the case of proper names, one individual entry per candidate.

Example 1 - Construction of the current context.

▷ **query:** who is edna's boss?
  sentence context:
    [[[1.1,singular], → (segment.query number, syntactic number)
    [query,edna], → (candidate from query, word)
    [propn,temporary], → (proper name, temporary entry)
    [gender,-], → (gender feature not yet instantiated)
    [agreement,-], → (agreement feature not yet instantiated)
    [sem,lambda(p,p:'edna)], → (semantic value in PT)
    [domain,[EMP![name],string,animate]] → (domain type from data model)[2]
    [[1.1,singular], [query,boss], [noun,fixed], **[gender**,neut],
    [agreement,[[num,sing],[pers,3]]], **[sem**,'boss]
    [domain,[EMP![name],string,animate]]]]
▷ **dbanswer:** [malcolm]
  current context:
    [[[1.1,singular], [query,edna], [propn,temporary], **[gender**,fem],
    [agreement,[[num,sing],[pers,3]]], **[sem**,lambda(p,p:'edna)]
    [domain,[EMP![name],string,animate]]]
    [[1.1,singular], [query,boss], [noun,fixed], **[gender**,neut],
    [agreement,[[num,sing],[pers,3]]], **[sem**,'boss]
    [domain,[EMP![name],string,animate]]]
    [[1.1,singular], [answer,malcolm], [propn,temporary], [gender,masc],
    [agreement,[[num,sing], [pers,3]]], [sem,lambda(p,p:'malcolm)]
    [domain,[EMP![name],string,animate]]]]

Construction of a Consultation's Context. The *Discourse Module* deals with two contexts at a time: the *current context*, which is local to the current query and its answer, and the *previous context*, with entries obtained from all previous queries of the consultation still available, that is, the *context list* of the consultation to the present moment (*cf.* Fig. 1).

When the current query succeeds, the *current context* is combined with the *previous context*, resulting in the query's *final context*. The elements of the *previous context* which reoccur in the *current context* are eliminated. This simple

---

[2] EMP![name] denotes a name from the EMP (employee) table.

mechanism establishes the candidates' priority in the resolution process. The *final context* of the current query becomes the *previous context* for the subsequent query of the consultation.

3.2   Context Structuring

The *context list* is segmented in order to mirror the behaviour of the user-interface dialogue, where each segment should correspond to a topic of such dialogue. The question is *how to implement this principle?*

The lack of linguistic clues in how to segment the *context list* (*e.g.*, cue words), and also in how to identify the relationships between such segments, restricts the possible solutions. Therefore, the whole process is based upon (the very restricted) domain information available in the Data Model.

The segmentation process deployed here relies on two potential sources for identifying coherence in relational queries. First of all, 'meaningful' queries are always associated with a complete *access path* covering relations and attributes in the database. As such, if we represent the Data Model as a graph, a meaningful query will always cover a connected (partial) subgraph – the *query's covered domain*.

Secondly, in a coherent consultation, two queries which are concerned with the same topic will cover, in part, the same area in the database. That is, two queries are related when their access paths intersect. Furthermore, the area of intersection offers information regarding the identification of *focus*. Building on this, the *discourse domain* covered by successive related queries is defined as the union of their access paths.

Candidates for anaphoric reference are grouped into segments, where a segment contains all successive queries which share part of an access path. The first query starts the first segment of the *context list*. When a new query is entered, its covered domain is matched against that of the segment on top of the *context list*. If the intersection is not empty, candidates from the query are added to this segment. In case the intersection is empty, the system identifies a change of topic on the consultation, and a new segment is started. The segment's *topic* is defined as the discourse domain covered by a segment – the union of its queries' access paths.

Following [8], segments occur in sequence, or hold an embedding relation, to allow users to elaborate on a change of *focus* before returning to the previous topic. In order to deal with this, the *context list* maintains a number of segments available. This number is subject to customisation, and is currently set to three, the minimum necessary to simulate embedding.

Within a segment, candidates are grouped by query number. When a candidate re-occurs, it is placed on the top of the *context list*, and its previous occurrence is deleted, regardless what segment it belongs to. The antecedent of a resolved anaphor is also added to the top (*cf.* Fig. 2).

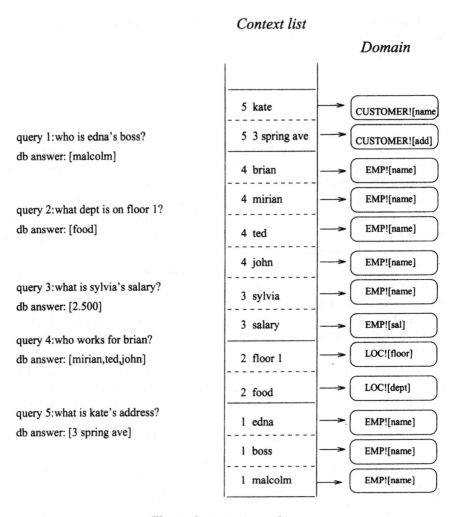

Context list

Domain

query 1:who is edna's boss?
db answer: [malcolm]

query 2:what dept is on floor 1?
db answer: [food]

query 3:what is sylvia's salary?
db answer: [2.500]

query 4:who works for brian?
db answer: [mirian,ted,john]

query 5:what is kate's address?
db answer: [3 spring ave]

Fig. 2. Context structuring.

3.3 The Resolution and Binding Phases

The resolution phase results in the formation of the *foci list*, to be presented to
the user during the binding phase.

As with any other noun phrase, the anaphora will have their associated domain fixed during the sentence's interpretation. This information, together with
gender and number, is used to select the suitable candidates from the *context
list*. When an anaphoric expression is found in a query, all candidates in the
current segment are considered as potential antecedents. In this way, the *context*
structuring restricts the options via the segmentation process. From these potential antecedents, the selection of suitable candidates for binding is guided by

the constraints number, gender and domain type. All candidates complying with these constraints are placed in the *foci list* (*cf.* Fig. 3), which will be presented to the user for selection, confirmation or rejection during the binding phase.

The *foci list* is used to track focus. The current segment is the most relevant to the binding of anaphora, and is therefore the first to be searched. The following example illustrates the resolution mechanism.

Example 2 - The resolution mechanism.

```
query: who is edna's boss?
db answer: [malcolm]
query: who is sylvia's boss?
db answer: [edna]
query: who works for her?
** USER, please choose a substitute for 'her':
1 - sylvia
2 - edna
3 - none above            number: 2
db answer: [mary, sylvia, ted]
```

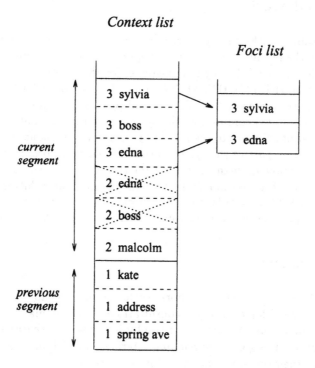

Fig. 3. Foci list formation.

In this example, the system has no means to disambiguate between the two possible candidates for binding the pronoun 'her' (*sylvia, edna*), since both have the same properties: female gender, EMP! [name] as domain type, and both belong to the same segment. The system has exhausted all the information it can draw on. Note that humans would not be able to select one either.

We are presented with an ambiguity, and a choice between competing candidates must be made, since the interpretation of the current query will affect the *context* for the rest of the consultation. In keeping with the principle of system transparency, the *foci list* is presented to the user, who must confirm the binding to one candidate (even if only one candidate is offered) or reject all options.

Once a candidate is chosen, it substitutes the anaphor in the query's representation, which is finally released to the database. The candidate's entry is then moved to the top of the *context list*, to assure its priority in the selection process.

When no suitable candidate is found in the current segment to form the *foci list*, or in the case when the user rejects all of the possibilities offered, the routine which allows access to the previous segments still in the *context list* is called by the system. The algorithms which control the *Discourse Module* functioning can be found in [1].

4   Related Work

Several portable NLFEs equipped with discourse modules were carefully investigated during the production of the work reported here (see [1, pp 9–34]). Among those, I highlight the following four systems, for their better achievements: INTELLECT [10], IRUS [3], DATALOG [7] and DATENBANK-DIALOG [11].

While some of these systems offer a broad coverage of anaphora, the deployed mechanisms either (1) compromise the system's overall portability and/or reliability, or (2) limit reference to the preceding query only, without even considering the DB *answer* as part of the system's context. Furthermore, none of them offers a segmentation mechanism to control the *discourse context*. Either they keep a stack which grows indefinitely, or they impose an arbitrary limit (*e.g.,* five queries in DATALOG) lacking theoretical or empirical motivation. Finally, none of them provides a comprehensive treatment of anaphoric plurals.

5   Conclusions

I presented here a module for anaphora resolution in a portable NLFE - SQUIRREL, which allows for continuous consultations, however maintaining the system's portability. The motivation for combining these two features comes from the same source: the goal of developing interfaces for helping non-expert users in consulting their, possibly varied, database systems.

The SQUIRREL front end was originally designed with a single-query based mode of consultation, setting portability as its main priority. Nontheless, because of its high degree of modularity, it presents a suitable base-line for the current extension.

Although the current application works only with NP heads, nothing prevents the possibility of dealing with candidates of different syntactic categories. This could be achieved by modifying the context rules in the system's grammar. In the case of DB answers, the category of the answer would have to be stored in the database, and would be retrieved in a similar manner as gender information.

I have demonstrated that it is possible to include reliable, user-controlled features of discourse phenomena (including comprehensive coverage of plurals) in modular NLFEs without recourse to world models, thus safeguarding portability.

References

1. Barros, F.A.: *A Teatment of Anaphora in Portable Natural Language Front Ends to Data Bases*. PhD thesis. University of Essex, U.K. (1995)
2. Barros, F.A. and DeRoeck, A.: Resolving Anaphora in a Portable Natural Language Front End to Databases. *Proc. of the 4th Conference on Applied Natural Language Processing – ANLP'94*. Stuttgart, Germany. (1994) 119–124
3. Bates, M., Moser, M.G. and Stallar, D.: The IRUS Transportable Natural Language Database Interface. *Expert Database Systems*. (1986) 617–630
4. Date, C.J.: *An Introduction to Database Systems*. 1 (1990) Addison-Wesley systems programming series.
5. DeRoeck A., Fox C., Lowden B., Turner R. and Walls B.: A Natural Language System Based on Formal Semantics. *Proc of the International Conference on Current Issues in Computational Linguistics*. Penang, Malaysia. (1991)
6. Gazdar G., Klein E., Pullum G. and Sag I.: *Generalised Phrase Structure Grammar*. Blackwell. (1985)
7. Godden, K.: Computing Pronoun Antecedents in an English Query System. *Proc. of the Eleventh Int. Joint Conference on AI – IJCAI'89*. 2 (1989) 1498–1503
8. Grosz B., Sidner C.: Attention, Intention, and the Structure of Discourse. *Computational Linguistics*. 12 (1986) 175–204
9. Grosz B., Appelt, D., Martin, P., Pereira, F.: TEAM: An Experiment in the Design of Transportable Natural-Language Interfaces. *Artificial Intelligence*. 32 (1987) 173–243
10. Harris L.: Experience with INTELLECT: Artificial Intelligence Technology Transfer. *The AI Magazine*. 2(2) (1984) 43-50
11. Heinz, W., Matiasek, J., Trost, H., Buchberger, E.: Comparison in NLIs - Habitability and Database Reality. *Proc. of the 10th European Conference on Artificial Intelligence – ECAI'92*. (1992) 548–552
12. Hendrix G., Sacerdoti E., Sagalowowicz D., Slocum J.: Developing a Natural Language Interface to Complex Data. *ACM Transac. on database Systems*. 3(2) (1978) 105–147
13. Turner R.: A Theory of Properties. *Journal of Symbolic Logic*. 52(2) (1987)
14. Woods, W.A.: Progress in Natural Language Understanding: An Application to Lunar Geology. *Proc. of AFIPS National Computer Conference.*. (1973) 441-450

A Discourse Model for Gist Preservation

Lucia Helena Machado Rino
DC - UFSCar
Caixa Postal 676
13565-905 São Carlos - SP, Brazil
Fax: (016) 2748233
lucia@dc.ufscar.br

Donia Scott
ITRI - University of Brighton
Lewes Road
Brighton BN2 4AT, UK
Fax: (00-44-1273) 642908
Donia.Scott@itri.bton.ac.uk

Abstract. This paper describes an approach to gist preservation during automatic summarization whereby the source is a complex information structure which must be "pruned" and organized in such a way as to make it appropriate for textual expression. Based on a discourse model, we propose a process whereby gist is guaranteed at the deep level according to communicative and rhetorical settings. The main function of such a goal-driven summarization model is to map intentions onto coherence relations whilst still observing the semantic dependency indicated by the message source. The discourse model is thus based on an association of intentionality, coherence and semantics, which guides the production of summary message sources that highlight the central proposition of the discourse.

Keywords: Automatic summarization, discourse modeling, text generation.

Introduction

This paper addresses the processes underlying automatic summarization within the context of natural language generation. In particular, the main problem under focus is how to derive the text plan of a summary of a complex information structure, i.e., a reduced but suitably enhanced structure that eliminates redundant or less relevant information while preserving the gist of its source. This problem can be viewed within the context of a traditional natural language generation system to which we add a summarization component. Since the focus of this work is in the underlying processes, a summarizer is simply seen here as the text structurer. In this special context, the input (i.e., the complex information structure) is referred to as *primary message source*, and the output is a new, concise, text plan derived from a subset of such a structure and overlaid with a discourse structure, henceforth named *summary message source*. This source can then be passed to a realization component for textual expression.

In this paper, we will not address the later stage of linguistic realization. Instead, we will discuss two main issues concerning the production of summaries in the specified context:

- the required characteristics of the primary message source for it to be amenable to the derivation of coherent and accurate summaries that are gist-preserving;

- the nature of the process required to derive summary message sources.

Main concepts

A discourse is typically viewed within the computational linguistics community as a hierarchical composition of discourse segments represented linguistically by a structured collection of clauses (Grosz and Sidner, 1986; Hobbs, 1985; Hovy, 1993). Discourse segments are seen as units of meaning (e.g., sentences or propositions), each having a specific function in the discourse, established by the inter-relationship among its elements. In general, each discourse segment reflects a subtopic of the global discourse topic and its relation to the overall communicative goal by means of its own communicative function in the discourse.

At the deep level of processing, the main elements manipulated or produced by our summarizer are the following:

The communicative goal. This is the primary intention of the writer in producing the text.

The central proposition. This is the "kernel" of the discourse (Levelt, 1989), i.e., the information around which the discourse is organized to satisfy the communicative goal. This information can be highly complex. For the purpose of this paper, however, we restrict it to a single component of the primary message source, i.e., a leaf of its information structure, as it will be shown shortly.

The primary message source. This is a complex information structure composed of three distinct kinds of information: a communicative goal, a central proposition, and a knowledge base. This base is a hierarchical structure of semantically inter-related content units, as illustrated in Fig. 1 (underlined words stand for the super-components of the knowledge base), and is the only component of the primary message source that is available for condensation. Such a structure can be "pruned" by extracting those propositions that are superfluous in the specific context determined by the communicative goal and the central proposition. Fig. 1 shows the structure of the knowledge base for the following example text (numbered clauses are propositions, but not all of them have been exhaustively dismembered. Occurrences of, e.g., X, Y or Z in the message source stand for implicit concepts whose content could not be retrieved from the text surface):

Example text:

1. This paper presents the results of measurements on the keyhole structure produced during the laser processing of materials.

2. A cw CO_2 laser was used to produce keyhole structures in water and measurements were made of the depth of the keyhole as a function of laser power and the force due to gravity.

3. The data show that as the laser power is increased, the keyhole depth also increases.

4. However, changes in the force due to gravity seem to have little effect on the depth.

5a. The data for the different power conditions are compared with calculations using the Andrews and Atthey expression for the hole shape
5b. and good agreement is achieved.
6. There is however no term in the theoretical description which accounts for the downward flow of liquid around the keyhole.
7a. This flow is estimated at 20 cm/s
7b. and is thought to be an important factor
7c. which it is planned to include in more detailed calculations.
8. Further measurements are also planned.

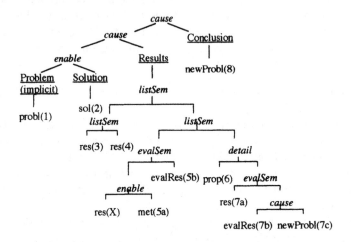

Fig. 1. A knowledge base of a primary message source

The summary message source. This is a discourse structure which reflects the logical chaining of ideas and propositions built around the central proposition by means of subthemes, or subtheses. It is derived from the primary source by selecting only the relevant material contained within it and organizing that material coherently. Selection and organization are pipelined, so that first the knowledge base is pruned and then the discourse of the summary is organized according to the resulting knowledge base, the communicative goal and the central proposition. Fig. 2 and Fig. 3 show, respectively, the condensed knowledge base and the summary message source to describe a result in a summarizing process whereby the primary message source is composed of the communicative goal **Describe** and the central proposition *result "7a"* (or *res(7a)*, as shown). Bold branches in the summary message source indicate nuclear subtrees, according to the *Rhetorical Structure Theory* (RST) (Mann and Thompson, 1987). In the model presented here, the propositions of the condensed knowledge base will be used to complement or emphasize the central proposition, at the same time that they contribute to the communicative goal (Grosz and Sidner, 1986; Scott and Souza, 1990).

According to the above, the central proposition of a discourse will be one of the leaves of both, the primary and the summary message sources. If the summary is gist-preserving, the central proposition of both sources will be identical. A possible hand-generated summary based upon the illustrated summary message source is given below.

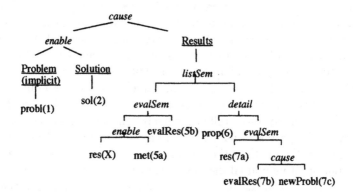

Fig. 2. A condensed knowledge base

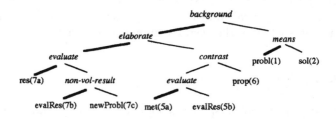

Fig. 3. A summary message source of a description

Example summary: A possible description of a result

The downward flow of liquid around a keyhole structure produced during the laser processing of materials has been estimated at 20 cm/s, an important factor which must be included in more detailed calculations. Although good agreement is achieved with a comparison between data for the different power conditions and calculations using the Andrews and Atthey expression for the hole shape, there is no term in the theoretical description which accounts for such a flow.

Strategic account

The results described in this paper are based on the analysis of a corpus of scientific journal articles from a single technical domain (physics). Given the highly stereotyped nature of this genre, our analysis revealed a well-known pattern of discourse organization, known as Problem-Solution (P-S) (Hoey, 1983). This pattern reveals the set of common semantic relations used in the primary message source (Rino and Scott, 1994). Many of them can be fairly straightforwardly mapped onto coherence relations drawn from existing theories of discourse organization, e.g., RST and Hobbs' coherence relations. The analysis also identified the most frequent communicative goals (Describe, Relate, and Discuss). For an intentional account, we add to our model the *Grosz and Sidner Discourse Theory* (GSDT) (Grosz and Sidner, 1986), whose dominance and precedence relations are independent of a linguistic behavior and characterize the search for a communicative setting at a high level of abstraction.

GSDT and RST are complementary and both allow for a functional approach. RST specifies the intended effects of a coherence relation on the behavior of the reader and expresses (albeit coarsely) the underlying discourse intentions, conveying the propositional content in a relational form that is essential for coherence. GSDT, on the other hand, focuses fundamentally on the intentional contribution of individual discourse segments to the overall discourse by allowing for structural relations between intentions. We show here that this theory can lead to the choice of specific coherence relations, complementing the lack of a clear specification of communicative purposes of the RST. At the same time, chosen coherence relations cannot violate the conceptual dependence specified in the primary message source. The inter-relationship between intentions and coherence relations is critical to summarization: it is this that provides the basis for determining the partial contribution of content information to gist preservation and the satisfaction of the overall communicative goal.

Modeling discourse

Formal and functional perspectives both hold in our discourse modeling: we make use of a formalism that summarizes the primary message source by considering the functional perspective, responsible for the discourse internal structure and for the relationship between the intentional and coherence levels. Therefore, discourse functionality determines discourse organization by mapping intentionality onto coherence, while still observing the semantics of the knowledge base to provide the informative means of the discourse.

Modeled in such a way, discourse is organized considering three distinct levels of structural relations: the functional one, which combines intentions and coherence relations, the informative one, given by the knowledge base, and the formal one, which addresses linguistic resources based upon the interaction between informativity and functionality. This formal method of producing discourse is illustrated in Table 1. For example, in Case 5 there is a formal correspondence that reads: *If a "symmetry" intentional relation holds between discourse segments X and Y, and if both segments are in a "listSem" (i.e., a parallel) relation in the knowledge base, then the preferrable coherence relations between X and Y are either* LIST *or* CONTRAST.

Semantic relations	Coherence relations	Structural intentions among intentions	Cases
enable(Y,X)	purpose[1](X,Y) means(Y,X)	X <u>sat-precedes</u> Y Y <u>dom</u> X	1
rationale(X,Y)	purpose[2](X,Y) justify[1](X,Y)	Y <u>supports</u> X X <u>dom</u> Y not X <u>sat-precedes</u> Y	2
proof(X,Y)	evidence(X,Y) justify[2](X,Y)	Y <u>sat-precedes</u> X X <u>dom</u> Y Y <u>supports</u> X	3
cause(X,Y)	non-vol-result(Y,X) non-vol-cause(X,Y)	Y <u>sat-precedes</u> X X <u>dom</u> Y Y <u>generates</u> X	4
listSem(X,Y)	list(X,Y) contrast(X,Y)	X <u>symmetr</u> Y	5
attribute(X,Y) *detail*(X,Y) *exemplify*(X,Y)	elaborate(X,Y)	Y <u>supports</u> X	6
evaluateSem(X,Y)	evaluate(X,Y)	X <u>dom</u> Y	7
reason(X,Y)	explain(X,Y)	Y <u>generates</u> X	8
sequence(X,Y)	sequence(X,Y)	X <u>sat-precedes</u> Y	9
background(X,Y)	background(X,Y)	not X <u>sat-precedes</u> Y Y <u>supports</u> X	10

Table 1. Mapping of intentions and semantic relations onto coherence relations

Table 1 addresses all the possible mappings of our current discourse model, i.e., all three sets of relations are necessary and sufficient for summary planning. Semantic relations are naturally depicted in the English language. Coherence relations are determined through the propositional delimitation of spans of sample texts. Structural relations between intentions follow the GSDT. In addition to these, we find it necessary to include the relation **symmetry**, which holds between two intentions when one contributes to the other and vice-versa. Of the coherence relations relevant to our task, only two present a symmetric account at the intentional level: LIST (Scott and Souza, 1990) and CONTRAST (Mann and Thompson, 1987), as shown in Case 5.

Along with the main communicative goals, there are other subgoals whose interplay display a complex interaction among different text types. For example, narratives exchange features with expositions when they narrate facts of an explanation of plans. Such a complex interplay can provide a *systemic network*, which allows for the mapping between communicative goals and coherence relations in a special way, as partly shown in Fig. 4.

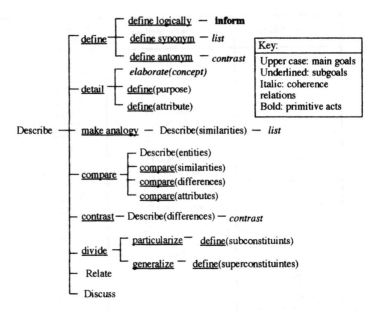

Fig. 4. Communicative goals and their interaction with coherence relations

Conceptual classes found in the corpus analysis determine another kind of network, i.e., a *communicative inheritance network*, which details further the communicative goals. For example, an entity description can be a description of a **solution** or a **problem**, which are two conceptual classes of the scientific discourse model. Such classes are used to annotate the content units of a knowledge base, e.g., "Result" produces the annotation "res" in Fig. 1.

Computational account

Both inheritance and systemic networks allow for the definition of discourse schemata (McKeown, 1985) and plan operators (Moore and Paris, 1993). A schema guarantees that the proper communicative setting is initially established, in order to preserve gist. For example, given that a super-structure of a summary can be represented by the logical sequence *Situation-Problem-Solution-Results-Discussion and evaluation of results* (Hoey, 1983), to **describe a specific result** a schema is chosen which emphasizes either the subpath *Describe-Feature,Describe-Attribute,Describe-ValueOfResult* or the subpath *Describe-Object,Describe-Result*. Plan operators allow for distinct rhetorical settings based upon different choices of rhetorical strategies (see Fig. 4).

Gist preservation is addressed at all levels of discourse processing. The most important resources to address this issue are the plan operators, which are responsible for discourse organization, in that they map intentional and semantic relations onto coherence relations, according to the correspondence shown in Table 1. Graduallly, the summary message source is constrained to present the central proposition as the "most nuclear" unit.

We follow Moore and Paris to specify our plan language. Communicative goals can be represented, for example, by *Describe, Interpret, or Discuss*, and can be associated to the writer's intention to make the reader believe, or act according to, a proposition. A discourse is successfully produced when it achieves the intended change of the mental state of the reader. Linguistic goals to support these intentions can be primitive acts (only inform in our current model) or rhetorical goals (e.g., evidence, or justify), which are directly expressed as coherence relations.

Plan operators handle both types of goals. However, only those that explicitly post linguistic goals can modify the discourse structure under construction. Planning is complete when all the active plan operators are successfully applied, generating all the leaves of the discourse structure, i.e., the primitive acts given by *inform* nodes. At this point, the proof space resulting from the recursive and progressive account of constrained discourse organization registers not only the thread of discourse, but also the space of contribution of each discourse segment to the overall discourse, in terms of the purpose of each particular segment.

Each plan operator is a modified RST plan (embedding functional aspects of discourse organization) whose satellites can be essential or optional. Essential satellites affect the purpose of the nucleus and, consequently, the contribution of the corresponding discourse segment to the overall communicative purpose. For this reason, they must be further developed in the plan. Optional ones, on the other hand, may elucidate the nucleus, but are not crucial. The decision to include them in a summary plan depends on the constraints (for example, the degree of detail required). Such satellites are responsible for varying degrees of conciseness at the deep level of summarization.

Since subgoals can be either communicative or linguistic, coherence relations are determined only when a plan operator applies to a context that provides appropriate conditions for the mapping between intentions and semantic relations. This approach proves appropriate for summarization in that it provides the flexibility to choose plan operators that can convey and organize information in varied ways, provided that the central proposition is preserved and is guaranteed to be available to the realization phase. Moreover, built on a constraint satisfaction model, the final discourse structure is guaranteed to achieve the communicative goal because it operates on partial information, gradually constraining the range of possible choices of new information to compose such a structure.

Discussion and Conclusion

Other work has explored a similar communicative account to the one presented here, e.g., in text generation by Cawsey (1990) and Maybury (1992), and in automatic summarization by Sparck Jones (1993). However, none have addressed the crucial problem of preserving gist in the context of condensing the message to be conveyed. Pursuing this view, we add to Moore and Paris' discourse model the specific constraints for gist preservation and prominence, assigning the position of the central proposition of a summary message source to the "most nuclear" leaf of an RST-like discourse structure. In addition, we trigger the planning process by narrowing the possible paths to achieve the communicative goal based on the typical semantic organization of the primary message source. The consistency provided by the highly stereotyped discourse under investigation allows us to identify the possible super-components that involve the central proposition of the discourse to be constructed. In this respect, the Problem-Solution pattern is particularly interesting, allowing for schemata definitions that indicate the possible ways of satisfying the summarization constraints.

The correspondence between semantics and coherence described here is based on an empirical study. From Table 1, we can see that the mapping of semantic relations to coherence relations can be one-to-many or many-to-one, and that coherence relations do not necessarily map to the same structural relations at the intentional level (e.g., PURPOSE and JUSTIFY). This is fortuitously advantageous for summarization, in that it provides the necessary flexibility to produce different discourse structures for the same message and also varying degrees of conciseness or informativeness.

Compared to other approaches based on schemata (e.g., (McKeown, 1985)), the approach described here provides more flexibility through the addition of plan operators which combine in a single formalism the interdependence between three distinct levels of discourse representation, namely intentionality, coherence and semantics. None of these structural levels taken alone is able to address any of the others (Sparck Jones, 1993), e.g., a communicative setting does not completely account for a rhetorical one; semantic relations do not express intentions by themselves. Besides such advantages, "reasoning" provided by plan operators is not predetermined: special cases where the choice of a specific discourse relation runs the risk of obscuring the central proposition can be handled by the constraints field of any plan operator.

Our approach relies on the active identification of information that can complement the central proposition to be conveyed. However, it takes an inverse view to that proposed by Robin (1994). Whereas we identify less relevant propositions, *omitting* them from the primary message source and reorganizing them, Robin identifies relevant propositions, *adding* them to a given proposition in order to build up a text. In our approach, automatic summarization is based on conventional text generation processes for modeling discourse, to which we add a severe constraint: the preservation of the gist of a message source. We show that a communicative account is essential to determine the space of contribution of discourse segments to both gist preservation and the overall communicative goal. In this, our work supports the insights provided by Sparck Jones.

In carrying out this work, we have provided a specification of the correspondence between intentions and coherence relations on the basis of the highly stereotyped discourse of science. We have applied our discourse model to a small number of scientific domains and to another genre (technical texts) (Rino, 1996). Our results so far show that gist can be preserved in summary generation provided that the corresponding primary message sources are structured according to the Problem-Solution pattern. This pattern is not specific to scientific texts, but can be found in a number of other genres, e.g., (Jordan, 1992), suggesting that our discourse model for gist preservation may be more generally applicable to a wider context of natural language generation.

Acknowledgments. The research described in this paper was partially supported by the Conselho Nacional de Desenvolvimento Científico e Tecnológico (CNPq), Project No. 201610/92-2.

References

Cawsey, A. Generating Explanatory Discourse. In R.Dale; C. Mellish and M. Zock (eds.), *Current Research in Natural Language Generation*, pp. 75-101. London, Academic Press, 1990.

Grosz, B. and Sidner, C. Attention, Intentions, and the Structure of Discourse. *Computational Linguistics*, Vol. 12, No. 3, 1986.

Hobbs, J.R. *On the Coherence and Structure of Discourse*. Technical Report CSLI-85-37, Center for the Study of Language and Information, Stanford University, 1985.

Hoey, M. *On the Surface of Discourse*. George Allen & Unwin (Publishers) Ltd., 1983.

Hovy, E. Automated Discourse Generation Using Discourse Structure Relations. *Artificial Intelligence* 63, pp. 341-385, 1993.

Jordan, M.P. An Integrated Three-pronged Analysis. In W.C. Mann and S.A. Thompson (eds.), *Discourse Description: Diverse Linguistic Analyses of a Fund-Raising Text*. John Benjamins Publishing Co., 1992.

Levelt, W.J.M. *Speaking: From Intention to Articulation*. The MIT Press, Cambridge. 1989.

Mann, W.C. and Thompson, S.A. *Rhetorical Structure Theory: A Theory of Text Organization*. Technical Report ISI/RS-87-190, June 1987.

Maybury, M.T. Communicative Acts for Explanation Generation. *Int. Journal of Man-Machine Studies* 37, pp. 135-172, 1992.

McKeown, K.R. *Text Generation: Using Discourse Strategies and Focus Constraints to Generate Natural Language Text*. Cambridge University Press, 1985.

Moore, J.D. and Paris, C. Planning Text for Advisory Dialogues: Capturing Intentional and Rhetorical Information. *Computational Linguistics*, Vol.19, No. 4, pp. 651-694, 1993.

Robin, J. *Revision-Based Generation of Natural Language Summaries Providing Historical Background: Corpus-Based Analysis, Design, Implementation and Evaluation*. PhD. Thesis. Columbia University, December 1994.

Rino, L.H.M. *Modelagem de Discurso para o Tratamento da Concisão e Preservação da Idéia Central na Geração de Textos*. PhD. Thesis. Universidade de São Paulo, Brasil. Abril 1996.

Rino, L.H.M. and Scott, D. Content selection in summary generation. *XI Simpósio Brasileiro de Inteligência Artificial*. Fortaleza, Brazil, October 1994.

Scott, D.R. and Souza, C.S. Getting the Message Across in RST-Based Text Generation. In R.Dale; C.Mellish and M. Zock (eds.), *Current Research in Natural Language Generation*. London, Academic Press, pp. 47-73, 1990.

Sparck Jones, K. *Discourse Modelling for Automatic Summarising*. Tech. Rep. No. 290. University of Cambridge, Feb 1993.

Iterative Curve Organisation with the EM Algorithm

J. A. F. Leite and E. R. Hancock
Department of Computer Science
University of York, York, Y01 5DD, UK.

Abstract. This paper describes how the early visual process of contour organisation can be realised using the EM algorithm of Dempster, Laird and Rubin [2]. The underlying computational representation is based on Zucker's idea of fine spline coverings [17]. According to our EM approach the adjustment of spline parameters draws on an iterative weighted least-squares fitting process. The expectation step of our EM procedure computes the likelihood of the data using a mixture model defined over the set of spline coverings. These splines are limited in their spatial extent using Gaussian windowing functions. The maximisation of the likelihood leads to a set of linear equations in the spline parameters which solve the weighted least squares problem. We evaluate the technique on the localisation of road structures in aerial infra-red images.

1 Introduction

Dempster, Laird and Rubin's EM (expectation and maximisation) [2] algorithm was originally introduced as a means of finding maximum likelihood solutions to problems posed in terms of incomplete data. Despite its relatively poor convergence properties, the algorithm provides a powerful statistical framework for fitting sparse data that has many features in common with robust parameter estimation [10]. Recently, the algorithm has attracted renewed interest in the domain of artificial neural networks where it has not only been shown to have an intimate relationship with mean-field annealing [1], but also to provide a convenient framework for hierarchical data processing [7]. The basic idea underlying the algorithm is to iterate between the expectation and maximisation modes until convergence is reached. Expectation involves computing a weighted likelihood function using a mixture density specified in terms of a series of model parameters. In the maximisation phase, the model parameters are recomputed to maximise the expected value of the incomplete data likelihood. In fact, when viewed from this perspective, the updating of data likelihoods in the expectation phase would appear to have much in common with the probabilistic relaxation process extensively exploited in low and intermediate level vision [12, 5]. Maximisation of the incomplete data likelihood is reminiscent of robust estimation where outlier reject is employed in the iterative re-computation of model parameters [10].

It is these observations that motivate the study reported in this paper. We are interested in the organisation of the output of local feature enhancement operators into meaningful global contour structures [17, 5]. Despite providing one of the classical applications of relaxation labelling in low-level vision [12], successful solutions to the iterative curve reinforcement problem have proved to be surprisingly elusive [11, 16, 5]. Recently, two contrasting ideas have offered practical relaxation operators. Zucker *et al* [17] have sought biologically plausible operators which draw on the idea of computing a global curve organisation potential and locating consistent structure using a form of local snake dynamics [15]. In essence this biologically inspired model delivers a fine arrangement of local splines that minimise the curve organisation potential. Hancock and Kittler [5], on the other hand, appealed to a more information theoretic motivation [8]. In an attempt to overcome some of the well documented limitations of the original Rosenfeld, Hummel and Zucker relaxation operator [12] they have developed a Bayesian framework for relaxation labelling [8]. Of particular significance for the low-level curve enhancement problem is the underlying statistical framework which makes a clear-cut distinction between the roles of uncertain image data and prior knowledge of contour structure. This framework has allowed the output of local image operators to be represented in terms of Gaussian measurement densities, while curve structure is represented by a dictionary of consistent contour structures [5, 4, 14].

While both the fine-spline coverings of Zucker [17] and the dictionary-based relaxation operator of Hancock and Kittler [5] have delivered practical solutions to the curve reinforcement problem, they each suffer a number of shortcomings. For instance, although the fine spline operator can achieve quasi-global curve organisation, it is based on an essentially *ad hoc* local compatibility model. While being more information theoretic, the dictionary-based relaxation operator is limited by virtue of the fact that in most practical applications the dictionary can only realistically be evaluated over at most a 3x3 pixel neighbourhood. Our aim in this paper is to bridge the methodological divide between the biologically inspired fine-spline operator and the statistical framework of dictionary-based relaxation. We develop an iterative spline fitting process using the EM algorithm of Dempster *et al* [2]. In doing this we retain the statistical framework for representing filter responses that has been used to great effect in the initialisation of dictionary-based relaxation. However, we overcome the limited contour representation of the dictionary by drawing on local cubic splines.

2 Expectation

The practical goal in this paper is the detection of line-features which manifest themselves as intensity ridges of variable width in raw image data. Each pixel is characterised by a vector of measurements, z_i where i is the pixel-index. This measurement vector captures multi-scale line appearance by applying a battery of directional second derivative of Gaussian filters of various widths and orientations to the raw image. Suppose that the image data is indexed by the pixel-set I. Associated with each image pixel is a cubic spline parameterisation which represents the best-fit contour that couples it to adjacent feature pixels. The spline is represented by a vector of parameters denoted by $q_i = (q_i^0, q_i^1, q_i^2, q_i^3)^T$. Let (x_i, y_i) represent the position co-ordinates of the pixel indexed i. The spline variable, $s_{i,j} = x_i - x_j$ associated with the contour connecting the pixel indexed j is the horizontal displacement between the pixels indexed i and j. We can write the cubic spline as an inner product $F(s_{i,j}, \underline{q}_i) = \underline{q}_i^T \cdot \underline{S}_{i,j}$ where $\underline{S}_{i,j} = (1, s_{i,j}, s_{i,j}^2, s_{i,j}^3)^T$. Central to our EM algorithm will be the comparison of the predicted vertical spline displacement with its measured value $r_{i,j} = y_i - y_j$.

In order to initialise the EM algorithm, we require a set of initial spline probabilities which we denote by $\pi(\underline{q}_i^{(0)})$. Here we use the multi-channel combination model recently reported by Leite and Hancock [9] to compute an initial multi-scale line-feature probability. Accordingly, if Σ is the variance-covariance matrix for the components of the filter bank, then

$$\pi(\underline{q}_i^{(0)}) = 1 - \exp\left[-\frac{1}{2}z_i^T \Sigma^{-1} z_i\right] \tag{1}$$

Our basic model of the spline organisation process is as follows. Associated with each image pixel is a spline parameterisation. Key to our philosophy of exploiting a mixture model to describe the global contour structure of the image is the idea that every image point can in principle associate to each of the putative splines residing in a Gaussian window. This spline representation of the raw image data, i.e. the vectors of line filter responses, is incomplete in the sense that we do not know a priori the spline-data associations required to explain the underlying image structure. Accordingly we turn to the EM algorithm to compute the parameters of the mixture model which maximise an incomplete data likelihood function.

We commence by developing a mixture model for the conditional probability density for the filter response z_i given the current global spline description of the image data. If $\Phi^{(n)} = \{\underline{q}_i^{(n)}, \forall i \in I\}$ is the global spline description at iteration n of the EM process, then we can expand the mixture distribution over a set of putative splines that may associate with the image pixel indexed i

$$p(z_i | \Phi^{(n)}) = \sum_{j \in I} p(z_i | \underline{q}_j^{(n)}) \pi(\underline{q}_j^{(n)}) \tag{2}$$

The components of the above mixture density are the conditional measurement densities $p(z_i | \underline{q}_j^{(n)})$ and the spline mixing proportions $\pi(\underline{q}_j^{(n)})$. The conditional measurement densities represent the likelihood that the datum z_i originates from the spline centred on pixel j. The mixing proportions, on the other hand, represent the fractional contribution to the data arising from the jth parameter vector i.e. $\underline{q}_j^{(n)}$. Since we are interested in the maximum likelihood estimation of spline parameters, we turn our attention to the global likelihood of the raw image data, i.e.

$$p(z_i, \forall i \in I | \Phi^{(n)}) = \prod_{i \in I} p(z_i | \Phi^{(n)}) \tag{3}$$

The expectation step of the EM algorithm is aimed at estimating the log-likelihood using the parameters of the mixture distribution. In other words, we need to average the likelihood over the space of potential pixel-spline assignments. In fact, it was Dempster, Laird and Rubin [2] who observed that maximising the weighted log-likelihood was equivalent to iteratively maximising the conditional expectation of the likelihood for a new parameter set given an old parameter set. For our spline fitting problem, maximisation of the expectation of the conditional likelihood is equivalent to maximising the weighted log-likelihood function

$$Q(\Phi^{(n+1)}|\Phi^{(n)}) = \sum_{i \in I} \sum_{j \in I} P(\underline{q}_j^{(n)}|\underline{z}_i) \ln p(\underline{z}_i|\underline{q}_j^{(n+1)}) \tag{4}$$

The *a posteriori* probabilities $P(\underline{q}_j^{(n)}|\underline{x}_i)$ may be computed from the corresponding components of the mixture density $p(\underline{z}_i|q_j^{(n)})$ using the Bayes formula

$$P(\underline{q}_j^{(n)}|\underline{z}_i) = \frac{p(\underline{z}_i|\underline{q}_j^{(n)})\pi(\underline{q}_j^{(n)})}{\sum_{k \in I} p(\underline{z}_i|\underline{q}_k^{(n)})\pi(\underline{q}_k^{(n)})} \tag{5}$$

For notational convenience, and to make the weighting role of the *a posteriori* probabilities explicit we use the shorthand $w_{i,j}^{(n)} = P(\underline{q}_j^{(n)}|\underline{z}_i)$.

In order to proceed with the development of a spline fitting process we require a model for the mixture components, i.e. $p(\underline{z}_i|\underline{q}_j^{(n)})$. Here we assume that the required model can be specified in terms of Gaussian distribution functions. In other words, we confine our attention to Gaussian mixtures. The physical variable of these distributions is the squared error residual for the position prediction of the ith datum delivered by the jth spline. Accordingly we write

$$p(\underline{z}_i|\underline{q}_j^{(n)}) = \sqrt{\frac{\beta}{2\pi}} \exp\left[-\frac{1}{2}\beta\left(r_{i,j} - F(s_{i,j}, \underline{q}_j^{(n)})\right)^2\right] \tag{6}$$

where β is the inverse variance of the fit residuals. Rather than estimating β, we use it in the spirit of a control variable to regulate the effect of fit residuals. The expectation step of the EM algorithm simply reduces to computing the weighted squared error criterion

$$Q(\Phi^{(n+1)}|\Phi^{(n)}) = -\sum_{i \in I} \sum_{j \in I} w_{i,j}^{(n)}\left(r_{i,j} - F(s_{i,j}, \underline{q}_i^{(n+1)})\right)^2 \tag{7}$$

The EM incomplete data likelihood function defined above effectively implies that the splines are global in extent. For realistic curve organisation problems this is not only an over-ambitious goal it is also computationally over-demanding. We therefore impose a Gaussian window on each spline representation. This effectively limits the extent of each curve to a feasible local window. Although this imposes a restriction on the global organisation process, experience with dictionary-based relaxation [5, 4] and fine-spline coverings [17] suggests that the process of iteration can overcome the locality of representation. Global organisation is achieved through a process of iterative and co-operative contour re-enforcement. We therefore modify our expected log-likelihood function to include a windowing weight $g_{i,j}$ as follows

$$Q(\Phi^{(n+1)}|\Phi^{(n)}) = -\sum_{i \in I} \sum_{j \in N_i} g_{i,j} w_{i,j}^{(n)} \epsilon_{i,j}(q_j^{(n+1)})^2 \tag{8}$$

where $\epsilon_{i,j}(\underline{q}_j^{(n+1)}) = r_{i,j} - F(s_{i,j}, \underline{q}_j^{(n+1)})$ and N_i is the neighbourhood window. Typically, the neighbourhood consists of a 5x5, 7x7 or 9x9 pixel window. In fact in Section 5, we use a 9x9 window for the bulk of our experiments. The window weight is defined as follows

$$g_{i,j} = \frac{h_{i,j}}{\sum_{j \in N_i} h_{i,j}} \tag{9}$$

where $h_{i,j}$ is windowing function which limits the extent of the spline. Here we use a Gaussian function of the form

$$h_{i,j} = \exp\left[-k\left((x_i - x_j)^2 + (y_i - y_j)^2\right)\right] \tag{10}$$

where the scale parameter k is chosen to concentrate the available probability-mass over an appropriately sized support window. Once updated parameter estimates $\underline{q}_i^{(n)}$ become available through the maximisation of this criterion, improved estimates of the mixture components may be obtained by substitution into equation (6). The updated mixing proportions, $\pi(\underline{q}_i^{(n+1)})$, required to determine the new weights $w_{i,j}^{(n)}$ are computed from the newly available density components using the following estimator

$$\pi(\underline{q}_i^{(n+1)}) = \sum_{j \in N_i} \frac{g_{i,j} p(z_j | \underline{q}_i^{(n)}) \pi(\underline{q}_i^{(n)})}{\sum_{k \in I} g_{i,j} p(z_j | \underline{q}_k^{(n)}) \pi(\underline{q}_k^{(n)})} \tag{11}$$

Equations (5), (6) and (11) therefore specify a recursive procedure that iterates the weighted residuals to compute a new mixing proportions based on the quality of the spline fit.

3 Maximisation

The maximisation step aims to optimize the quantity $Q(\Phi^{(n+1)}|\Phi^{(n)})$ with respect to the spline parameters. Formally this corresponds to finding the set of spline parameters which satisfy the condition

$$\Phi^{(n+1)} = \arg\max_{\Phi} Q(\Phi|\Phi^{(n)}) \tag{12}$$

We find a local approximation to this condition by solving the following set of linear equations

$$\frac{\partial Q(\Phi^{(n+1)}|\Phi^{(n)})}{\partial (q_i^k)^{(n+1)}} = 0 \tag{13}$$

for each spline parameter $(q_i^k)^{(n+1)}$ in turn, i.e. for k=0,1,2,3. In other words upon substituting for $Q(\Phi^{(n+1)}|\Phi^{(n)})$ from equation (8) the maximisation step reduces to solving the following set of four linear equations for the spline parameters

$$\sum_{j \in N_i} g_{i,j} w_{i,j}^{(n)} (r_{i,j} - F(s_{i,j}, \underline{q}_i^{(n+1)})) \frac{\partial F(s_{i,j}, \underline{q}_i^{(n+1)})}{\partial (q_i^k)^{(n+1)}} = 0 \tag{14}$$

Recovery of the splines is most conveniently expressed in terms of the following matrix equation for the components of the parameter-vector $\underline{q}_i^{(n)}$

$$\underline{q}_i^{(n+1)} = (A_i^{(n)})^{-1} \underline{X}_i^{(n)} \tag{15}$$

The elements of the vector $X^{(n)}$ are weighted cross-moments between the parallel and perpendicular spline distances in the Gaussian window, i.e.

$$\underline{X}_i^{(n)} = \begin{pmatrix} \sum_{j \in N_i} g_{i,j} w_{i,j}^{(n)} r_{i,j} \\ \sum_{j \in N_i} g_{i,j} w_{i,j}^{(n)} r_{i,j} s_{i,j} \\ \sum_{j \in N_i} g_{i,j} w_{i,j}^{(n)} r_{i,j} s_{i,j}^2 \\ \sum_{j \in N_i} g_{i,j} w_{i,j}^{(n)} r_{i,j} s_{i,j}^3 \end{pmatrix} \tag{16}$$

The elements of the matrix $A_i^{(n)}$, on the other hand, are weighted moments computed purely in terms of the parallel distance $s_{i,j}$. If k and l are the row and column indices, then the (k,l)th element of the matrix $A_i^{(n)}$ is

$$[A_i^{(n)}]_{k,l} = \sum_{j \in N_i} g_{i,j} w_{i,j}^{(n)} s_{i,j}^{k+l-2} \tag{17}$$

4 Experiments

We have evaluated our iterative spline fitting algorithm on the detection of line-features in aerial infra-red images. Figure 1a shows the original picture. The initial feature probabilities assigned according to equation (1) are shown in Figure 1b.

We illustrate the iterative properties of our algorithm in Figure 1c using a 9x9 Gaussian window. The sequence shows the feature probabilities as a function of iteration number for the EM algorithm. There are a number of points that merit comment. The initial result is very noisy and the genuine contours are submersed in clutter. As the algorithm iterates the salient image structure is organised into meaningful contours by the spline fitting process. The final result is relatively noise free and the detected contours display impressive continuity. It is important to stress that this final contour configuration is stable.

Our next sequence of experiments are aimed at illustrating some of the properties of the recovered splines. Figure 2 shows a second infra-red image together with both the initial feature probabilities and the final contour-map after the EM algorithm has converged. We have highlighted a subregion of the original image. There are two features in this subregion to which we would like to draw attention. The first of these is centred on the junction structure. The second feature is a neighbouring point on the descending branch of the road.

Figure 3 shows the iterative evolution of the cubic spline at these two locations. In the case of the junction feature the spline adjusts to fit the upper pair of road segments. Notice also that although initially displaced, the final spline passes directly through the junction. In the case of the descending road-branch

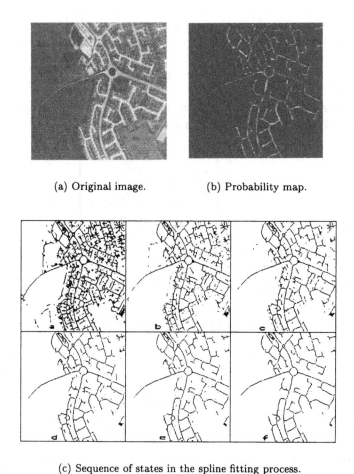

(a) Original image.　　　　(b) Probability map.

(c) Sequence of states in the spline fitting process.

Fig. 1. Applying the spline-fitting process to an aerial infra-red image.

the spline recovers from an initially poor orientation estimate to align itself with the underlying road structure.

Finally, we provide some comparison with the application of dictionary-based relaxation to the multi-scale filter responses. Here we adopt identical initial probabilities but use a dictionary of local contour structures for a 3x3 neighbourhood rather than a variable window spline model. We present our results as a sensitivity curve. Figure 4 shows the fraction of genuine line pixels correctly identified in a sample of synthetic images of known signal-to-noise ratio measured in decibels (dB). The added noise in these images is Gaussian with zero mean and controlled variance. The dotted curve is the result of spline fitting while the solid curve is the result of dictionary-based relaxation. Provided that the signal-to-noise ratio exceeds 5 dB, then there is little to distinguish the results of applying

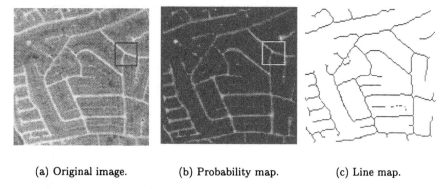

(a) Original image. (b) Probability map. (c) Line map.

Fig. 2. Infra-red aerial picture with corresponding probability map showing region containing pixel under study and correspondent line map.

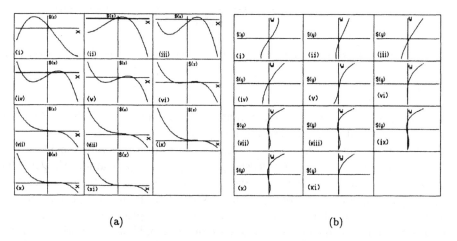

(a) (b)

Fig. 3. Evolution of the spline in the fitting process. The image in (a) is the junction spline while the image in (b) is the branch spline. The first spline is shown in (i), and the subsequent ones from (ii) to (xi).

the two schemes. However, once the SNR falls below this value, then the spline fitting method outperforms dictionary-based relaxation. For instance when the SNR is zero dB, then spline fitting recovers 85% of the genuine line pixels, while dictionary-based relaxation recovers only 40% correctly.

5 Conclusions

We have demonstrated how the process of parallel iterative contour refinement can be realised using the classical EM algorithm of Dempster, Laird and Rubin [2]. The refinement of curves by relaxation operations has been a preoccupation in the literature since the seminal work of Rosenfeld, Hummel and Zucker [12]. However, it is only recently that successful algorithms have been developed by

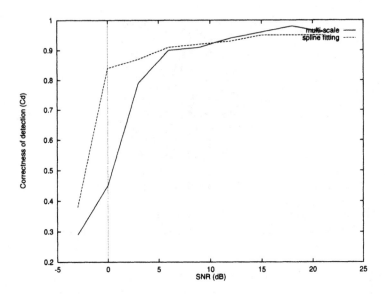

Fig. 4. Noise sensitivity of spline fitting and dictionary-based relaxation compared.

appealing to more sophisticated modelling methodologies [17, 5, 4]. Our EM approach not only delivers comparable performance, it does so using a very simple contour model. Moreover, it allows the contour re-enforcement process to be understood in a weighted least-squares optimisation framework which has many features in common with snake dynamics [15] without being sensitive on the initial positioning of control points. Viewed from the perspective of classical relaxation labelling [12, 8], the EM framework provides a natural way of evaluating support beyond the immediate object neighbourhood. Moreover, the framework for spline fitting in 2D is readily extendible to the reconstruction of surface patches in 3D [13, 3].

References

1. Becker S. and Hinton G.E, "Learning mixture models of spatial coherence", Neural Computation, **5**, pp 267–277, 1992.

2. Dempster N.M. and Rubin D.B., "Maximum-likelihood from incomplete data via the EM algorithm", J. Royal Statistical Soc. Ser. B (methodological),**39**, pp 1-38, 1977.

3. Ferrie F.P., Lagarde J. and Whaite P., "Darboux frames, snakes, and superquadratics: geometry from the bottom up", IEEE PAMI, **15**, pp. 771-784, 1993

4. Hancock E.R., "Resolving edge-line ambiguities using probabilistic relaxation", *Proceedings of the IEEE Conference on Computer Vision and Pattern Recognition*, pp. 300-306, 1993.

5. Hancock E.R. and Kittler J., "Edge labelling using dictionary-based probabilistic relaxation", IEEE PAMI, **12**, pp. 161-185, 1990.

6. Hummel R.A. and Zucker S.W., "On the foundations of relaxation labelling processes", IEEE PAMI, **5**, pp267-287, 1987.

7. Jordan M.I. and Jacobs R.A, "Hierarchical mixtures of experts and the EM algorithm", *Neural Computation*, **6**, pp. 181-214, 1994.

8. Kittler J. and Hancock, E.R., "Combining evidence in probabilistic relaxation", International Journal of Pattern Recognition and Artificial Intelligence, **3**, N1, pp 29-51, 1989.

9. Leite J.A.F. and Hancock, E.R., " Statistically combining and refining multichannel information", *Progress in Image Analysis and Processing III: Edited by S Impedovo, World Scientific*, pp. 193-200, 1994

10. Meer P., Mintz D., Rosenfeld A. and Kim D.Y., "Robust regression methods for computer vision - A review", *International Journal of Computer vision*, **6**, pp. 59–70, 1991.

11. Peleg S. and Rosenfeld A., "Determining compatibility coefficients for curve enhancement relaxation processes", *IEEE SMC*, **8**, pp. 548–555, 1978.

12. Rosenfeld A., Hummel R.A. and Zucker S.W., "Scene labelling by relaxation operations", IEEE Transactions SMC, SMC-6, pp400-433, 1976.

13. Sander P.T. and Zucker S.W., "Inferring surface structure and differential structure from 3D images", IEEE PAMI, **12**, pp 833-854, 1990.

14. Sharp N.G. and Hancock E.R., "Feature tracking by multi-frame relaxation", Image and Vision Computing, **13**, pp. 637–644, 1995.

15. Terzopoulos D., "Regularisation of inverse problems involving discontinuities", IEEE PAMI, **8**, pp 129-139, 1986.

16. Zucker, S.W., Hummel R.A., and Rosenfeld A., "An application of relaxation labelling to line and curve enhancement", *IEEE TC*, **C-26**, pp. 394–403, 1977.

17. Zucker S., David C., Dobbins A. and Iverson L., "The organisation of curve detection: coarse tangent fields and fine spline coverings", *Proceedings of the Second International Conference on Computer Vision*, pp. 577–586, 1988.

Model-Based Pose Proposal for 2-D Object Recognition

Hemant Tagare and Drew McDermott

Computer Science Department
Yale University
P.O. Box 208285
New Haven, CT 06520-8285
{tagare-hemant,mcdermott-drew}@yale.edu

Abstract

We consider the problem of finding a known two-dimensional object in an image, or verifying that it does not appear in the image. We adopt the strategy of doing a fast scan for potential places in the image where the object could be; we call this scan pose proposal. *Each pose hypothesis is a set of edges that correspond to a subset of the transformed object boundary. Our algorithm works by finding U-shaped segments of object boundaries, doing a quick match process between U-shaped segments in the image and the model, and combining the matches into overall pose hypotheses. Analysis and experiments show that the algorithm runs efficiently, and does a good job of discarding all but a few spots in the image as possible pose hypotheses.*

1 Introduction

In this paper we consider the problem of finding a known, rigid two-dimensional object in a cluttered scene, or deciding that the object is not present. This problem can be broken into two phases: a fast check for places where the object might occur in the image, followed by a slow phase to investigate each such place to see if the object is really there. Our focus is on Phase 1. We will be making two other assumptions: that there is just one object being sought, and that there are no color or texture cues to the object we are looking for. The second assumption is implausible, but the first, we believe, is reasonable for a variety of applications.

With these restrictions in mind, we can state our problem formally thus:

> Given a closed two-dimensional contour, called the *model,* and a series of scenes, each containing zero or one instance of the model at some

translation, scale, and rotation, and occluded to a greater or lesser degree, quickly find zero to two candidate poses for the object to be checked by a slow and careful algorithm (unspecified) to see if the object is present, subject to the requirement that if an instance of the model is actually present, then its actual pose is among the poses returned.

We will call this process *pose proposal*, and the candidate poses it finds *pose hypotheses*. For each pose hypothesis there is a set of image edges that are postulated to belong to the contour if so posed, and these are called the *edge set selected by* the pose hypothesis.

proposal [8, 6, 1, 9], it is assumed that the model is represented as a set of "features," where a feature is typically a curvature extremum of the model's boundary. The image is also represented as a set of features, which requires grouping its edges into curves, and looking for curvature extrema, or other points of interest, in them. There are, of course, a lot more image features than model features, because the image contains several objects. The problem is to find *matches* of one to the other, that is, to find which image features correspond to which features in the model. Any proposed match of one kind of feature to the other constrains the pose we are looking for. if we knew all the correct correspondences then the pose would be sharply constrained, and we'd be done.

The most common framework for solving this combinatorial problem is pose clustering, most often referred to by the most famous method for doing the clustering, the Hough transform[5][7]. Pose clustering operates by accumulating votes for a model match from low-level feature matches. One can then locate peaks in the histogram of votes, and discard all features that do not participate in these clusters. Each cluster corresponds to a pose hypothesis. Such a strategy is used, for example, by Grimson [4]. Hough-transform-like winner-take-all networks are also used by Bolle et. al. [3] to limit the combinatorics of search in the model recognition system.

Pose clustering is often expensive and error-prone because each match constrains the possible poses only a little bit, so that many matches have to be accumulated before a clear cluster emerges. The reason each match means so little is that most work in the field [2, 8, 6, 1, 9], takes features to be point-like entities, or small groups of such entities. But many features look alike; and any given feature match doesn't constrain the pose very much. The reason why previous researchers have focused on point-like features is their fear that larger features will be destroyed by occlusion [6, 8]. Our claim is that pose proposal can be made much simpler and more efficient by using features that are of medium size, midway between point features that don't constrain the pose much, and global features that require that a large chunk of the entire contour be visible. Each such feature will have a good probability of being at least partially visible, and a match will give so much information about the pose that only a few matches will be required to constrain it completely. (See Fig. 1.) In our experience, one is unlikely to find features in the clutter with exactly the right transformation parameters so that a group of two or more of them can be consistently interpreted as coming from a single instance of the model. Two feature matches that are consistent suffice to pick out a pose for closer examination, at least in the absence of a competing candidate pose.

Fig. 1. Medium-Complexity Feature

2 Finding Features in Object Contours

In our implementation to date, we have used just one kind of feature, a U-shaped segment of the model boundary called, anticlimactically, a "U." The precise definition of a "U" is as follows: Edge elements in the image are linked into continuous curves and tokens are placed at the corners and the end points of the curve. (A *corner* is a point of maximum curvature.) A U is the portion of a curve that encompasses three successive tokens. Fig. 2a shows an example of a curve parsed into a sequence of U's. Note that concave Us alternate with convex ones. Fig. 2b shows the corner and arms of a U. By orienting the line of sight from the corner along the bisector of the acute angle between the two arms, we can identify one arm as the left arm and the other arm as the right arm.

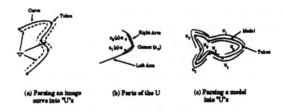

Fig. 2. The Feature

The object model as well as image data are parsed into U's. Fig. 2b shows an instance of a parsing of an object model. To distinguish between image and model U's, we denote the former with the letter U and the latter with the letter $\mathcal{U}$.

Finding U's in an image takes little time. The edge elements are linked together into continuous curves and the corners of the curves are found as the extrema of curvature. Space prevents us from describing the details. The processing time for finding U's is low — typically about 2 secs on a Sun SPARCStation 2 for processing images with 5 to 15 objects in view.

It is easy to make an intuitive arguments that U's are at about the right level of complexity. It is of key importance that partial occlusion does not make it impossible to find U's. So long as a few high-curvature points are visible, some U's will be extractable from an image. Even if an arm of a U is partially occluded, it is still possible, as we shall show, to match it with model $\mathcal{U}$'s fairly reliably. Of course, it's also true that occlusion creates spurious U's, by creating corners formed from segmets of physically distinct boundaries.However, these spurious U's are unlikely to give rise to consistent pose hypotheses, and their presence is only a minor nuisance.

As suggested in Fig. 2(c), matching one U to another tightly constrains the transformation: the corners of the two Us have to line up, which constrains the translation, and the arms of the U's have to line up, which constrains the possible rotation and scale. But we need a fast check that the two can be put into alignment, and this is provided by comparing the angle of the average deviation of the arms of the two. This angle is defined as follows. If $\mathbf{x}_c$ is the corner of a $\mathcal{U}$, $\mathbf{x}_1(s_1)$ is a point at a distance s_1 from the corner on the left arm, and $\mathbf{x}_2(s_2)$ is a point at a distance s_2 from the corner on the right arm, then (Fig. 2b)

$$\mathbf{v}_1 = \frac{1}{L} \int_0^L (\mathbf{x}_1(s) - \mathbf{x}_c)\, ds, \qquad \mathbf{v}_2 = \frac{1}{L} \int_0^L (\mathbf{x}_2(s) - \mathbf{x}_c)\, ds,$$

where L is the length of the smaller arm, are taken to be the "average" arm vectors and $\theta = \angle(\mathbf{v}_1, \mathbf{v}_2)$, where $\angle()$ is the smaller of the two angles between $\mathbf{v}_1$ and $\mathbf{v}_2$, is taken to be the angle of deviation between the two arms. Note that $\mathbf{v}_1$ and $\mathbf{v}_2$ are computed by integrating over the same arc length on both the arms. So we characterize the l'th image U by the "signature" $\langle \theta_l, L_l \rangle$.

If we were sure that the image U was completely unoccluded, we could match it against the corresponding signature for a model $\mathcal{U}$. But we can't be sure of that, so, for every model $\mathcal{U}$, we must compute a set of angles of deviation. We define the *partial arm vectors for fraction μ* $(0 < \mu \le 1)$ as

$$\mathbf{w}_1(\mu) = \frac{1}{\mu L} \int_0^{\mu L} (\mathbf{x}_1(s) - \mathbf{x}_c)\, ds, \qquad \mathbf{w}_2(\mu) = \frac{1}{\mu L} \int_0^{\mu L} (\mathbf{x}_2(s) - \mathbf{x}_c)\, ds,$$

Here L refers to the length of the smaller of the two arms, and $1 - \mu$ indicates the level of occlusion. The deviation angles $\phi(\mu)$ are given by $\phi(\mu) = \angle(\mathbf{w}_1(\mu), \mathbf{w}_2(\mu))$. The signature of a model $\mathcal{U}$ is then stored as a set of pairs giving the value of $\phi(\mu)$ and μL for a representative range of μ:

$$\langle \langle \phi(\mu_1), \mu_1 L \rangle, \langle \phi(\mu_2), \mu_2 L \rangle, \ldots \langle \phi(\mu_p), \mu_p L \rangle \rangle$$

with $0 < \mu_1 < \mu_2 < \ldots < \mu_p = 1$. In our implementation, we store 10 pairs, with $\mu_n = 0.1n$. For the k'th model $\mathcal{U}$, we will write the n'th such pair as $\langle \phi_{k,n}, L_{k,n} \rangle$.

A model $\mathcal{U}$ (say the kth $\mathcal{U}$) is considered a feasible match of an image U (say the lth U) if for some level of occlusion n, the deviation angles of the two U's are similar and the change of scale required to match the shorter of the two model $\mathcal{U}$ arms to the shorter of the two image U arms is within prerequired bounds, i.e.,

$$\|\phi_{k,n} - \theta_l\| \leq \Delta_\theta, \text{ and} \tag{1}$$
$$\alpha_{min} - \Delta_\alpha \leq \frac{L_l}{L_{k,n}} \leq \alpha_{max} + \Delta_\alpha,$$

where, Δ_θ is the allowable range of angle mismatch and Δ_α is the allowable range of scale mismatch. α_{max} and α_{min} are the maximum and minimum values for allowable scale transformations.

If $\mathcal{U}_k$ can be feasibly matched to U_l, then the ranges of scale and rotation for the match can also be found. The range of the scale is obtained as the interval $S = [\frac{L_l}{L_{k,n}} - \Delta_\alpha, \frac{L_l}{L_{k,n}} + \Delta_\alpha]$. The range of rotation is obtained as the intersection of the range of the rotation parameter for the left arm and the range of the rotation parameter for the right arm, i.e., if $\mathbf{w}_1$ and $\mathbf{w}_2$ are the left and right arms of the model and $\mathbf{v}_1$ and $\mathbf{v}_2$ the left arm and right arms of the image U, the range of rotations is the interval

$$R = [\angle(\mathbf{w}_1, \mathbf{v}_1) - \Delta_\theta, \angle(\mathbf{w}_1, \mathbf{v}_1) + \Delta_\theta] \bigcap [\angle(\mathbf{w}_2, \mathbf{v}_2) - \Delta_\theta, \angle(\mathbf{w}_2, \mathbf{v}_2) + \Delta_\theta] \tag{2}$$

A feasible match is denoted by $(\mathcal{U}_m \overset{[R,S]}{\leftrightarrow} U_n)$.

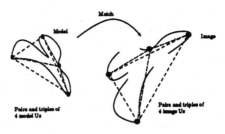

Fig. 3. Combinations of U's.

Multiple feasible matches can be grouped into a *feasible interpretation* if they have a consistent range of scale and rotation parameters and if no model $\mathcal{U}$ or image U occurs more than once in the interpretation. Note that when feasible matches are grouped together additional information is available from combinations of matches that can further reduce the range of the transformation parameters. In our case, it is easy to see that comparing the distances between the corners of all pairs of model $\mathcal{U}$'s in the feasible interpretation to the distances between the corners of corresponding pairs of image U's (Fig. 3) gives more information about scale. Also, by comparing triples of model $\mathcal{U}$ corners in the feasible interpretation to corresponding image U corners (Fig. 3) further information about the rotation range can be obtained.

3 Forming Feasible Interpretations

Finding feasible interpretations can be thought of as a two-stage process, where all feasible matches are found in the first step and in the second stage the feasible matches are combinatorially grouped into different sets and sets that are not feasible interpretations deleted. At the end of the first stage, there is a list for every model U containing all of its feasible matches. The current version of the algorithm creates the lists by comparing every image U with every model U for a potential match.

In this paper, we focus on a greedy constraint-propagation algorithm for doing the grouping in the second stage:

```
Interps ← {};
For each U
    (For each I ∈ Interps

        If there is an unused match M = (U ⟷[R,S] U),
                that can be consistently added to I
            then (I ← I ∪ {M};
                Mark M used in the list of matches with U);
        For each unused match M = (U ⟷[R,S] U)
            Interps ← Interps ∪ {M})
```

The procedure begins by initializing the feasible-interpretations list Interps to the empty list. Then the feasible-interpretations list is merged with each feasible-match list starting from the list for the first model U and proceeding to the last. Every merge proceeds as follows: Beginning from the first feasible interpretation, each feasible interpretation I is considered for grouping with each feasible match in the feasible-matches list. As soon as a match is found which can be merged with I to make an enlarged feasible interpretation, the merge is carried out, and the feasible match is marked "used." The algorithm does not even consider alternative consistent ways of using this U to augment I, but goes on to consider ways of combining other matches of U with other partial interpretations. Once all feasible interpretations are compared with elements of a feasible matches list, there may remain unused feasible matches in the list for U that are not compatible with any of the current feasible interpretations. They are added to the end of the list Interps as new feasible interpretations.

Note that for the first U considered, Interps is empty, so each $M = (U \leftrightarrow U)$ will be unused and Interps will be initialized to the set of all matches to U. On the next iteration, each such "seed" match will be extended, and so forth. The greedy nature of the algorithm lies in the choice to remove a feasible match from its list as soon as it fits into a feasible interpretation; and to enlarge a feasible interpretation with the first feasible match that fits it.

At the end of the grouping step a set of feasible interpretations is obtained. Some of these interpretations must be discarded, for reasons that are familiar to others who have studied pose proposal:

- Those consisting of sets of matches in which every model $\mathcal{U}$ has 80% or higher occlusion. (Under severe occlusion all U's tend to look the same.)

- Those which contain only single feasible matches. (These are often wrong, and even when correct they don't tell us much.)

Our algorithm is somewhat heuristic and hard to analyze. For example, the complexity of the U-matching phase depends not just on how many edges there are, but on how many U's they make. We observe empirically that there are on the order of 100 U's in a typical image. They must all be matched against model $\mathcal{U}$'s, but the matching process is very fast, because it involves comparison of two numbers, θ_U and $\theta_{\mathcal{U}}$.

We should also say a few words about the probability of a mismatch. Let's consider the probability that two randomly chosen image U's will form a feasible interpretation given two model $\mathcal{U}$'s. The probability can be computed as the probability of the following conjunction:

U_1 matches $\mathcal{U}_1$ and U_2 matches $\mathcal{U}_2$
and match orientations are consistent and match scales are consistent
and distance between U_1 and U_2 is consistent with match scale

Getting meaningful probabilities for all these conjuncts is not easy, and it is not likely that the probabilities are independent. Space does not allow us to present the details, but we estimate the combined probability to be about 10^{-6} of two U's being explained by two $\mathcal{U}$'s. In a typical model, there are about 10 $\mathcal{U}$'s, and in a typical image about 100 U's, so there are $10 \times 9 \times 100 \times 99 \approx 10^6$ combinations to count (the order is significant). Hence we should expect zero to two accidental matches. This level of false positive is tolerable for pose proposal, because it is acceptable to have to weed out a couple of bogus feasible interpretations.

4 Experimental Results

As we discussed before, pose proposal is useful only if on the average it can quickly find the object in the presence of dissimilar clutter. To evaluate the performance of our algorithm we performed experiments on 50 images containing an instance of a model and 25 images containing no instance of the model. The model used was the cardboard cutout of a fish as shown in Fig. 4. It has 6 $\mathcal{U}$'s.

We discuss the images containing the model first. Each image was created as follows: the model was placed on a rectangular area approximately 1 foot long by 1 foot wide. Between 5 and 15 commonly occurring laboratory tools and other objects were randomly tossed onto the above area. These provided the clutter. Since the model was always placed before the clutter was introduced, in all cases the model was partially occluded. The camera zoom was randomly varied so

Fig. 4. The Model.

that the apparent magnification of the model in the scene (compared to the size of the model in the image used to acquire the model) was between 2 and 0.5. No special lighting was introduced. A single image of each scene was recorded.

Fig. 5. A Correct Feasible Interpretation.

Once an image was obtained it was preprocessed to extract U's, on the average 105 of the them. After image U's were found, they were compared with the model $\mathcal{U}$'s and feasible matches were formed. The greedy grouping algorithm was used to find feasible interpretations. The values of all of the parameters used in the algorithm are as follows:

- Deviation Angle Mismatch (Δ_θ): 10°

- Scale Mismatch (Δ_α): 0.1

- Scale Range ($\alpha_{min}, \alpha_{max}$): 0.333, 3.0

- Error in dist. between two corners (Δ_d): 7 pixels

Since the model has 6 $\mathcal{U}$'s, potentially there are 105 × 6 feasible matches. On the average only 7.5 of these survive, validating the argument that medium-occcomplexity features can provide the appropriate pruning. As a further valida-tion of the heuristic, we note that on the average only 2.16 feasible interpretations are created. Correct interpretations were the ones whose image U's came from an occurrence of the model in the image. An example of a correct interpretation is shown in Fig. 5. The figure shows the model in the clutter. The edges of the model which formed the image U's of the correct feasible interpretation are outlined in the figure. In the 50 images we processed, at least one correct interpretation was found in 44 cases giving a success rate of 88%.

We also attempted to validate the use of the greedy algorithm. Once a feasible interpretation is formed by a greedy algorithm, it cannot be dismantled and its feasible matches cannot be used elsewhere. Therefore if a feasible match from the occurrence of the model is assigned to an incorrect feasible interpretation, it will not be present in the correct feasible interpretation thereby reducing the "strength" of the correct feasible interpretation. We measured the strength of correct interpretations to evaluate how serious this effect is. We counted the number of image pixels every feasible interpretation accounted for and ranked all of the feasible interpretations in each image according to the edge pixel count, so that when more than one feasible interpretation was present, the relative strength of any interpretation could be measured by its rank. In the 44 images which contained at least one correct feasible interpretation, Our results are that 98% of the time the correct interpretation was either the strongest or the next strongest interpretation. This validates the use of the greedy algorithm.

The six images where no correct feasible interpretation was found were also examined. In all cases, the failure could be attributed to one of the following reasons: (1) The object was so heavily occluded so that at most one corner (and hence at most one U) was visible, or (2) The edge detector or the corner detector failed to locate a relevant U.

For each image, timing statistics were also gathered. The whole process, not counting the time to find edges in the first place, took on the order of 3 seconds.

The procedure for creating the images with the model was repeated additionally 25 times without the model. The greedy algorithm was executed with these images as data and the same statistics were gathered as before. The number of U's found, and the time required to find them, were very similar.

It was found that the algorithm indicated at least one feasible interpretation in 60% of the cases (i.e. no feasible interpretations were found in 40% of the cases). Only 16% of cases had more than one feasible interpretation These statistics are consistent with the analysis of Sect. 3. Visual inspection of all feasible interpretations revealed that most feasible interpretations could easily be rejected by a more detailed model-matching stage.

5 Conclusion

A special case of object recognition arises when just one object is being searched for, and when there is prior reason to believe that the current image contains no more than one occurrence of the object. In this case it makes sense to use the model of the object for *pose proposal*, the goal of which is to find quickly a small set of possible poses for the object, and the parts of the image that would have to match it if that were the actual pose. If the set is empty, we can conclude that the object is not present. If a few possible poses are found, we can look at them more carefully with slower but more selective algorithms.

In the case of two-dimensional objects subject to arbitrary rotations and translations, we have argued that a specific medium-complexity feature called a U can be used to propose poses. A U is a U-shaped segment of the object's contour. It has two key advantages: (1) There are fast, reasonably selective tests for whether a U in the image matches a $\mathcal{U}$ in the model, and these tests are insensitive to occlusion; (2) A small number of matches is sufficient to tightly constrain the possible poses of the object.

In our experiments, when the object was present the algorithm found it 88% of the time. When the algorithm fails, it does so either because the object is very heavily occluded, or because our U detector fails to find a U that appears visible to the human eye. Spurious pose proposals occur 60% of the time when the object is absent, and 16% of the time when it is present. These would have to be tested and rejected by a more comprehensive shape-matching algorithm.

We believe that finding U's is useful for a large variety of two-dimensional objects. For three-dimensional objects we will have to explore other types of features, because U's do not tend to remain stable as viewpoints change; or represent a three-dimensional object as a collection of two-dimensional views Another open problem is a principled approach to the second phase of object finding, pose-hypothesis verification.

References

1. Breuel, T.M., "Fast Recognition using Adaptive Subdivisions of Transformation Space," *Proc. IEEE Conf. on Computer Vision and Pattern Recognition*, pp. 445–451, 1992.
2. Bolles R. C., Cain R. A., "Recognizing and Locating Partially Visible Objects: The local-feature-focus Method," Intl. Journ. Robotics Research, 1(3), 1982.
3. R. M. Bolle, Califano A., Kjeldsen,"A Complete and Extendable Approach to Visual Recognition," I.E.E.E. Trans. Pat. Recog. Mach. Intell., Vol. 14, No. 5, May 1992.
4. W. Eric L. Grimson, T. Lozano-Perez, "Localizing Overlapping Parts by Searching the Interpretation Tree," IEEE Trans. Pattern Anal. Machine Inell., vol. PAMI-9, no. 4, pp. 469-482, July 1987.
5. P. V. C. Hough, "A Method and Means for Recognizing Complex Patterns," US Patent No. 3,069,654, 1962.
6. Huttenlocher, D.P. and Ullman, S., "Recognizing Solid Objects by Alignment with an Image," *Int. J. or Computer Vision*, vol. 5, no. 2, pp. 195–212
7. J. Illingworth, J. Kittler, "A Survey of the Hough Transform," Comput. Vision, Graphics, Image Proc., vol. 44, pp. 87-116, 1988.
8. Lamdan, Y., Schwartz, J.T., and Wolfson, H.J. "Affine Invariant Model-Based Object Recognition," I.E.E.E. Trans. on Robotics and Automation, Vol. 6, no. 5, pp. 578–589, 1990.
9. Olson, C.F., "Time and Space Efficient Pose Clustering," I.E.E.E. Trans. on Pattern Analysis and Machine Intellligence, pp. 251–258, 1994

TARCA - An Integrated System for Diagnosis and Treatment of Cardiac Arrhythmias

António José Ferreira da Silva[1] and Eugénio Oliveira[2]

[1]Department of Mechanical Engineering, Instituto Superior de Engenharia do Porto,
Rua de S. Tomé, 4200 Porto, Portugal
Email: toze@fe.up.pt

[2]Department of Electrical Engineering and Computers, Faculdade de Engenharia da
Universidade do Porto, Rua dos Bragas - 4099 Porto CODEX, Portugal.
Email: eco@fe.up.pt

Abstract. TARCA is an Integrated Computer System which includes an Expert System for diagnosis, prevention, therapy planning, as well as monitoring, of cardiac arrhythmias. TARCA is under development at Oporto University in cooperation with S. João Hospital.
TARCA aims towards an autonomous medical aid system for the treatment of cardiac patients from the automatic extraction of the electrocardiogram (ECG) signal to the final diagnosis, followed by a possible preventive medical advice and specifying a therapeutic prescription plan and posterior patient monitoring.
It is known that any system in this domain has to deal with many different kinds of knowledge and information sources and to use different types of inference processes. Production rules, frames, probabilistic and mathematical models are among different knowledge representation formalisms which have been used to encode the domain knowledge. The functional architecture of TARCA is based on the blackboard control architecture model, perhaps the most suitable framework for building medical knowledge-based systems fulfilling the requirement of integrating different knowledge representation formalisms.
The automatic ECG acquisition and processing module of TARCA, plus the diagnosis module is already being used at S. João Hospital, while the therapy planning module undergoes the testing state of development.

1 - Introduction

Patient care management usually requires to perform different, but interrelated, fundamental medical tasks : diagnosis, prevention, therapy planning and monitoring are indicated as the most important. Although being different, these tasks share a common characteristic: they all are very complex tasks accessible only to specialists.

Artificial Intelligence (AI) in Medicine, has given special attention to the construction of knowledge-based systems (KBS) which are the realm of the integrated systems capable of displaying all these features.

The great majority of systems developed until now refer almost exclusively to the diagnostic part. In fact, Diagnostic Expert Systems only deal with a passive phase of all patient care problems - the interpretation phase.

Although the diagnostic phase is fundamental to the success of any medical action, it is the competence of other more active modules - therapy planning and monitoring - to find the best therapeutic action to be applied to the patient as well as to follow up all implications. This means that our system gave an important and difficult step from a passive to an active one.

Almost all medical planning problems, are particularly difficult because of three main reasons: First, because a physician can't be absolutely sure about his own diagnosis. Second, because physicians can rarely be sure of the effects of any therapy. Both this characteristics of medical problems fall under the domain of the uncertainty knowledge. A third degree of complexity involved in medical planning process is that an attempt to satisfy one medical goal tends sometimes to prevent other goals from being met. For instance, an antiarrhythmic drug can cure an arrhythmia, but can also activate another different kind of arrhythmia. All these supply the search for tradeoffs. Solutions are not adopted without a careful analysis of two trends: on one hand maximization of patients benefits and on the other hand costs minimization.

It was also accepted that medical treatment is not completed without the inclusion of two other important steps: prevention and monitoring.

At the prevention phase, the skill of the physician should be enough to detect the significant signs and symptoms that could indicate future patient clinical problems and provide the necessary actions to avoid them. Relying inference in early symptoms, although important, involves a high degree of uncertainty and complexity.

The monitoring phase is usually the last one, but nevertheless remains important and complex. Monitoring, in this context, means observing the course of a patient's condition who is following a specific therapy, and verifying whether the selected therapeutic action proves to be effective improving patients health condition..

Despite the above mentioned complexities, it is a fact of reality that physicians usually solve patient-care problems with remarkable regularity and skill.

The sophistication of the problems involved in all the process and the necessity for an adequate solution adjusted to the characteristics and personal needs of each particular patient, becomes the main motivation to understand, design and integrate all the steps that constitute medical treatment of cardiac arrhythmia in one system: TARCA.

The methodologies that will be described here, claim to make easier the conception and construction of models that translate in a pragmatic way all the medical tasks referred here. TARCA as well as other systems of the same kind indeed constitute a tool of great importance to help all kinds of physicians, experts and non-experts, on making well-founded decisions that reveal particular importance to the patients cure.

The fundamental aims of TARCA are the following :

- to provide the non-experts with an easy way of detecting the existence of cardiac arrhythmias (and their type);
- to improve the skill of those responsible for clinical diagnosis, providing a tool including an approach that is systematic and complete;

- to improve the understanding of the process of clinical decisions, namely not allowing the influence of similar cases, but not identical (frequent cause of errors among clinicians) and giving place to a explicit criteria of decision making that will be therefore reproducible;
- to increase the efficiency of the tests to perform and of the therapies to advise, recollecting to that purpose, information that reveals itself important to the resolution of future problems. The system must also be sensible to the inconveniences and make a careful balance between risks and benefits to the patient before proposing any action.

It was considered that the most viable and practical way of achieving these objectives would be to build up a completely automated integrated system which starting from the ECG signal acquisition finds possible diagnostics and leads to the therapeutic prescription (including if necessary, prevention and monitoring).

2 - The TARCA System

TARCA is made up of several different modules, including an electrocardiogram signal acquisition and processing module, an Expert System which is responsible for the diagnosis and a Planning module responsible for the therapeutic prescription.

In order to be completely automated, the system includes an hard/soft interface which achieves an automatic acquisition of the ECG and supplies a PROLOG file, with the necessary quantitative data for the posterior inference and diagnosis. Once this diagnosis is found, another process starts, trying to give advice about possible therapies.

Figure 1 shows the information flow at TARCA system.

2.1 - ECG Acquisition and Processing

The ECG acquisition and processing subsystem allows ECG signal extraction from an ordinary electrocardiograph. It supplies a data file that is read and interpreted by the expert system.

In a first stage, the most important characteristics of the acquired waves (those who have been considered of interest for the arrhythmia diagnosis) are processed (Wartak, 1978).

Frank's ECG model of three leads in used and is transformed into the derived ECG (leads AVR and D2) by mathematical manipulations. Specialists find these transformations adequate for pathological cardiac diagnosis, at least in the case of adults.

From the AVR and D2 leads, 11 and 5 parameters are extracted respectively for each of the considered cardiac cycles.

They mainly concern temporal positions and duration's as well as amplitudes of P and T waves and QRS complexes. Other important information is also gathered, like the possible existence of a baseline and cardiac and P wave frequencies.

The automatic ECG acquisition and processing module ("Sistema de Electrocardiografia Computorizada do Porto" - Oporto Computerized

Electrocardiograph System) (Abreu-Lima and Marques de Sá, 1988) is installed in
Oporto S. João Hospital as well as ARCA [Oliveira, Rocha 1990].

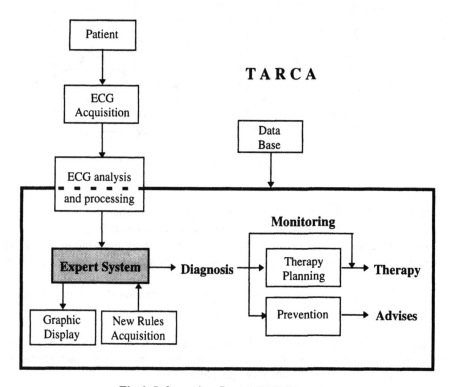

Fig 1. Information flow at TARCA system

2.2- Diagnosis

Arrhythmia constitute a group of physiological cardiac states characterized by
alterations in the depolarization and re-polarization process of the heart. This
phenomenon doesn't always indicate a heart disease. The relevant parameters for the
detection of cardiac arrhythmias (Wartak, 1978) are represented in figure 2.

Morphology and timing of the QRS complexes are the most reliable data in
diagnosing arrhythmias. They are employed early in our evaluation of the
electrocardiogram.

It is also possible to discuss how long (1 hour, 1 day,...) and in which situation (stress,
rest, ...) the ECG's should be recorded in order to provide the initial data for further
analysis.

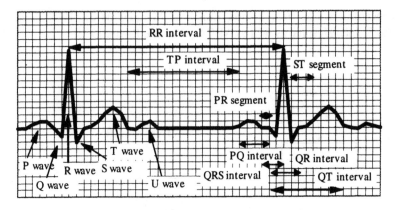

Fig 2. ECG parameters used by TARCA

The domain knowledge is basically represented in three different forms :
- production rules also incorporating inexact reasoning capabilities;
- semantic networks including specific domain concepts, all the relationships among them and other useful attached information (concept meanings, domain values, etc.);
- ECG measurements asserted as facts with an associated certainty factor in PROLOG clauses.

To assemble small pieces of expert reasoning into rules to explicit the existing knowledge in the domain, is somewhat difficult, due to the large number of patterns necessary for a realistic approach in any area of medicine.

An aspect also considered of vital importance, is the attempt to establish rules at the lowest possible level. These fine grained rules explicit all inference steps from the ECG data to the more elaborated and higher level diagnostic rules.

These lower level rules together with more sophisticated knowledge also embedded in the same form (rules), make the knowledge base completely modular and easy to increment. They avoid the use of implicit knowledge in procedures that are not completely visible neither easily modified.

The established model divides the arrhythmias into classes defined in Wartak, 1978 (Table 1).

Each of these classes is considered independently, thus constituting the superior level of chaining of the diagnosis. Therefore, the initial characteristics taken from the ECG, trigger knowledge sources that are activated in backward chaining conduct to the diagnosis. These rules make in practice, the rules used by the physicians to determine and that don't involve directly (in the sense that they don't involve calculation or determination of values), the manipulation of data from the ECG and have a simple translation to a language understood by the users.

- regular rhythms
    - tachycardias
    - normal or shifted pacemaker
    - blocks and AV dissociation
- periodically irregular rhythms
- completely irregular rhythms
- beats outside the dominant run
    - extrasystoles
    - blocked beats

Table 1 - Classes of arrhythmias considered in TARCA.

2.3- Graphic Capabilities

To enable on-line visualization of the ECG which is being analyzed, the system is able to present the ECG graphic, including different derivation, on the screen.

It is also possible to display an individual QRS complex, including all important calculations made up by the system (for example PR interval, QRS interval, P wave amplitude, etc.).

2.4 - Prevention

Prevention is a task that could be implemented with minimal costs and permits avoiding or at least reducing the probability of a certain disease. In the case of cardiac arrhythmias that is also true. Avoid risk factors that may unchain or aggravate an arrhythmia, will be of more benefit to the patient than applying a therapy after the arrhythmia detection.

In medicine, prevention of a disease still is the main goal.

2.5 - Therapy planning and Monitoring

The design of a KBS for therapy planning and monitoring may benefit from an epistemological analysis of such generic medical task.

An epistemological model of medical reasoning requires the combination of an ontology and an inference model. Ontology represents the conceptual model of entities and relationships composing the domain knowledge, while the inference model is the conceptual representation of the inference structure employed to execute a generic medical task by managing that ontology. [Quaglini 1992].

This paper extends the same approach towards therapy planning and monitoring, where ontological entities are patient's general history, signs and symptoms, diseases, therapies, side effects and health outcomes.

The complexity and diversity of knowledge involved in these tasks, imply the necessity of different forms of knowledge representation. These considerations lead to the notion of a hybrid system where formalisms typical of AI, such as frames and production rules, and formalisms typical of probability and utility theories, such as decision trees, are conveniently mixed together. Therefore we decided to use an architecture that is able, not only to efficiently integrate this formalisms, as well as an explicit representation of the problem at two different levels : *epistemological level* and *computational level.*

At the computational level, a blackboard control architecture has been exploited. It allows the developer of the KBS to represent separately control knowledge and domain knowledge, and to organize knowledge into several independent rule sets. These features have been exploited, respectively, to explicitly represent the epistemological model of therapy planning and to choose the most suited representation formalism for each knowledge source.

An epistemological model of therapy planning (figure 3)

The data-request task shown in the epistemological model is activated when the initial information is not sufficient to begin therapy planning. From this information, it is possible to make a concise and essential portrait of the situation consisting of a list of therapeutic problems which could be relevant for the given patient. It is also worth to make a distinction between *simple* and *complex problems.* A simple problem is a problem where the solution arises immediately because the physician is familiar with it and the solution is well-accepted by the medical community. A complex problem is a problem where several therapeutic action need to be taken into consideration and their appropriateness cannot be established easily, due to both uncertainty of their outcomes and decision-maker's preferences. We use for the representation and solving this complex problem, decision trees.

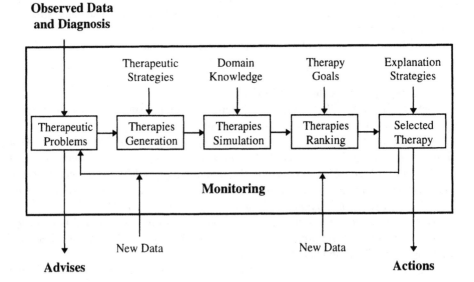

Fig. 3 - The epistemological model of therapeutic reasoning

Next phase, takes the set of therapeutic problems and infers a presumptive set of therapies which includes those treatments that deserve consideration as potentially useful in handling those problems. Far from being definitive, elements of this list are considered just as hypotheses which may need more focused consideration and testing. In fact, therapy planning proceeds with a ranking phase, which usually establishes priorities over current set of treatments. In this phase it is necessary focusing on a single therapy, or a restricted set of therapies, to predict possible effects on a patient's clinical course. On the basis of these predictions, some therapies may be excluded from the initial set. The remaining ones need to be compared in terms of their utilities. The therapy which has the best expected utility is the selected one.

The architecture chosen can be viewed, at an implementation level, from two perspectives: First, the functional view presents a blackboard control architecture. The second perspective is structural, it includes specifications of used knowledge representation formalisms, inference mechanisms, and control strategies.

The functional view

The functional architecture is based on the blackboard control architecture model.

As shown in Fig. 4, the medical knowledge and tasks involved in therapy planning are represented separately and explicitly. The network of therapeutic tasks defines the so called control knowledge. It indexes the medical knowledge, specifying when and how the system has to execute one of the tasks described above.

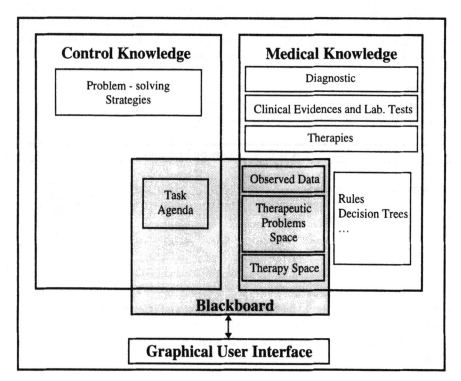

Fig 4. The functional view of the blackboard control architecture used in TARCA

The control knowledge
Figure 5 shows the system task agenda on the control blackboard.

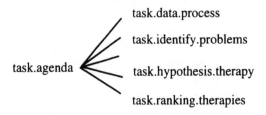

task.agenda

- task.data.process
- task.identify.problems
- task.hypothesis.therapy
- task.ranking.therapies

Fig. 5 - The system task agenda

The system also has a set of meta-rules for controlling tasks execution in the form:

meta-rule(Situation, NewSituation, Task).

The medical knowledge
The medical knowledge sources are encoded as taxonomies of entities, rules classes and decision trees. Each therapeutic problem is represented by a frame. Two of its slots contain the possible diagnostic context (the set of diseases that may cause the problem) and the rule class to be invoked for assessing its presence. Since applying these rules often requires new data, another slot of each problem frame contains the list of data to collect in order to confirm the presence of the problem itself. Finally, another slot represents the severity of the problem itself.

An example
Clinic situation of the patient : *a smoker woman with 43 years old, who has a very active profession. Diagnostic is ventricular extrasystoles.*

T A R C A - Therapy Planning

Diagnosis : *ventricular extrasystoles*

Prevention : *The patient must quit smoking.*

Therapy
Any of these therapies *amiodarone, beta-blocking* or *ansiolitics* could be indicated. Nevertheless, given the reduced aged of the patient (43 years old), *amiodarone* seems particularly indicated.
Given the patient has an active profession, it isn't particularly indicate the ministration of *ansiolitics*.

Note : See pharmacological indications about *amiodarone.*

3 - Conclusions and Perspectives

Part of this work referring to the diagnosis process, finds itself at a stage of validation at the S. João Hospital at Oporto. The part involving acquisition and graphic visualization of the ECG is already of routine utilization. In the future, we hope that all the system (comprising therapy, prevention and monitoring modules) might progressively be accepted and used by the medical community. This progressive acceptance by medical community of the work performed using AI methods, might contribute in a future that we wish will be near, to a bigger and easier acceptance of ES in medicine. This bigger acceptance, translated in a bigger cooperation by the medical part, will allow the development of new and better ES in this area.

One of the aspects that we wish to improve on the described system, implies better gathering and access to information about the population of patients existing in the geographical area where the system will be installed. This information will allow the creation of data bases about the population, allowing, the creation of a generic model of treatment of that same population.

Specific treatment of a patient will be understood as successive instanciations of this generic model, using the information available at that point in time.

This point of view will be more global and also the error factors connected to the attribution of probabilities would be substantially diminished.

Another important aspect, concerns new rules that may be inserted in the system. It would be of obvious interest, the creation of a module of true maintenance, allowing the control of the information introduced regarding its coherence.

To conclude, we may say that the system implemented performs with success all the tasks which it was built for. The final package constitutes an integrated system since the automatic acquisition of the ECG until the therapeutic prescription and monitoring. The system is provided with an interface that allows a simple and pleasant interaction with the users.

References

Abreu-Lima C.,Marques de Sá J. P.,"Novos aperfeiçoamentos do Sistema de Electrocardiografia Computadorizada do Porto". BioEng'88, Porto 1988, pp. 112-113

Oliveira, E., Rocha, "ARCA - An Integrated System for Cardiac Pathologies Diagnosis and Treatment" in Knowledge Based Systems in Medicine: Methods, Applications and Evaluation, Lecture Notes in Medical Informatics, n° 47, Spring Verlag, 1992

Quaglini S, et al, "Hybrid knowledge-based systems for therapy planning" in Artificial Intelligence in Medicine 4, Elsevier 1992, pp. 207-226

Wartk, J., "Processing of electrocardiograms by a computer", 1978.

Intelligent Distributed Environmental Decision Support System

Benedita Malheiro[1] and Eugénio Oliveira[2]

[1] Department of Electrical Engineering, Instituto Superior de Engenharia do Porto,
Rua de S. Tomé, 4200 Porto, Portugal, Telephone: +351 2 2041849
Email: mbnm@garfield.fe.up.pt
WWW URL: http://www.up.pt/~bene
[2] Department of Electrical Engineering and Computers, Faculdade de Engenharia da
Universidade do Porto, Rua dos Bragas, 4099 Porto CODEX, Portugal
Email: eco@garfield.fe.up.pt
WWW URL: http://garfield.fe.up.pt:8001/~eol/eco.html

Abstract. This article discusses the development of an Intelligent Distributed Environmental Decision Support System, built upon the association of a Multi-agent Belief Revision System with a Geographical Information System (GIS). The inherent multidisciplinary features of the involved expertises in the field of environmental management, the need to define clear policies that allow the synthesis of divergent perspectives, its systematic application, and the reduction of the costs and time that result from this integration, are the main reasons that motivate the proposal of this project.

This paper is organised in two parts: in the first part we present and discuss the developed *Distributed Belief Revision Test-bed - DiBeRT*; in the second part we analyse its application to the environmental decision support domain, with special emphasis on the interface with a GIS.

1 Introduction

The decision activity in the field of environmental management is highly complex and involves a great number of contradictory interests (socio-economic, ecological, etc.). The development of adequate tools that act as decision support systems contribute to the making of sensible, justifiable, and legally correct decisions. They prevent the making of gross errors, either by neglect or by miss-evaluation of the direct and side effects, while trying to reach a compromise between the pressure of the existing socio-economic interests and need to preserve the planet resources.

Frequently, different recommendations are produced by the interveniens of the process. In order to reach a final decision, these distinct perspectives and opinions have to be discussed and accommodated, through the application of some criteria. The criteria applied may vary largely, even within the same group, due to the lack of a systematic approach and to the inclusion of some 'ad-hoc' heuristics, allowing large discrepancies on the final decisions reached by the same committee. This activity presents a number of well defined features: (i) is distributed over the group of advisors; (ii) each individual performs autonomously his share of problem solving; (iii) the existing dependency between expertise domains establishes cooperative links among the members of the decision committee; and (iv) lacks a systematic methodology to accommodate divergent opinions. In this scenario, the modelling of the behaviour of the environmental management team can be appropriately achieved through an autonomous cooperative multi-agent system with consistency maintenance capabilities. Finally, the inclusion of a GIS will provide the multi-agent system with the adequate geographic data platform.

This paper is structured in two parts: (i) presentation of the developed distributed belief revision system, and (ii) discussion of its application to the environmental decision support field.

2 Distributed Belief Revision

Reasoning while maintaining the knowledge base's consistency in a distributed system presents many challenges (see [Huhns, 1991]). In a distributed system diverse levels of consistency occur: (i) when the sets of propositions of each one of the various agents are internally consistent the system is referred as *locally consistent*; (ii) when the reunion of these sets is consistent the system is classified as *globally consistent*. The selection of the adequate consistency level becomes one of the more important aspects of the design of a distributed system with consistency maintenance.

The adoption of a distributed system consistency policy has to take into account the system's type of control (centralised, decentralised), the characteristics of the tasks to be performed (tasks with hard or soft time constraints; granularity of the tasks), and the problem to be solved (some problems impose automatically the required consistency level).

2.1 Distributed Belief Revision with DiBeRT

The *Distributed Belief Revision Test-bed (DiBeRT)* developed is intended to study and model inherently distributed systems, with decentralised control, in which the available information is incomplete and dynamic and the time factor is relevant. A presentation and discussion of the architecture, the used knowledge representation, the multiple contexts management mechanism, the belief revision methodology, the inclusion and representation of external propositions, the applied belief status synthesis criteria, and the sharing of relevant inconsistencies follows.

Architecture The adopted multi-agent architecture is based on the architectural model proposed by the Esprit ARCHON project [Wittig, 1992]. The agents have a double layer architecture: the cooperation layer (CL) and the intelligent system (IS) layer. While the latter contains the agent's domain knowledge based system, the first, holds the functionalities needed for the establishment of the inter-agent cooperative actions.

The CL contains a model of the agent - the Self Model, as well as a model of its acquaintances - the Acquaintances Model. Based on these models, the CL determines when and what type of cooperative action to start, and guarantees that the data sent is relevant to the activity of the recipients through the use of a direct message passing mechanism.

In DiBeRT, the IS is a belief revision system composed of two modules: the problem solver and the assumption based truth maintenance system (ATMS) [de Kleer,1986]. The latter is responsible for maintaining the agent's IS knowledge base free of inconsistencies.

Knowledge Representation in the IS The IS knowledge base is a production rule system. The rules and propositions of each agent can be of several types. There are *inference rules* and *inconsistency detection rules* represented through the following structure:

$rule(Rule\_Id, Dep\_Lev, Type, Agent\_Id, Antecedents\_List, Consequent)$
$Rule\_Id$ - The rule's identification;
Dep_Lev - The rule's dependency level;
$Type$ - The rule's type ($Type \epsilon \{inference, inconsistency\_detection\}$);
$Agent\_Id$ - The identification of agent owner of the rule;
$Antecedents\_List$ - The list of the rule premises;
$Consequent$ - The rule conclusion.

The propositions are of the type $prop(Attribute, Value)$, $prop(Concept, Attribute, Value)$ and can represent *axioms*, *assumptions* or *ordinary inferred propositions*.
The rules and propositions are internally represented at the assumption based truth maintenance system (ATMS) as arbitrary identifiers called *nodes*. The node structure has the following fields:

$node(Node\_Id, Type, Label, Scope, Agent\_Id, Status)$
$Node\_Id$ - The node's identifier;
$Type$ - The node's type ($Type \epsilon \{axiom, assumption, ordinary\}$);
$Label$ - The node's set of support assumptions;
$Scope$ - The scope of the node ($Scope \epsilon \{private, shared\}$);
$Agent\_Id$ - The identification of the agent owner of the node;
$Status$ - The node's belief status ($Status \epsilon \{believed, unbelieved\}$).

Knowledge Representation in the CL The CL is responsible for the interface between the IS and the remaining agents of the multi-agent system, establishing, automatically, cooperative actions whenever the IS: (i) needs help - it asks for external help to accomplish the undergoing tasks (task sharing); (ii) provides voluntary help - it sends, voluntarily, results relevant to the problem solving activity of the recipients (result sharing); (iii) performs belief revision over shared propositions - it automatically resends to every agent with whom the revised proposition is shared the updated belief status [Malheiro, 1994].
The agent that starts a cooperative action is called organiser and the agent that

responds to the *organiser agent* is named the *respondent agent*.

According to the different kinds and possible stages of the cooperative actions a high level communication protocol with adequate primitives was developed [Malheiro, 1994]. The data exchanged between agents contains beliefs. Typically, and since the beliefs are internally represented by nodes, a structure very similar to the node structure (proposition + label) would be expected for the exchanged data. However, in the DiBeRT the structure adopted is composed of a reduced version of the node structure: *proposition + belief status* (see subsection Belief Sharing Format).

Multiple Context Management The DiBeRT prototype was meant as a modelling tool for inherently distributed systems in which the available information is incomplete and dynamic. To be well adjusted to this setting, DiBeRT's main inference mechanism is forward chaining or data-driven, in order to accommodate as fast as possible the perceived or communicated world changes. This operative mode has some disadvantages, namely, the possibility of being easily distracted from the main goal - staying absorbed in processing data which is not relevant to the current system's focus.

To allow meta-control over the system's activity, a multiple context management mechanism was designed and implemented. This control is achieved through the classification of the knowledge domain into sub-domains. A sub-domain is a pre-defined set of rules and propositions that can be distributed over a group of agents. The control is performed through the enabling of the relevant sub-domains and the disabling of the less interesting sub-domains. This mechanism is based on the attribution of belief status to the rules of the system according to the current focus of the system: (i) the rules that belong to the relevant sub-domains are believed - represented by assumption nodes, and thus ready to be triggered; (ii) the rules that belong to the irrelevant sub-domains are not believed - represented by ordinary nodes without valid foundations, and thus disabled. The change of focus of interest is specified by the User. This meta-control uses, exclusively, the already available ATMS functionalities.

Belief Revision The belief revision task is based on the prior classification of the propositions. An agent's group of propositions is divided into two sets: (i) the set of *private propositions* - propositions only used by this agent; and (ii) the set of *shared propositions* - propositions that are shared with some acquaintance. The belief revision of the private propositions is automatically performed by the local agent's ATMS. The belief revision of the shared propositions is accomplished by the shared propositions' owner agent. An agent, upon revising the belief status of a shared proposition, immediately communicates its updated belief status to every recipient with whom it is shared, guaranteeing the system's physical consistency (see [Mason, 1994]).

Inclusion of External Beliefs The decision of how and when to include external beliefs in an agent's knowledge base is fundamental to the characterisation of a distributed belief revision system [Malheiro, 1996]. The DiBeRT agents act in "good faith" and exchange messages using the direct message passing mechanism, thus guaranteeing, that the information received by a recipient agent is, not only, relevant for its activity, but also, truthful from the sender's perspective. A wide range of different methodologies for the inclusion of incoming beliefs can be adopted by the recipient agents: unconditional acceptance, conditional acceptance, rejection, etc.. From this spectra DiBeRT has chosen two policies for the local inclusion of communicated beliefs:

• *local consistency of the shared propositions* - the local beliefs prevail over the communicated beliefs, i.e., the adoption of an external belief is conditioned by the existence or absence of the belief in the agent's local knowledge base. A previously incorporated external proposition is abandoned as soon as the agent infers it by itself. In the absence of a locally deduced belief, a shared proposition for which there are several external belief status is represented by as many nodes as there are external beliefs;

• *global consistency of the shared propositions* - every communicated belief is unconditionally added to the local knowledge base of the recipient agent. A shared proposition owned by different agents has a multiple node representation: is represented by as many nodes as there are agents with beliefs concerning the shared proposition. While the first consistency methodology for the shared propositions is an instance of a conditional acceptance - a communicated belief is included, if and only if, there is no local belief concerning the shared proposition, the second, is an example of unconditional acceptance - a received external belief is always added to the local knowledge base.

Local Representation of the External Propositions The actual representation of the adopted external propositions is based on the available ATMS functionalities [Malheiro, 1995], and depends on the belief status of the external propositions: (i) *an externally believed proposition* - is locally represented by an assumption node; (ii) *an externally unbelieved proposition* - is locally represented by an ordinary node without valid foundations (the contents of the node's label is the empty set).

The accommodation of external propositions' belief status update from: (i) *believed to unbelieved* - corresponds, locally, to the removal of the previous assumption node representation, and to the creation of a new ordinary node without valid foundations to hold the external belief; (ii) *unbelieved to believed* - corresponds, locally, to the removal of the prior ordinary node with empty label representation, and to the creation of a new assumption node in agreement with the external belief update.

Belief Status Synthesis Criteria Upon accepting a set of external beliefs, an agent may find itself with conflicting belief status for the same proposition. In such circumstances which belief status to adopt? The synthesis of the different belief status attributed by the involved agents to the same shared proposition can be performed using diverse criteria, such as unanimity, majority, negotiation, and many others.

In DiBeRT two distinct synthesis criteria were implemented guaranteeing the assignment of an unique belief status to every shared proposition:
- *the disjunctive (OR) synthesis criterion* - a shared proposition is believed as long as there is some agent where it is believed;
- *the conjunctive (AND) synthesis criterion* - a shared proposition is believed, if and only if, it is believed by every agent that share the proposition.

These two synthesis criteria reflect different levels of demand: in the case of the OR synthesis, the belief in a shared proposition by one of the involved agents is enough to make it believed by the system, while, in the case of the AND synthesis, only the consensus among the involved agents makes a shared proposition believed by the system.

The interpretation of the two adopted synthesis criteria is similar to the notions behind the necessary truth and possible truth operators of the standard Modal Logic. The necessary truth operator translates the idea of truth in every accessible contexts (worlds), and the possible truth operator conveys the idea of truth in at least one accessible context.

Belief Sharing Format The information exchanged among agents is, as was previously explained, mainly composed of beliefs. Supposing the code is optimised, the total execution time can only be reduced through the minimisation of the time and amount of beliefs exchanged. Typically, and since the beliefs are internally represented by nodes, a structure very similar to the node structure (proposition + label) should be expected. The adoption of the node-like structure would imply, not only, the future update messages of the proposition and its label, as well as, the update messages regarding the assumptions contained in the label.

In an effort to reduce the number and size of inter-agent messages, the structure selected for the exchange of beliefs was reduced to the (proposition, belief status) pair. Since this format does not include the label, not only, is obviously shorter, but also, avoids the subsequent updating messages of the assumptions contained in the label. However, the reduced belief exchange format no longer allows the receiver agent to verify if there are inconsistencies between its local beliefs and the foundations of the incoming belief.

Sharing of Relevant Inconsistencies This limitation imposed by the selected reduced belief exchange format led to the sharing of detected inconsistencies (invalid environments or *nogoods*) among the agents that share propositions. The intention is to guarantee that the shared propositions hold valid foundations at all times.

An agent upon the detection of a local inconsistency, removes it from every valid context, registers it in its ATMS, and, inspects the *nogood*. If the nogood affects any shared beliefs, the agent immediately sends it to the concerned agents. The receiver removes the communicated nogood from its contexts and records it in its ATMS. The sharing of the inconsistencies relevant to the activity of the agents results in the maintenance of valid foundations for the shared beliefs.

DiBeRT functionalities In DiBeRT, the user is asked, at launch time, to select from the available set of agents the sub-set to be run, the synthesis criterion
to be applied, and the level of consistency desired. The user chooses one from
the following four available distributed consistency modes for execution:
- *shared beliefs local consistency and conjunctive belief status synthesis criterion;*
- *shared beliefs local consistency and conjunctive belief status synthesis criterion;*
- *shared beliefs global consistency and conjunctive belief status synthesis criterion;*
- *shared beliefs global consistency and disjunctive belief status synthesis criterion.*

The private beliefs consistency level is unique: they are always locally consistent.
After launching the community of multi-agents, the interaction between DiBeRT
and the User is performed by a specialised agent called User Interface Agent. The
User Interface Agent architecture is identical to the remaining system agents,
being the IS role played by User. This interface allows, during runtime: (i) the
addition of new assumptions; (ii) the multiple contexts management; (ii) the
attribution of specific belief status; (iv) the querying of the system about any
beliefs.

3 Distributed Environmental Decision Support

So far, the DiBeRT prototype has been tested with simplified problems based
on simulated data. The need to evaluate its performance and adequacy in face
of a real world problem solving suggested its application to the environmental
decision support field. This second part is focused on the analysis of the diverse
aspects of the association of DiBeRT with a GIS.

3.1 Geographical Information Systems

The main characteristics of a GIS are the storing, processing and analysis capabilities of the spatial and alphanumeric data representing a geographic area
(see [Burrough, 1992]). On one hand, a GIS constitutes a resourceful geographic
data bank, encapsulating the capabilities of a relational database management
system (RDBMS) together with a spatial database, allowing the simultaneous
representation of inter-related graphic entities and respective alphanumeric attributes. On the other hand, it contains a large variety of geographical data
processing and handling functions to be used on the stored data, to produce its
classification and analysis.

The spatial database is structured in layers, where each layer can contain one of
two different spatial data representations: raster or vector data. Both data types
are geo-referenced, permitting the simultaneous consultation and overlaying of
the desired thematic layers. Raster data is based on a grid cell matrix representation, while vector data approach is based on the graphic entity concept. The
vector data is made of sets of geo-referenced space points, which, define, recursively, more complex graphic entities (e.g. a line is an ordered list of points, and

polygon is an ordered list of lines). Associated with every graphic entity (point, line, arc or polygon) exists an unique identifier, which can act as a relational database key to access the entity's existing alphanumeric attributes (vegetation type, area, altitude, etc.). Finally, the multitude of raster and vector data handling, processing and classification functions, the automatic availability of the generated results, the constant data accessibility, and the countless possible studies that can be performed, make GISs powerful integrated geographic data tools.

3.2 Multi-agent Systems and Environmental Decision Support

Distribution over different domains and expertises exhibited in the environmental management field led, naturally, to the idea of its modelling trough a multi-agent system. The environmental management task force can be viewed as a community of autonomous cooperative agents. The modelling of the experts cooperative activity through a distributed belief revision system is very adequate. The goal is to reproduce, in an integrated framework, the behaviour of the decision-making group, while trying to reach a conclusion.

The advantages of the integration of the advisors activity with the GIS, when compared with the stand alone operative mode, include: (i) the definition and systematic application of adequate synthesis criteria whenever conflicts arise, and (ii) the explicitation of the existing inter-agent dependency relations and domain overlap. A better understanding, clarification and optimisation of the current technical committee operative mode results in obvious benefits for the overall environmental decision making task (total time and cost reduction).

The distributed nature of the problem, the dynamic and incomplete features of the information, and the variety of expertise involved provide an adequate real world setting for the testing of the DiBeRT.

3.3 Development of a Distributed Environmental Decision Support System

The development of a distributed environmental decision support system presents two main aspects:

• *the specification of the generic interface between both applications* - (i) the detailed analysis of the GIS functionalities (expected inputs and produced outputs), and (ii) the definition of the interface between the two applications;

• *the modelling of the application domain* - (i) the knowledge elicitation phase to build each agent knowledge base, and (ii) the acquisition and introduction of the GIS data concerning the study area.

The specification of the interface between the GIS and DiBeRT is fundamental. It has to allow the agents to: (i) consult/query any spatial or alphanumeric data stored; (ii) to create and store new spatial and alphanumeric data; (iii) to alter/remove any spatial or alphanumeric data stored; (iv) to invoke the available GIS data processing procedures. Two approaches have been considered to act as interface:

- *the interface software agent approach* - the agent collects every request made to the GIS, translates it into GIS inputs, submits it to the GIS, and, finally, sends the produced outputs back to DIBeRT.
- *the DiBeRT agent approach* - the agent's Intelligent System Layer corresponds to the GIS (domain knowledge database), and the Cooperation Layer constitutes the interface between the IS and the rest of the community. The translation of the requests presented to the GIS into GIS commands will be executed by a Convergence Layer (CvL), according to ARCHON architecture proposal (see [Wittig, 1992]), turning DIBeRT into a heterogeneous multi-agent system.

3.4 Proposed Interface Specification

After a careful analysis of both proposals (the implementation of an interface software agent or the modelling of the GIS as a DiBeRT agent) the DiBeRT agent proposal was selected. Not only it interfaces both naturally and automatically with the DiBeRT prototype, but, it will also constitute another heterogeneous application of the ARCHON architecture. In this case, the specification of the interface includes:

- *the CL of the GIS agent* - the CL contains the Self Model, the Acquaintances Model, and a Cooperation and Communication Module. The Acquaintances Model is built at launch time, and enumerates, not only, the acquaintances and situations in which help can be provided to each specific agent, but also, when each specific agent is able to voluntary supply help to others. The Self Model describes the tasks each agent knows how to perform, as well as the knowledge it is capable of inferring. In the case of the GIS agent, the Self Model has to specify: (i) the concepts and attributes existing within the GIS - suppose that every graphic entity of a vector data layer l has n different attributes in a RDBMS table. It is represented in the Self Model by the structure of the type $(Layer_l, [Attribute_1, ..., Attribute_n])$. If the theme of layer l is vegetation, and the attributes for the vegetation layer include, among others, *type* and *area* this structure may hold the following data $(vegetation, [type, ..., area])$. There will be one such structure for each existing vector data layer with associated attributes; Raster data will be represented accordingly - every raster layer represents an attribute (e.g. *soil cover type*) where each pixel value corresponds to a known soil cover type (e.g. $1 - grass, 2 - corn, ...,$ etc.) and constitutes the value of the attribute for that pixel; (ii) the high level GIS functionalities relevant to the application domain, and their decomposition in more elementary GIS procedures;
- *the CvL of the GIS agent* - the convergence layer (CvL) role is to act as a translator between the CL and the IS, converting the CL requests into GIS commands. It is highly dependent of the selected GIS and it contains the necessary knowledge to act as an intelligent translator.
- *the IS of the GIS agent* - the IS is the actual GIS: contains the domain knowledge base (a model of geographic area is in the spatial and alphanumeric databases), as well as a set of procedures to transform, analyse, and extract the necessary data.

4 Conclusion

The motivation behind the Intelligent Distributed Environmental Decision Support System was, not only, the intrinsic appeal and importance of the nature of the problem domain, but also, its particular suitability for the evaluation and testing the distributed belief revision methodologies developed for the DiBeRT prototype [Malheiro, 1996]. The application domain setting is naturally distributed over a set of domain experts and the exchanged data is dynamic and incomplete, making, therefore, the belief revision activity essential to perform opinion synthesis and to guarantee knowledge consistency. Finally, the selected application domain is sufficiently complex to provide a large set of challenging and motivating problems.

Although the development of the system is still in an early stage the presentation of the ideas behind the project seemed interesting enough to motivate this paper. Currently, the project is in the design and specification phase of the CL and CvL for the GIS agent.

References

[Burrough, 1992]   P. A. Burrough, "Principles of Geographical Information Systems for Land Resources Assessment", Monographs on Soil and Resources Survey N. 12, Oxford Science Publications, 1992.

[de Kleer, 1986]   J. de Kleer, "An Assumption-based TMS", Artificial Intelligence, 28 (2), 1986.

[Huhns, 1991]   M. N. Huhns and D. M. Bridgeland, "Multi-Agent Truth Maintenance", IEEE Transactions on Systems, Man and Cybernetics 21 (6), 1991.

[Malheiro, 1994]   B. Malheiro, N. Jennings e E. Oliveira, "Belief Revision in Multi-Agent Systems", Proceedings of the 11th European Conference on Artificial Intelligence - ECAI94, Amsterdam, Holland, 1994.

[Malheiro, 1995]   B. Malheiro e E. Oliveira, "An Intelligent Distributed System for Environmental Management", Environmental Informatics, Methodology and Applications of Environmental Information Processing, Eds. Nicholas M. Avouris and Bernd Page, Computer and Information Science, Vol. 6, Kluwer Academic Publishers, 1995.

[Malheiro, 1996]   B. Malheiro e E. Oliveira, Consistency and Context Management in a Multi-Agent Belief Revision Testbed, Agent Theories, Architectures, and Languages, Eds. Michael Wooldridge, Joerg P. Muller and Milind Tambe, Springer-Verlag, Lecture Notes in Artificial Intelligence, Vol: 1037, 1996.

[Mason, 1994]   C. Mason, "ROO: A Distributed AI Toolkit For Belief Based Reasoning Agents", Proceedings of the 2nd International Working Conference on Cooperating Knowledge Based Systems, Keele, UK, 1994.

[Wittig, 1992]   T. Wittig (ed.), "ARCHON: An Architecture for Cooperative Multi-Agent Systems", Ellis Horwood, 1992.

Object-Oriented Algorithm for Combining Dichotomic Belief Functions

Wagner Teixeira da Silva
e-mail: wagner@cic.unb.br
Pedro Antônio Dourado de Rezende
e-mail: rezende@cic.unb.br

The problem of combining dichotomic belief functions over a hierarchical structure of propositions can be viewed as a problem of updating local data in objects and exchanging messages among objects. Such approach is proposed in this paper. A set of propositions is given in a hierarchical structure so that each node represents a proposition. Nodes in the same level represent disjunctive propositions. A node proposition is given by the union of its node proposition children. Evidences for and against propositions in the hierarchy are translated into dichotomic belief functions. In this form they are combined and propagated to and over nodes of the hierarchy. In this approach, each node is an object. There are three classes of objects: root, internal and external nodes. The objects can receive message, update their local data and send messages to their father and children. For each piece of evidence, the effort to combine and propagate has time complexity linearly proportional to the number of propositions and to the branch factor of the hierarchical tree.

Keywords: Artificial intelligence, Knowledge representation, Dempster-Shafer theory, dichotomic belief functions, Hierarchy of propositions, Object-oriented, Algorithms.

1 INTRODUCTION

This paper specifies an algorithm for combining evidences in a hierarchy of propositions. Let Θ be a set of mutually exclusive propositions, and $\mathcal{A} = (V, E)$ a hierarchy for Θ. For each piece of evidence, the algorithm must add its impact on each node of $\mathcal{A}$. A piece of evidence is initially combined with other evidences already processed in a node X which is the most compatible with the present evidence. Next, this evidence is indirectly combined with the evidences in each one of X's neighboring nodes. The neighbors of these latter nodes also receive and combine this evidence, and the process continues until all nodes in $\mathcal{A}$ have received and combined the evidence. The propagating process certifies that each node in hierarchy $\mathcal{A}$ receives each piece of evidence only once. Therefore the effort of propagating evidences on a tree of propositions is of order nb in the worst case, where $n = |\Theta|$ and b is branch factor of tree $\mathcal{A}$.

Shafer and Logan (1987) proposed an algorithm to combine dichotomic belief functions over a hierarchy of propositions. They claim that their algorithm is linear in the number of propositions in the tree, but this is not obvious. It leaves the impression that its time complexity is linear in n and quadratic in b. They use Barnett(1981) algorithm only to rise in the tree, but not to descend it.

2 DEMPSTER-SHAFER THEORY

Let Θ be a finite set of propositions. Assume that just one proposition is true, but we do not know which one. In this case we call Θ a frame of discernment. Let Pr be a probability distribution on random non-empty subsets S of Θ. The function m(A)=Pr[S=A] for each non-empty subset A⊆Θ, is called a basic probability assignment (bpa). It measures one's belief in the hypothesis that proposition A⊆Θ is true, without accounting for the mass of belief distributed among the subpropositions of A. This function has the properties: $m(\phi) = 0$; and $\Sigma\{m(A)|A\subseteq\Theta\} = 1$.

Whereas m(A) measures the portion of belief specific to **A**, and of none of the proper subsets of **A**, how would Pr[S⊆A] and Pr[S∩A≠φ] be interpreted? These measures are respectively known as degree of belief in **A**, denoted by Bel(A), and degree of plausibility in **A**, denoted by Pl(A). The belief function Bel is given by (1). It attributes degrees of belief to every non-empty subset of Θ.

$$Bel(A) = Pr[S\subseteq A] = \Sigma\{Pr[S=B]|\ B\subseteq A\} = \Sigma\{m(B)|B\subseteq A,\} \qquad (1)$$

$$Pl(A) = Pr[S\cap A\neq\phi] = \Sigma\{Pr[S=B]|\ B\cap A\neq\phi\}= \Sigma\{m(B)|\ B\cap A\neq\phi\} \qquad (2)$$

Bel(A) is interpreted as the total belief mass ascribed to subset A. The Pl function, given by (2) attributes degrees of plausibility to every subset of Θ. Pl(A) is the belief that does not contradict the hypothesis of **A** containing a true proposition. The set $\mathbb{F}=\{A\subseteq\Theta|m(A)>0\}$ is called the focal set of Bel and its elements are the focal elements of Bel. The set $\mathscr{C} = \cup\mathbb{F}$ is the core of Bel and $Bel(\mathscr{C}) = 1$.

Let Ω be a partition of Θ, and let σ(Ω) denote the set consisting of all unions of elements of Ω. The set σ(Ω) is a σ-algebra of subsets of Θ, and Ω is a base for σ(Ω). If Bel is a belief function over Θ, and $\mathbb{F} \subseteq \sigma(\Omega)$ is Bel's focal set, then we say that Bel is carried by Ω. Since σ(Ω) is isomorphic to 2^Ω and belief functions can be all defined in terms of their focal set, if we are working with belief function carried by Ω, then we can think of them as belief function over Ω (Shafer, Shenoy & Mellouli, 1987).

Let Bel be a belief function over Θ, let $\mathbb{F}$ be its focal set, and let $\mathscr{C}$ be its core. If $\mathscr{C}\in\mathbb{F}$, then Bel is called a support function. Let Bel be a support function. If $\mathbb{F} = \{\Theta\}$, then Bel is called a vacuous belief function. Let Bel be a support function over Θ, and let **A** be a non-empty proper subset of Θ. If $\mathbb{F} \subseteq \{A,\Theta\}$, then Bel is called a simple support function, and **A** is the focus of Bel. Let Bel be a belief function over Θ, and let **A** be a non-empty proper subset of Θ. If $\mathbb{F} \subseteq \{A, A^c, \Theta\}$, then Bel is called a dichotomic belief function with dichotomy $\{A, A^c\}$ (henceforth called a DBF).

Let S_1 and S_2 be a random non-empty subset of the frame Θ. Suppose that S_1 and S_2 are probabilistically independent, and that $Pr[S_1\cap S_2\neq\phi]>0$. Let Bel_1 and Bel_2 be belief functions respectively with bpa m_1 and m_2 given by $m_1(A_1)=Pr[S_1=A_1]$, for each $A_1\subseteq\Theta$; and $m_2(A_2) = Pr[S_2=A_2]$, for each $A_2\subseteq\Theta$. Then the orthogonal sum $Bel = Bel_1\oplus Bel_2$ has bpa m given by $m(A) = Pr[S_1\cap S_2=A|\ S_1\cap S_2\neq\phi]$, for each A⊆Θ.

Let Bel_1 be vacuous belief function. Then $Bel = Bel_1\oplus Bel = Bel \oplus Bel_1$.

3 BASIC RESULTS

We use Θ hereafter to mean an original frame of discernment. Each partition of Θ can be viewed as another frame of discernment. In fact, we are interested in partitions of Θ whose refinement relationships form a qualitative Markov tree. In such tree, it is possible to propagate DBFs in polynomial time complexity (see Shafer & Logan, 1987; Shafer, Shenoy & Mellouli, 1987).

Definition 1: The directed tree $\mathcal{A}=(V,\mathbb{E})$ is a hierarchy for Θ if the following are true: a) $V \subseteq 2^{\Theta}$; b) Θ is the root of $\mathcal{A}$; c) C_x is the set of the X's children with at least two elements, if $X \in V$ and X is an internal node of $\mathcal{A}$. C_x is also a partition of X; d) $C_x = \phi$, if X is an external node of $\mathcal{A}$; e) If $X \in V$ and $X \neq \Theta$, then there is only one node $f(X) \in V$ such that $(f(X), X) \in \mathbb{E}$, $f(X)$ is the X's father; f) $A(X)=\{Z|Z=f(X)$ or $Z \in A(f(X))\}$ is the set of ancestors of X, where $X \in V$, $X \neq \Theta$, and $A(\Theta)=\phi$; g) $\mathbb{D}(X) =\{Z| X \in A(Z)\}$ is the set of descendants of X, for all $X \in V$ (Note $\mathbb{D}(X)=\phi$ if X is an external node in $\mathcal{A}$); h) $\mathbb{I}=\{X|X \in V, C_x \neq \phi \}$ is a set of internal nodes of $\mathcal{A}$.

Ex. 1: Figure 1 illustrates a hierarchical tree $\mathcal{A}=(V,\mathbb{E})$ for frame $\Theta=\{a,b,c,d,e,f\}$.

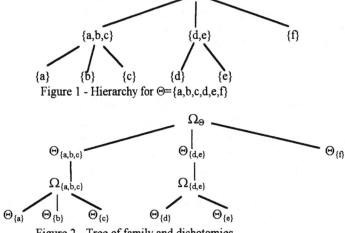

Figure 1 - Hierarchy for $\Theta=\{a,b,c,d,e,f\}$

Figure 2 - Tree of family and dichotomies

We define a subtree of $\mathcal{A}$, containing only the node X and its descendants, by $\mathcal{A}_x=(V_x,\mathbb{E}_x)$, where $V_x=\{X\}\cup\mathbb{D}(X)$. Taking $X=\{a,b,c\}$, then the tree $\mathcal{A}_x$, has $V_x=\{\{a,b,c\},\{a\},\{b\},\{c\}\}$. We also denote the subtree of $\mathcal{A}$ which excludes the subtree $\mathcal{A}_x$ by $\mathcal{A}^x = (V^x,\mathbb{E}^x)$, where $V^x = V-V_x$. Associated with a hierarchical tree $\mathcal{A}$ for Θ there is another tree $\mathcal{A}^d = (V^d,\mathbb{E}^d)$ called "tree of family and dichotomies". For each $X \in V$, $X \neq \Theta$, there is a partition $\Theta_x=\{X, X^c\}$ and for each $X \in \mathbb{I}$ a partition $\Omega_x=C_x\cup\{X^c\}$, both belonging to V^d. Ω_x is the coarsest common refinement among partitions Θ_x and Θ_t, for $t \in C_x$. $\mathcal{A}^d$ has its sets $V^d=\{\Theta_x|X \in V, X \neq \Theta\}\cup\{\Omega_x \mid X \in \mathbb{I}\}$; and $\mathbb{E}^d=\{(\Theta_x,\Omega_x)| X \in \mathbb{I}, X \neq \Theta\} \cup \{(\Omega_x,\Theta_t)| X \in \mathbb{I}, t \in C_x \}$. $\mathcal{A}^d$ is a Qualitative Markov tree (Shafer, Shenoy & Mellouli, 1987). In tree $\mathcal{A}^d$, for each $X \in \mathbb{I}$, $X \neq \Theta$, partitions Θ_x and Θ_t, for $t \in C_x$ are qualitatively independent given Ω_x. The partitions Θ_t are also qualitatively independent given Ω_Θ, for all $t \in C_\Theta$.

Ex. 2: Figure 2 illustrates a tree $\mathcal{A}^d$ associated to the tree $\mathcal{A}$ on example 1.

Definition 2: Let Ω_1 and Ω_2 be partitions of Θ, then $\Omega_1\oplus\Omega_2 = \{A\cap B \neq \phi \mid A\in\Omega_1, B\in\Omega_2\}$ is the coarsest common refinement of Ω_1 and Ω_2.

Lemma 1: In a hierarchical tree $\mathcal{A}$ for Θ, $\forall X \in \mathbb{I}$, suppose that C_x is a partition of X, then for each $t \in C_x$, $\Theta_t = \{t, t^c\}$ is a partition of Θ, and for $X \neq \Theta$, $\Omega_x = C_x \cup \{X^c\}$ is the coarsest common refinement of Θ_x and partitions Θ_t, for $t \in C_x$.

Proof. For any node X in tree $\mathcal{A}$, $X \neq \Theta$, we have by definition 1 that $\Theta_x = \{X, X^c\}$ is a partition of Θ, because $X \subseteq \Theta$, $X \cap X^c = \phi$ and $X \cup X^c = \Theta$. Therefore for $t \in C_x$, $\Theta_t = \{t, t^c\}$ is a partition of Θ. Now, by applying repeatedly definition 2, we have that $\Theta_x \oplus (\oplus \{\Theta_t | t \in C_x\}) = C_x \cup \{X^c\}$. Consequently Ω_x is the coarsest common refinement of Θ_x and partitions Θ_t, for $t \in C_x$. $\square$

The partitions Ω_x, $\forall X \in V$, and Θ_t, $t \in C_x$ have a refinement relationship that yield a qualitative Markov tree (Shafer, Shenoy & Mellouli, 1987).

Lemma 2: Let B_1 and B_2 be DBFs over Θ and carried by a partition Ω of Θ, both with the same dichotomy $\{A, A^c\}$, $A \in \Omega$. Then the orthogonal sum Bel $= B_1 \oplus B_2$ is also a DBF with dichotomy $\{A, A^c\}$, and can be given by

Bel$(A) = 1 - K(1 - B_1(A))(1 - B_2(A))$ and   Bel$(A^c) = 1 - K(1 - B_1(A^c))(1 - B_2(A^c))$;

where $K^{-1} = 1 - B_1(A)B_2(A^c) - B_1(A^c)B_2(A)$

Proof. Following directly from the orthogonal sum. $\square$

We are supposing that all DBFs treated here have belief mass in their focal elements less than 1, except perhaps, the belief mass in their frame, which can have value 1.

Lemma 3: Let Ω be a partition of Θ, and suppose that $\forall t \in \Omega$, there is a DBF B_t with dichotomy $\{t, t^c\}$. Suppose also that Bel $= \oplus \{B_t | t \in \Omega\}$. Then $\forall A \in \sigma(\Omega)$,

Bel$(A) = K[\Pi\{(1 - B_t(t)) \, | \, t \in \Omega\}.\Sigma\{B_t(t)/(1 - B_t(t)) \, | \, t \subseteq A, \, t \in \Omega\} +$

$\Pi\{B_t(t^c) \, | \, t \not\subseteq A, \, t \in \Omega\}.\Pi\{(1 - B_t(t)) \, | \, t \subseteq A, \, t \in \Omega\} - \Pi\{B_t(t^c) \, | \, t \in \Omega\}]$,

where $K^{-1} = \Pi\{(1 - B_t(t)) \, | \, t \in \Omega\}.(1 + \Sigma\{B_t(t)/(1 - B_t(t)) \, | \, t \in \Omega\}) - \Pi\{B_t(t^c) \, | \, t \in \Omega\}$,

Proof.: This lemma constitutes the results of Barnett's paper (Barnett, 1981). $\square$

Lemma 4: Given a hierarchical tree $\mathcal{A}$ for Θ, $\forall X \in \mathbb{I}$, and $X \neq \Theta$, suppose that F_x and S_t are DBFs carried by Θ_x and Θ_t respectively. Then F_x and S_t, $t \in C_x$, are carried by Ω_x.

Proof. By lemma 1, Ω_x is a common refinement of Θ_x and Θ_t, $t \in C_x$. This implies $\sigma(\Theta_x)$, $\sigma(\Theta_t) \subseteq \sigma(\Omega_x)$, $\forall t \in C_x$. In this way the focal set of all these functions are subsets of $\sigma(\Omega_x)$. Therefore the DBFs F_x and S_t, $t \in C_x$, are all carried by Ω_x $\square$

Lemma 5: Given a hierarchical tree $\mathcal{A} = (V, \mathbb{E})$ for Θ, suppose that there exists a DBF S_t, for each $t \in C_x$, $X \in \mathbb{I}$, $X \neq \Theta$. Then the orthogonal sum $\oplus \{S_t \, | \, t \in C_x\}$ projected into frame Θ_x is given by $C_x(X) = 1 - K_x$ and $C_x(X^c) = K_x.P_x$, where

$K_x = 1/(1 + \Sigma\{S_t(t)/(1 - S_t(t)) \, | \, t \in C_x\})$ and $P_x = \Pi\{S_t(t^c)/(1 - S_t(t)) \, | \, t \in C_x\}$.

Proof. By lemma 4, a DBF carried by either Θ_x or Θ_t, $t \in C_x$, is also carried by Ω_x. Being Ω_x a partition of Θ and considering the vacuous belief function S_x^c, then lemma 3 can be applied here to combine dbf's S_t, $t \in C_x$, with S_x^c. By taking Ω and B_t in lemma 3 as Ω_x and S_t, $\forall t \in \Omega_x \cup \{X^c\}$ respectively, we have

$C_x(X) = K[\Pi\{1 - S_t(t) \, | \, t \in C_x\}.\Sigma\{S_t(t)/(1 - S_t(t)) \, | \, t \subseteq C_x\}]$, $C_x(X^c) = K[\Pi\{S_t(t^c) \, | \, t \in C_x\}]$

where $K^{-1} = \Pi\{1 - S_t(t) \, | \, t \in C_x\}.(1 + \Sigma\{S_t(t)/(1 - S_t(t)) \, | \, t \in C_x\})$.

Taking $K_x = 1/[1 + \Sigma\{S_t(t)/(1 - S_t(t)) | \, t \in C_x\}]$ and $P_x = \Pi\{S_t(t^c)/(1 - S_t(t)) | \, t \in C_x\}$ we obtain $C_x(X) = 1 - K_x$, and $C_x(X^c) = K_x.P_x$. $\square$

Lemma 6: Given a hierarchical tree $\mathcal{A} = (V, \mathbb{E})$ for Θ, suppose that there exists a DBF F_x, for $X \in \mathbb{I}$, $X \neq \Theta$, and DBFs S_t, for each $t \in C_x$. Let $Z \in C_x$. Then the orthogonal sum $F_x \oplus (\oplus \{S_t \mid t \in C_x, t \neq Z\})$ projected into Θ_Z is given by

$$D_z(Z) = 1 - K_z; \text{ and } D_z(Z^c) = K_z.P_z$$

where $K_z = 1/[1 + \Sigma\{S_t(t)/(1 - S_t(t))\mid t \in C_x, t \neq Z\} + F_x(X^c)/(1 - F_x(X^c))]$;

$$P_z = F_x(X)/(1-F_x(X^c)).\Pi\{S_t(t^c)/(1-S_t(t))\mid t \in C_x, t \neq Z\}.$$

Proof. The argument used on proof of lemma 5 can also be applied here, except that the vacuous belief function is associated to Z instead of X^c, and $S_x{}^c = F_x$ $\square$

Lemma 7: The factor of normalization K_z in lemma 6 can be computed from K_x in lemma 5 by the formula $K_z = 1/[1/K_x - S_z(Z)/(1-S_z(Z))+F_x(X^c)/(1-F_x(X^c))]$

Proof. Following from lemmas 5 and 6 by comparing their expressions for K_x and K_z respectively $\square$

Lemma 8: The productory P_z on lemma 6 can be computed from P_x on lemma 5 by

$$P_z = 0, \text{ if more than one } t \in C_x \text{ such that } S_t(t^c) = 0 \text{ exist.}$$
$$= [F_x(X)/(1-F_x(X^c))][(1 - S_z(Z))/S_z(Z^c)].P_x, \text{ if } S_z(Z^c)>0$$
$$= F_x(X)/(1-F_x(X^c)).[\Pi\{S_t(t^c)/(1-S_t(t))\mid t \in C_x, t \neq Z\}], \text{ if } S_z(Z) = 0$$

Proof:. Following from lemmas 5 and 6.

4. DICHOTOMY PROPAGATION

4.1 DEFINITION PROBLEM

In a hierarchical tree $\mathcal{A} = (V, \mathbb{E})$ for Θ, suppose that each $X \in V$, $X \neq \Theta$, has a DBF L_x with dichotomy $\{X, X^c\}$. Our problem consists of finding the degrees of belief $Bel(X)$ and $Bel(X^c)$, where Bel is the combined belief function as defined by

$$Bel = \oplus\{L_x \mid X \in V, X \neq \Theta\} \qquad (4)$$

This function assigns a degree of belief $Bel(A)$ for each subset A of Θ. However we are interested only in those subsets $A \in V$, except $A = \Theta$. This method could be used to calculate the combination of all the DBFs L_x over Θ, but with exponential time complexity on the size of Θ. Consequently we must find a more economical solution.

4.2 PROPOSED SOLUTION

In a hierarchical tree $\mathcal{A}$ for Θ, $\forall X \in V$, $X \neq \Theta$, one has to consider the following:

a) We are interested only on values $Bel(X)$ and $Bel(X^c)$; since DBFs carried by Θ_x and Θ_t, $t \in C_x$, are also carried by Ω_x, according to lemma 4, we can combine functions on Ω_x and project the combined belief function onto Θ_x (according to lemma 5) or Θ_t, $t \in C_x$ (according to lemma 6); b) The relationships among Ω_x, Θ_x, and the partitions Θ_t associated with the children of X yield a tree of family and dichotomies, like a tree in figure 2; c) Since the tree of family and dichotomies $\mathcal{A}^d$ is a qualitative Markov tree, we can project functions, carried by a given partition on this tree, between this partition and a coarser (or finer) partition, or combine functions on any common refinement of partitions that carry these functions (Shafer, Shenoy & Mellouli, 1987).

Based on above considerations, figure 3 illustrates combinations of DBFs on the nodes and projections of DBFs among the nodes of a tree of family and dichotomies $\mathcal{A}^d$, associated with a hierarchical tree $\mathcal{A}$ for the original frame Θ.

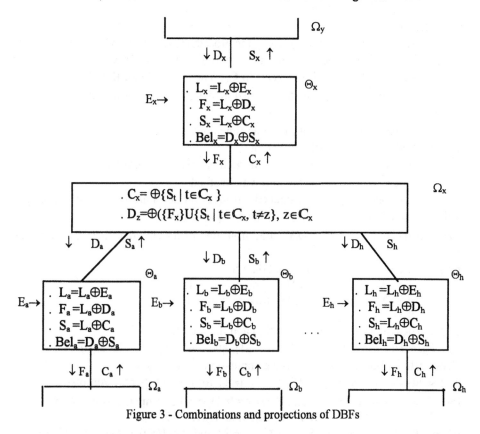

Figure 3 - Combinations and projections of DBFs

In terms of tree $\mathcal{A}$, the propagation of DBFs consists in computing: a) the influence S_x from subtree $\mathcal{A}_x$, through X, to subtree $\mathcal{A}^x$; b) the influence D_x from subtree $\mathcal{A}^x$, through f(X), to subtree $\mathcal{A}_x$; c) the final DBF $Bel_x = S_x \oplus D_x$ on frame Θ_x, for all $X \in V$ except $X = \Theta$. The belief functions Bel_x has the following properties: $Bel_x(X) = Bel(X)$ and $Bel_x(X^c) = Bel(X^c)$, where Bel is as defined on equation 4 (see Shafer, Shenoy & Mellouli, 1987).

Using the object oriented paradigm (Booch, 1986 and 1990; Nguyen, 1988), we can think of each node X in V as an object. An object X can receive and send messages from and to its neighboring objects, or receive the external message E_x. (A message is a DBF with dichotomy $\{Y, Y^c\}$, where Y is the destination object). X's neighbor objects are X's father and X's children, and X's methods are formulas to evaluate the belief functions in partitions Θ_x and Ω_x associated with X. (see figures 2 and 3)

There are three classes of objects: root, internal, and external. There is only one object that can be instanced to the root class, the object associated with the root

Θ in $\mathscr{A}$. Each object associated with an internal node $X \in \mathbb{I}$ in $\mathscr{A}$, $X \neq \Theta$, is instanced to the internal class. Each object associated to an external node in $\mathscr{A}$ is instanced to the external class.

4.2.1 ROOT CLASS

The behavior of a root class is given by the procedures in a root node Ω_Θ of a tree $\mathscr{A}^d$. This class of object does not receive external message. This object exchanges messages only with its children objects in C_Θ. The local data for this objects are:

i) $S_t(t)$, $S_t(t^c)$: belief in t, given by external evidences that impacted nodes of subtree $\mathscr{A}_t$, $\forall t \in C_\Theta$;

ii) K_Θ: Normalization factor of the belief function C_Θ;

iii) P_Θ: Productory of the belief function C_Θ;

iv) cz: counter for the number of Θ's children having $S_t(t^c)=0$, $t \in C_\Theta$.

The root object owes the following methods:

a) when the root object Θ is instanced: all local variables are initialized: K_Θ equals 1.0; cz equals $|C_\Theta|$; all other local variables equal zero.

b) when the root receives a DBF mS_x from one of its children $X \in C_\Theta$, it does the following:

b.0) updates counter cz and the local data S_x:

   If $S_x(X^c)=0$ and $mS_x(X^c)>0$ then cz = cz - 1;
   if $S_x(X^c)>0$ and $mS_x(X^c)=0$ then cz = cz + 1;
   $S_x = mS_x$;

b.1) updates the factor of normalization and the productory:

   $K_\Theta = 1/[1 + \Sigma\{S_t(t)/(1 - S_t(t))| \, t \in C_\Theta\}]$; and, $P_\Theta = \Pi\{S_t(t^c)/(1 - S_t(t))| \, t \in C_\Theta\}$

These values allow us minimize the computation of message D_z.

b.2) sends the message $D_z = \oplus\{S_t| \, t \in C_\Theta, t \neq Z\}$ for each of its children object $Z \in C_\Theta$, for $Z \neq X$. Taking $F_\Theta(\Theta) = 1$ and $F_\Theta(\Theta^c) = 0$, D_z can be computed as in lemma 6 by

   $$D_z(Z) = 1 - K_z; \text{ and } D_z(Z^c) = K_z.P_z$$

where $K_z = 1/[1 + \Sigma\{S_t(t)/(1-S_t(t))|t \in C_\Theta, t \neq Z\}$ and $P_z = \Pi\{S_t(t^c)/(1-S_t(t))|t \in C_\Theta, t \neq Z\}$

Lemmas 7 and 8 minimize computations for D_z. By lemma 7 we have that

   $$K_z = 1/[1/K_\Theta - S_z(Z)/(1 - S_z(Z^c))$$

and by lemma 8 we have that

   $P_z = 0$, if cz>1 (there is more than one $t \in C_\Theta$, such that $S_t(t^c) = 0$)

   $= [(1 - S_z(Z))/S_z(Z^c)].P_\Theta$, if $S_z(Z^c)>0$

   $= [\Pi\{S_t(t^c)/(1-S_t(t))| \, t \in C_\Theta, t \neq Z\}]$, if $S_z(Z^c) = 0$.

Note that when there is only one $t \in C_\Theta$ such that $S_t(t^c) = 0$ we have: if $t \neq Z$ then $P_z = [(1-S_z(Z))/S_z(Z^c)].P_\Theta$ otherwise $P_z = [\Pi\{S_t(t^c)/(1-S_t(t))| \, t \in C_x, t \neq Z\}]$.

The analysis of time complexity for the computations made by the root object shows that the computational effort made in item "a" is of order $O(|C_\Theta|)$; and the computational effort made in "b" is also of order $O(|C_\Theta|)$ when the lemmas 7 and 8 are used to compute messages D_z. The computational effort in "b" could be expensive. We can cut this cost significantly by observing that P_z needs to be recomputed for only one Z in C_Θ. This recomputational effort is of order $O(|C_\Theta|)$.

For its $|C_\Theta|$-1 other children the maximum effort is constant. Hence adding the efforts in "a" and in "b" we have the total computational effort made by root object, which is of order $O(|C_\Theta|)$.

4.2.2 INTERNAL CLASS

The behavior of an internal X object is given by the function evaluations in the internal nodes Θ_x and Ω_x of a tree of family and dichotomy $\mathscr{A}^d$ (figure 3). An internal object is associated to the internal node X of $\mathscr{A}$. This exchanges messages with its father and children, and receive external messages from the environment. When this class of object receive a message it spreads the effects of a received message to all neighbors, except for that one who sent it the message. The local data for this class of objects are given by:

i) $Bel_x(X)$, $Bel_x(X^c)$: belief in X, given by external evidences that impact some node in $\mathscr{A}$;

ii) $C_x(X)$, $C_x(X^c)$: belief in X, given by external evidences which impact some node in $\mathscr{A}_x$, excluded the root X;

iii) $D_x(X)$, $D_x(X^c)$: belief in X, given by external evidences which impact some node in $\mathscr{A}^x$;

v) $F_x(X)$, $F_x(X^c)$: belief in X, given by external evidences which impact some node in $\mathscr{A}^x$ and inclusive X;

v) $L_x(X)$, $L_x(X^c)$: belief in X, given by external evidences impacting X directly;

vi) $S_t(t)$, $S_t(t^c)$: belief in t, given by external evidences which impacted nodes of subtree $\mathscr{A}_t$, $\forall t \in C_x$;

vii) cz: counter for the number of X's children having $S_t(t^c) = 0$, $t \in C_x$.

Suppose X's father is Y, as in figure 3. Then X carries out the following:

a) when X is instanced: all local variables but cz are initialized to 0; cz = $|C_x|$.

b) when X receives an external message E_x from the environment:

b.1) updates local function $L_x = L_x \oplus E_x$. The updated L_x is computed as in lemma 2;

b.2) sends the message $S_x = L_x \oplus C_x$ to its father Y. S_x is computed as in lemma 2;

b.3) updates its global belief, $Bel_x = D_x \oplus S_x$, as given in lemma 2, where D_x is the last message received from X's father Y.

b.4) computes DBF $F_x = L_x \oplus D_x$ as in lemma 2.

b.5) Sends the message $D_z = F_x \oplus (\oplus \{S_t \mid t \in C_x, t \neq Z\}$ to each child object $Z \in C_x$. D_z is computed according to lemma 6. However, lemmas 7 and 8 minimize this computational effort. In the last case we compute D_z by

$$D_z(Z) = 1 - K_z \text{ and } D_z(Z^c) = K_z.P_z, \text{ where}$$
$$K_z = 1/[1/K_x - S_z(Z)/(1-S_z(Z^c)) + F_x(X^c)/(1-F_x(X^c));$$
$$P_z = 0, \text{ if } nz>1 \text{ (there is more than one } t \in C_x, \text{ such that } S_t(t^c) = 0); \text{ or}$$
$$P_z = [F_x(X)/(1-F_x(X^c))].[(1 - S_z(Z))/S_z(Z^c)].P_x, \text{ if } S_z(Z^c)>0; \text{ or}$$
$$= F_x(X)/(1-F_x(X^c)).[\Pi\{S_t(t^c)/(1-S_t(t))|t \in C_x, t \neq Z\}], \text{ if } S_z(Z^c) = 0;$$
$$K_x = 1 - C_x(X); \text{ and, } P_x = C_x(X^c)/K_x$$

c) when X receives the message mD_x from its father Y, then X:

c.1) updates the local data $D_x = mD_x$;

c.2) updates its global belief, $Bel_x = D_x \oplus S_x$, as in lemma 2.

c.3) computes DBF $F_x = L_x \oplus D_x$ as in lemma 2.

c.4) Sends the message $D_z = F_x \oplus (\oplus \{S_t | t \in C_x, t \neq Z\}$ to each child object $Z \in C_x$. Uses the same procedure of item b.5 of Internal Class.

d) when X receives the message mS_z from its child Z, then X:

d.0) updates counter cz and the local data S_z.

$\quad\quad\quad$ If $S_z(Z^c) = 0$ and $mS_z(Z^c) > 0$ then $cz = cz - 1$;

$\quad\quad\quad$ if $S_z(Z^c) > 0$ and $mS_z(Z^c) = 0$ then $cz = cz + 1$;

$\quad\quad\quad$ $S_z = mS_z$;

d.1) computes the DBF $C_x = \oplus \{S_t | t \in C_x\}$ according to lemma 5.

d.2) sends the message $S_x = L_x \oplus C_x$ to its father Y, according to item b.2 of this class.

d.3) updates its global belief, $Bel_x = D_x \oplus S_x$, as in lemma 2.

d.4) computes DBF $F_x = L_x \oplus D_x$ according to lemma 2.

d.5) Sends the message $D_w = F_x \oplus (\oplus \{S_t | t \in C_x, t \neq W\}$ to each child object $W \in (C_x \setminus \{Z\})$. D_w is computed according to lemma 6. However, lemmas 7 and 8 minimize this computational effort, in which case we compute D_z by

$\quad\quad\quad$ $D_w(W) = 1 - K_w$ and $D_w(Z^c) = K_w . P_w$,

where $\quad K_w = 1/[1/K_x - S_w(W)/(1-S_w(W)) + F_x(X^c)/(1-F_x(X^c))$;

$\quad\quad\quad$ $P_w = 0$, if $cz > 1$ (there is more than one $t \in C_x$, such that $S_t(t^c) = 0$); or

$\quad\quad\quad\quad$ $= [F_x(X)/(1-F_x(X^c))] . [(1 - S_w(W))/S_w(W^c)] . P_x$, if $S_w(W^c) > 0$; or

$\quad\quad\quad\quad$ $= F_x(X)/(1-F_x(X^c)) . [\Pi \{S_t(t^c)/(1-S_t(t)) | t \in C_x, t \neq W\}]$, if $S_w(W^c) = 0$;

$\quad\quad\quad$ $K_x = 1 - C_x(X)$; and, $P_x = C_x(X^c)/K_x$

For each one of the three types of messages received (itens b, c and d) by an internal node, the time complexity, on worst case, is linearly proportional to $|C_x|$, $O(|C_x|)$. Observe that the evaluation $P_w = F_x(X)/(1-F_x(X^c)) . [\Pi \{S_t(t^c)/(1-S_t(t)) | t \in C_x, t \neq W\}]$ in item d.5 is made only when $S_w(W^c) = 0$ and $cz = 1$. This effort is made only for one of the children of X.

4.2.3 EXTERNAL CLASS

The external class behavior is given by evaluations in a leaf node Θ_z of a tree $\mathscr{A}^d$, (figure 3). An external object Z corresponds to an external node in tree $\mathscr{A}$. The local data for this class of object is:

i) $Bel_x(X)$, $Bel_x(X^c)$: belief in X, given by external evidences which impact some node in $\mathscr{A}$;

iii) $D_x(X)$, $D_x(X^c)$: belief in X, given by external evidences which impact some node in $\mathscr{A}^{x}$;

v) $L_x(X)$, $L_x(X^c)$: belief in X, given by external evidences impacting X directly.

If X is father of Z, then $Z \in C_x$ in tree $\mathscr{A}$ and Z carries out the following:

a) when Z receives an external message E_z (external evidence):

a.1) updates the local function $L_z = L_z \oplus E_z$, according lemma 2.

a.2) sends the message L_z to its father object X.

a.3) updates its global belief, $Bel_z = D_z \oplus L_z$, conform lemma 2;

b) when Z receives message D_z from its father object X: updates its global belief $Bel_z = D_z \oplus L_z$. This orthogonal sum is made according to lemma 2.

The effort, at the worst case, except for receiving and sending messages, made by an external node can be measured by ten assignments, fourteen products, and sixteen subtractions. Consequently the operations made in an external object has constant time complexity, $O(1)$.

5. CONCLUSION

A linear time complexity algorithm has been proposed for combing DBFs over a hierarchy of propositions. The DBFs are supported by evidences for and against propositions in the hierarchy. The algorithm follows an object-oriented design. Each node of the hierarchy is represented by an object. There are three classes of objects: root, internal and external. By the mechanism of updating local data and receiving/sending messages among objects, this algorithm combines evidences and updates the degree of belief and plausibility to each proposition on the hierarchy. No node receives impact from the same evidence more than once. Since each node sends messages to all its neighbors, then the computational complexity for each piece of evidence is linear in the number of propositions and in the branch factor in the hierarchy of propositions.

This algorithm differs from the Shafer and Logan(1987) algorithm in that it uses Barnett's(1981) algorithm both to rise and descend in the hierarchy of propositions, while propagating belief functions over the hierarchical tree. Another important difference is this algorithm's object-oriented design, which clarify its computational complexity.

REFERENCE

BARNETT, J.A. Computational methods for a mathematical theory of evidence. In: Proceedings IJCAI-81, Vancouver, BC, 1981. pp 868-75.

BOOCH, G. Object-Oriented Development. IEEE Transaction on Software Engineering, 12(2):211-21, Feb. 1986.

BOOCH, G. Object Oriented Design: with applications. Menlo Park, CA: Benjamim/ Cummings, 1994.

DEMPSTER, A. P. A generalization of bayesian inference. Journal of Royal Statistical Society, Series B, 30:205-47, 1968.

NGUYEN, Van et alii. A generalized Object Model. ACM SIGPLAN Notices, 21(10):78-87, Oct. 1988.

SHAFER, G. A mathematical theory of evidence. Princeton University Press, 1976.

SHAFER, G. & LOGAN, R. Implementing Dempster's Rule for hierarchical evidence. Artificial Intelligence, 33:271-98, 1987.

SHAFER, G., SHENOY, P.P. & MELLOULI, K. Propagating Belief Functions in Qualitative Markov Trees. International Journal of Approximate Reasoning, 1987, 1:349-400.

Automatic Bottom-Up Analysis and Transformation of Logic Programs*

Wamberto W. Vasconcelos

State Univ. of Ceará
Statistics & Computing Dept.
Fortaleza, Ce. – Brazil
wamb@fortal.uece.br

*Marcelo A. T. Aragão***

Federal Univ. of Ceará
A. I. Lab
Fortaleza, Ce. – Brazil
aragao@lia.ufc.br

Norbert E. Fuchs

Universität Zürich
Institut für Informatik
Zürich – Switzerland
fuchs@ifi.unizh.ch

Abstract. The comparatively small size and clean declarative semantics of logic programs hide performance issues that must be accounted for if the programs are to be executed using the currently available technology. Proposals have been made to tackle these computational issues by analysing a program and trying to optimise its code. We introduce a bottom-up method for analysing logic programs. The method incrementally builds self-contained subtheories of the initial program, starting from facts and then picking up more complex clauses that depend on simpler, previously analysed constructs. A transformation system is then applied to these subtheories yielding more efficient subprograms. Eventually a subtheory that encompasses the full initial program is obtained.

Keywords: Logic programming, automatic program transformation.

1   Introduction

The comparatively small size and clean declarative semantics of logic programs hide performance issues that must be accounted for if the programs are to be executed using the currently available technology. Methods have been proposed for devising programs with efficiency concerns [VF96b, Rob91]; proposals have also been made to deal with such computational issues after the program has been devised trying to optimise the existing code [LS90, FF92, PP92]. Our work fits into this second approach: we introduce a framework for the systematic analysis of a logic program, detecting opportunities to improve its efficiency.

Our method incorporates a bottom-up policy for gradually building more efficient subprograms of the initial program and extending them until the whole initial program is analysed. We aim at a fully automatic context within which a logic program can be thoroughly analysed and, if necessary, transformed in order to achieve a better computational performance.

In Section 2 we explain how transformations have been formalised and opportunistically employed in a realistic context for program analysis. In Section 3 we point out the drawbacks of the approach shown before and introduce our

---

* This work was partially carried out while the first author was visiting the Department of Artificial Intelligence, University of Edinburgh, Scotland, Great Britain.

** Sponsored by the Brazilian Research Council (CNPq), grant n° 300.968/95-7.

proposal to deal with such problems. In Section 4 we summarise, draw some conclusions and give directions for future work.

2 Enhanced Schema-Based Transformations and their Opportunistic Application

In [VF95, VF96a] an opportunistic approach is proposed for performing program analysis and optimisation: opportunities for improving a logic program are systematically attempted, either by examining its procedures in an isolated fashion, or by checking for conjunctions within clauses that can be used as joint specifications. Opportunities are represented as *enhanced schema-based transformations*, generic descriptions of inefficient programming constructs and of how these should be altered in order to confer a better computational behaviour on the program. The programming constructs are described in an abstract manner using an *enhanced schema language* which allows important features to be highlighted and irrelevant details to be disregarded.

A special schema language is used which enables the economic description of programs in an abstract fashion. The programming constructs are represented by means of *program schemata*, generic descriptions of a program in a suitable Horn-clause notation. The proposed schema language allows the description of large classes of constructs sharing particular features, ignoring unimportant variations. Ordinary Prolog constructs can be used within program schemata, in which case they are considered as constraints, since they are specific syntactic patterns. A number of other constructs are offered: the formal description of the enhanced schema language is presented in [VF95, VF96a].

Schema-based transformations are standard syntactic manipulations of portions of a given program. Such constructs can be seen as rewriting rules consisting of second-order program schemas, similar to the work depicted in [HL78]. Program schemata are used to depict both input programs and their improved output versions.

Two kinds of opportunities for program optimisation are formalised in [VF95, VF96a], one concerning individual procedures and how they can be improved singly, and the other concerning groups of procedures and how their joint use can be optimised. Both alternatives can be appropriately described using the enhanced schema-based transformations and pursued in an opportunistic approach, consisting of analysing a program Π in search of opportunities to employ these enhanced schema-based transformations. The following definition describes the opportunistic approach[3]:

$$transform(\Pi, \Pi^F) \longleftrightarrow apply(\Pi, T^{pred}, \Pi') \wedge transform(\Pi', \Pi^F)$$
$$transform(\Pi, \Pi^F) \longleftrightarrow apply(\Pi, T^{conj}, \Pi') \wedge transform(\Pi', \Pi^F)$$
$$transform(\Pi, \Pi)$$

---

[3] We have slightly altered the original formalisation shown in [VF95, VF96a].

Predicate *transform*/2 holds if both its arguments are programs such that the second argument is an equivalent, possibly more efficient, version of the first argument, in which the whole repertoire of transformations has been tried. The repertoire of transformations is divided into two subsets: $\mathcal{T}^{pred}$, the transformations applicable to predicates, and $\mathcal{T}^{conj}$, the transformations applicable to conjunctions. Initially, attempts are made at transforming isolated procedures: *apply*/3 transforms *one* isolated procedure of Π by applying one predicate transformation (first clause); when no more predicate transformations are applicable then the conjunction transformations (second clause) are applied. In either case *apply*/3 obtains a new version Π' with the appropriate alterations incorporated. This newly obtained program Π' is then recursively used in further transformations. When there are no more predicates or conjunctions to be transformed, we can say that the program Π has reached its optimal state with respect to the available repertoire of transformations and that no more improvements can be made – the third clause caters for this possibility. The ordering of the application of transformations (predicate transformations first, and then conjunction transformations) is, however, immaterial.

The termination of the process above is only possible when the transformed program eventually converges to a form in which no further transformations can be applied to it. This convergence depends on the nature of the syntactic alterations prescribed by the available transformations. Each schema-based transformation should be designed bearing in mind the iterative framework within which it will be employed.

3 Bottom-Up Analysis and Transformation

The exhaustive opportunistic approach proposed in [VF95, VF96a] and described in the previous section has a serious drawback. Let us suppose that Π, consisting of predicates $p_0, \ldots, p_n$, has a transformation applied to predicate p_i, after predicates p_0 to p_{i-1} have been exhaustively analysed, yielding Π'. When the opportunistic framework tries to transform Π', procedures p_0 to p_{i-1} are once again unnecessarily analysed. This re-processing is due to the non-separation between portions of the program that have already been exhaustively matched against the repertoire of transformations and portions of the program still to be checked for inefficiencies. The cost of matching a single transformation is proven in [VF95] to be exponential in the worst case, when different clause orderings must be tried. A substantial improvement can be conferred on the performance of the program analysis framework if we are able to properly separate the stable part of a program (*i.e.* no more transformations are applicable) and the portions yet to be analysed.

A program consisting of independent procedures can be analysed by having each predicate definition separately matched against the transformations. For each predicate, the applicable transformations are appropriately applied, one at a time: the outcome of the application of a transformation is further used in subsequent analyses. Since the predicates are all independent, their alterations will not affect each other. However, if there are dependencies among the procedures of a program, the analysis has to be performed in a more sophisticated fashion: we must devise a manner to properly partition a program into its already analysed portion and the part that still awaits to be checked for improvements. Since there are dependencies between procedures, the alterations carried out in one predicate definition may have to be considered when analysing other parts of the program.

We propose a bottom-up policy to discipline this process: firstly the basic independent procedures are analysed; then we handle those more complex procedures whose auxiliary procedures have already been analysed. The initial program is split into two portions, consisting of those procedures already analysed (possibly transformed into more efficient, equivalent versions of the original procedure) and those still to be analysed. The portion of the program that has already been analysed is a self-contained subtheory of the initial program, stable with respect to the repertoire of transformations.

3.1 Formalising Predicate Dependency

Some preliminary definitions are necessary to explain our framework. The first definition permits us to obtain the predicate symbol of subgoals:

Definition 1 The relationship $predicate(S, p/n)$ holds if subgoal S is of the form $p(t_0, \ldots, t_n)$, that is, S has predicate symbol p with n terms.

A procedure is a sequence of clauses whose head goals have the same predicate symbol p. The definition below can be used to obtain a procedure from a given program Π:

Definition 2 The relationship $procedure(p/n, \Pi, \Pi^{p/n})$ holds iff for each clause $H :- S_1, \ldots, S_m \in \Pi$ such that $predicate(H, p/n)$, then $H :- S_1, \ldots, S_m \in \Pi^{p/n}$.

We extend the *procedure* relation to cover *sets* of predicate symbols, that is, it is the case that $procedure(\{p_1, \ldots, p_n\}, \Pi, \Pi^{\{p_1, \ldots, p_n\}})$ holds iff $\Pi^{\{p_1, \ldots, p_n\}} = \Pi^{p_1} \cup \cdots \cup \Pi^{p_n}$, $procedure(p_1, \Pi, \Pi^{p_1})$, $\ldots$, $procedure(p_n, \Pi, \Pi^{p_n})$. Abusing our notation, and when no confusion arises, we may simply refer to a procedure by the predicate symbol p in the head goal of its clauses.

A program is analysed and possibly transformed through the methodic inspection of its procedures: they are analysed in a bottom-up fashion, starting from the simplest ones, *i.e.* facts and those procedures consisting of clauses employing only system predicates whose definitions are not required, then analysing those procedures whose auxiliary predicates have already been previously considered. Each procedure is considered in its turn: if its auxiliary predicates have already been previously analysed, then it is eligible for analysis as well.

In order to make sure that the procedures are analysed appropriately according to our approach, the dependencies among the different predicates of a program have to be represented. Each predicate symbol p of a program has a possibly empty set of dependencies, *i.e.* those predicates in terms of which p is defined. The definition below formalises this intuition:

Definition 3 The relationship $dependency(p, \Pi, \delta_\Pi^p)$ holds iff for each clause $(H \text{ :- } S_1, \ldots, S_n) \in \Pi^p$ such that $procedure(p, \Pi, \Pi^p)$, if $predicate(S_i, q_i)$, $q_i \notin \sigma^4$ and $q_i \neq p$, then $q_i \in \delta_\Pi^p$, $1 \leq i \leq n$.

System predicates and recursive calls are left out of our sets of dependencies, as formalised by the tests $q_i \notin \sigma$ and $q_i \neq p$, respectively, in the definition above. We shall assume that the set of dependencies of facts is always empty.

Mutually recursive procedures (directly or not) pose particular problems. Our proposed method aims at self-contained subtheories and hence mutually recursive procedures should be considered as a single construct at the same time. Furthermore, during the application of conjunction transformations the definition of auxiliary procedures also has to be taken into account: in the case of mutually recursive procedures it is not possible to define an ordering among them so that they can be analysed one at a time. Mutual recursions can be detected when we represent all the intra-procedural dependencies of a program and test for cycles. The definition below formalises the dependencies among the procedures of a program as a graph:

Definition 4 Given a program Π with predicate symbols $p_1, \ldots, p_n$, its *dependency graph* Γ_Π^δ is the set of edges $\{p_i \lhd q | q \in \delta_\Pi^{p_i}\}$, $dependency(p_i, \Pi, \delta_\Pi^{p_i})$.

One way of detecting the indirect recursions of a program Π is simply to traverse its dependency graph checking for cycles. A cyclic path is a sequence of edges in the graph such that its first and last nodes are the same:

Definition 5 Given a graph $\Gamma = \{x \lhd y, \ldots\}$ and a node z such that there is an edge $z \lhd w$ in Γ, a *dependency cycle* $\check{\delta}_\Gamma^z$ is the set $\{w_1, w_2, \ldots, w_{n-1}, w_n\}$ such that $z \lhd w_1 \in \Gamma, w_1 \lhd w_2 \in \Gamma, \ldots, w_{n-1} \lhd w_n \in \Gamma, w_n \lhd z \in \Gamma$ is a cyclic path.

In order to obtain the whole set of indirectly recursive procedures we can inspect the dependency graph of the program and check for all those cyclic paths in it. The indirect recursions of a predicate is the union of its cyclic paths:

Definition 6 Given a program Π and a predicate symbol p the relationship $ind\_rec(p, \Pi, \rho_\Pi^p)$ holds iff its dependency graph is Γ and for each $\check{\delta}_\Gamma^p$, $\check{\delta}_\Gamma^p \subseteq \rho_\Pi^p$.

The definitions for *dependency* and *ind_rec* can be extended to cope with sets of predicate symbols, as in the definition of *procedure* above.

The computational effort to obtain the set of dependencies of a predicate (relation *dependency*) is a linear function of the size of the program. The dependency cycles of a predicate can be obtained in polynomial time by examining the set of dependencies and checking for cyclic paths; the already analysed paths (cyclic or not) should be kept and used to test new candidates, so as to avoid loops. Although there might be an exponential number of candidate paths (2^n, where n is the number of edges), the search for cyclic paths can follow a more

---

[4] We shall assume the existence of a set σ of *system predicates* whose meaning is implicitly encoded in the program interpreter.

restricted and disciplined method, whereby different paths starting from an initial node (a predicate symbol) would be inspected; a linear search for an edge leading from the last predicate symbol to another predicate symbol then takes place. The set of all indirect recursions is obtained by collecting all those predicate symbols in the cyclic paths and removing repeated elements. A similar approach to model dependencies of strongly coupled predicates is described in [Gal95].

3.2 A Framework for Bottom-Up Program Analysis

The predicate dependency relations above are necessary to define our framework. A central part of our proposal consists of selecting the next procedure to be analysed. In order to properly choose a procedure we must check if its auxiliary procedures have already been analysed. If a number of procedures are indirectly recursive then they should all be analysed at the same time, provided their auxiliary procedures have already been analysed.

The *choose*/3 relation defined below formalises the bottom-up method to choose a procedure to be analysed. In order to appropriately choose procedure(s) $\Pi^{\{p_1,\dots,p_n\}}$ (it could be a single procedure Π^p or a cluster of indirectly recursive procedures $\Pi^{\{p_1,\dots,p_n\}}$ which must all be analysed at the same time) the original program Π must be examined and also the subprogram Π' (initially empty) consisting of those procedures already analysed:

$$
\begin{aligned}
choose(\Pi, \Pi', \Pi^{\{p_1,\dots,p_n\}}) \longleftrightarrow\ & procedure(\{p_1,\dots,p_n\}, \Pi, \Pi^{\{p_1,\dots,p_n\}}) \wedge \\
& ind\_rec(\{p_1,\dots,p_n\}, \Pi, \rho^{\{p_1,\dots,p_n\}}) \wedge \\
& (\rho^{\{p_1,\dots,p_n\}} = \emptyset \ \vee\ \rho^{\{p_1,\dots,p_n\}} = \{p_1,\dots,p_n\}) \wedge \\
& dependency(\{p_1,\dots,p_n\}, \Pi, \delta^{\{p_1,\dots,p_n\}}) \wedge \\
& \delta' = \delta^{\{p_1,\dots,p_n\}} - \{p_1,\dots,p_n\} \wedge \\
& procedure(\delta', \Pi, \Pi^{\delta'}) \wedge \Pi^{\delta'} \subseteq \Pi'
\end{aligned}
$$

Initially an appropriate portion of the program Π is chosen via the *procedure* relation. When choosing a portion of Π to be analysed we have to make sure that those indirectly recursive procedures are dealt with together, as a single construct. This is enforced in the framework above by the *ind_rec* relation: the set $\rho^{\{p_1,\dots,p_n\}}$ of all predicate symbols of indirectly recursive calls among procedures $p_1,\dots,p_n$ is either empty or is $p_1,\dots,p_n$ itself. In the former case there is no indirect recursion and $n = 1$, that is, we have only one procedure chosen. In the latter case all those indirectly recursive procedures, and only those, are considered together for analysis, as a single construct.

The definition above also makes sure that the non-indirectly recursive procedures in terms of which $p_1,\dots,p_n$ are defined have already been analysed. This is done via the *dependency* relation: the set $\delta^{\{p_1,\dots,p_n\}}$ contains all those predicate symbols in terms of which procedures $p_1,\dots,p_n$ are defined; we remove any of the predicate symbols $p_1,\dots,p_n$ from this set thus obtaining δ', the set of predicate symbols of those auxiliary procedures (non-indirectly recursive) of

$p_1, \ldots, p_n$. The definitions $\Pi^{\delta'}$ of those predicate symbols in δ' should all have been analysed previously, that is, they should be a subset of the subprogram analysed so far, $\Pi^{\delta'} \subseteq \Pi'$.

Our definitions are similar to the *transform/2* framework shown previously, but the application of the conjunction transformations is performed differently:

$$transform(\Pi, \Pi^A, \Pi^F) \longleftrightarrow apply(\Pi, \mathcal{T}^{pred}, \Pi') \wedge transform(\Pi', \Pi^A, \Pi^F)$$
$$transform(\Pi, \Pi^A, \Pi^F) \longleftrightarrow apply(\Pi, \mathcal{T}^{conj}, \Pi^A, \Pi') \wedge transform(\Pi', \Pi^A, \Pi^F)$$
$$transform(\Pi, \Pi^A, \Pi \cup \Pi^A)$$

The first clause applies one transformation of $\mathcal{T}^{pred}$ to one procedure in Π, yielding Π', which is then recursively used to obtain Π^F. The second clause covers the repertoire $\mathcal{T}^{conj}$ of conjunction transformations. The auxiliary procedures Π^A previously analysed (*i.e.* stable) must be supplied and treated separately: they are merely used in the matching process and should not be checked again. The result of the analysis of Π using Π^A is Π'. The third clause caters for the end of the recursion when no more transformations are applicable and also for those programs that have no applicable transformations. The final program is the union $\Pi \cup \Pi^A$: since the auxiliary procedures are manipulated separately, and we aim at self-contained subtheories, at the end of the process the procedures that had been used separately should be merged together so as to yield a single subprogram.

We can now establish the bottom-up framework itself. It is defined in terms of the original program Π, a subprogram Π^A consisting of those procedures of Π analysed (and possibly transformed) so far, a subprogram Π^L consisting of those procedures of Π waiting to be handled and the final transformed Π^F:

$$bottom\_up(\Pi, \Pi^F, \emptyset, \Pi^F)$$
$$bottom\_up(\Pi, \Pi^A, \Pi^L, \Pi^F) \longleftrightarrow choose(\Pi, \Pi^A, \Pi^{\{p_1, \ldots, p_n\}}) \wedge$$
$$transform(\Pi^{\{p_1, \ldots, p_n\}}, \Pi^A, \Pi^A_{new}) \wedge$$
$$\Pi^L_{new} = \Pi^L - \Pi^{\{p_1, \ldots, p_n\}} \wedge$$
$$bottom\_up(\Pi, \Pi^A_{new}, \Pi^L_{new}, \Pi^F).$$

Initially procedures $\Pi^{\{p_1, \ldots, p_n\}}$ are selected from Π according to the relation *choose* defined previously, using Π^A as the procedures analysed so far. The repertoire of predicate and conjunction transformations are appropriately applied to $\Pi^{\{p_1, \ldots, p_n\}}$ yielding Π^A_{new}, as defined in *transform/3* above. The new subprogram Π^L_{new} containing those procedures still to be analysed is obtained by removing $\Pi^{\{p_1, \ldots, p_n\}}$ from Π^L. The bottom-up analysis then recursively continues, using the newly obtained subprograms.

The above framework simply defines a more efficient way of checking the program for opportunities to apply transformations. The essential idea is to appropriately choose portions of the initial program and then apply the repertoire of transformations on them, ensuring that those portions already analysed and stable are not tested again, unnecessarily.

3.3 Comparative Performance Analysis

The performance of the bottom-up approach is sensitive to the kind of program submitted to it. Its worst scenario is that of a program in which all procedures are mutually recursive: the entire program would then be analysed and the complete repertoire of transformations exhaustively matched against it. This possibility is similar to the performance of the exhaustive approach (Section 2) when analysing any kind of program. The worst performance of our proposal equates the performance of the other approach surveyed.

The best situation is that in which the program is such that no transformations are applicable: here, both the bottom-up method and the exhaustive approach will perform equally. In both cases the transformations will all be matched against the constructs of the program; since no transformations will take place, there is no need to re-examine portions of the program. The analysis proceeds without the need of checking procedures already analysed since these will not have changed. If there are n procedures and m predicate and conjunction transformations, then the number of unsuccessful attempts will be mn in both bottom-up and exhaustive approaches.

The bottom-up approach can, however, outperform the exhaustive approach in more average settings. Let us suppose, for the sake of comparison, a simpler context in which the program has n procedures and m predicate and conjunction transformations such that only one transformation is applicable exactly once to each procedure. Let us assume further that only the last transformation is applicable to the procedures: $m - 1$ attempts must be made before the applicable transformation is actually reached. In such circumstances the exhaustive approach has the following number of successful and unsuccessful attempts:

Iterations/no. of attempts

Pred.	1	2	3	$\cdots$	n	$n+1$
p_1	m	m	m	$\ldots$	m	m
p_2		m	m	$\ldots$	m	m
p_3			m	$\ldots$	m	m
$\vdots$				$\ddots$	$\vdots$	$\vdots$
p_n					m	m

The exhaustive approach gradually transform each of the predicates. In order to analyse predicate p_i the whole repertoire of m transformations has to be unnecessarily matched against each of the preceding $i - 1$ predicates. The number of attempts of the exhaustive approach can be depicted by the equation $mn + \sum_{i=1}^{n} im$. The bottom-up framework on the other hand will only perform the framed number of attempts shown in the table above: once procedure p_i is analysed, it is no longer matched in posterior stages of the process. The number of attempts performed by the bottom-up method is $2mn$, which is always less than or equal to the previous equation.

A prototypical implementation confirmed the above analysis. We submitted a number of different programs to both approaches and examined the overall number of successful and unsuccessful attempts. A set of 30 schema-based transformations was used. Six sample programs with distinct features were chosen to highlight the difference between the performance of both approaches. We produced the following table of results:

Program	No. of Predicates	No. of Attempts Exhaustive	Bottom-Up
Π_1	10	300	300
Π_2	7	929	929
Π_3	10	1950	600
Π_4	37	6575	2021
Π_5	15	3246	546
Π_6	47	46592	1862

We chose program Π_1 to illustrate the best scenario explained above, when there are no applicable transformations: the same number of attempts is made in both approaches. The worst case for the bottom-up method is represented by program Π_2, whose predicates are all mutually recursive: it equates the performance of the exhaustive approach. Π_3 is the example discussed above, in which only the last transformation is applicable to each predicate of the program; the results are in accordance with the equations presented. Program Π_4 and Π_5 are of a more commmon kind, the former possessing a "cluster" of mutually recursive predicates. Program Π_6 has a reasonable number of predicates each of which with at least one applicable transformation and some of them with whole sequences of applicable transformations. Π_6 highlights the fact that the more applicable transformations a program has, the better is the performance of the bottom-up method compared with the exhaustive approach.

4 Summary, Conclusions and Directions of Research

We have proposed a program analysis and transformation system, as an improvement to the work described in [VF95, VF96a]. Our method incrementally builds self-contained subtheories of an initial program, starting from facts and then picking up more complex clauses that depend on simpler, previously analysed constructs. A transformation system is then applied to these subtheories yielding more efficient subprograms.

A program must have its predicate dependencies explicitly represented, in order to be analysed in our framework. We have devised a means to formally state the procedural interrelationships within a program and use this information to organise the analysis process in a bottom-up fashion.

The extra overhead involved in obtaining the predicate dependencies has to be considered in the light of the reduction of unsuccessful matchings during the transformation of the program. The formalisation and analysis of the predicate dependencies in a program has polynomial complexity. The complexity of matching a predicate to a transformation is exponential, in the worst case [VF95]. The initial overhead can be safely disregarded when we take into account that unnecessary exponential tests will not take place anymore.

Our work basically exploits the surveyed exhaustive approach, providing an organised way to analyse the procedures of a program. The bottom-up framework only avoids the unnecessary reprocessing of stable portions of the original program; the same transformations are applied albeit in a different order. We also believe we have formally characterised a program analysis method that can be profitably adopted by programmers in a manual context.

Transformations must preserve the *meaning* of those programs they are applied to [PP94]. Within our bottom-up context, each transformation must be individually verified; it must also be proved that their interplay will not disturb the meaning of those programs transformed or their termination status. There are attempts at proposing a mathematical framework [VAa96] to carry out such verification procedures, preferably in an automated or semi-automated fashion.

Acknowledgements: Thanks to Seumas Simpson for proofreading this text

References

[FF92]   N. E. Fuchs and M. P. J Fromherz. Schema-Based Transformations of Logic Programs. In *Proceedings of the International Workshop on Logic Program Synthesis and Transformation (LoPSTr'92)*. Springer-Verlag, 1992.

[Gal95] J. P. Gallagher. A Bottom-Up Analysis Toolkit. Technical report, Dept. Comp. Sci., Univ. of Bristol, 1995. Invited talk given at WAILL (Workshop on Abstract Interpretation of Logic Languages), Israel.

[HL78]   G. Huet and B. Lang. Proving and Applying Program Transformations Expressed with Second-Order Patterns. *Acta Informatica*, 11:31–55, 1978.

[LS90]   A. Lakhotia and L. Sterling. How to Control Unfolding when Specialising Interpreters. In L. Sterling, editor, *The Practice of Prolog*. MIT Press, 1990.

[PP92]   M. Proietti and A. Pettorossi. Best-first Strategies for Incremental Transformations of Logic Programs. In *Proceedings of the Second International Workshop on Logic Program Synthesis and Transformation (LoPSTr'92)*, 1992.

[PP94]   M. Proietti and A. Pettorossi. Transformations of Logic Programs: Foundations and Techniques. *Journal of Logic Programming*, 19, 20:261–320, 1994.

[Rob91] D. Robertson. A Simple Prolog Techniques Editor for Novice Users. In *3rd Annual Conference on Logic Programming*, Edinburgh, Scotland, April 1991. Springer-Verlag.

[VAa96] W. W. Vasconcelos and M. T. Aragão. Proving Schema-Based Transformations for Logic Programs. Extended Abstract, 1996. Available from authors.

[VF95]   W. W. Vasconcelos and N. E. Fuchs. Opportunistic Logic Program Analysis and Optimisation: Enhanced Schema-Based Transformations for Logic Programs and their Usage in an Opportunistic Framework for Program Analysis and Optimisation. Tech. Rep. 95.24, IFI, Univ. Zürich, 1995.

[VF96a] W. W. Vasconcelos and N. E. Fuchs. An Opportunistic Approach for Logic Program Analysis and Optimisation using Enhanced Schema-Based Transformations. In *Proc. 5th Int'l Workshop on Logic Program Synthesis and Transformation (LoPSTr'95)*, The Netherlands, 1996. Springer-Verlag.

[VF96b] W. W. Vasconcelos and N. E. Fuchs. Prolog Program Development via Enhanced Schema-Based Transformations. Technical report, Department of Artificial Intelligence, University of Edinburgh, 1996.

A Temporal Extension to the Parsimonious Covering Theory

Alexandre de Melo Rezende and Jacques Wainer
{arezende,wainer}@dcc.unicamp.br

Instituto de Computação, UNICAMP

Abstract. In this work we propose a temporal extension to the Parsimonious Covering Theory (PCT). PCT provides a theoretical foundation for the diagnostic reasoning process as an abductive reasoning based associations between causes with their consequences. Our temporal extension of PCT allows one to associate to a disease a temporal evolution of its symptoms.

The elimination of temporally inconsistent hypotheses minimizes one of the greatest problems of PCT: the solution for a particular diagnsotic problem may include a large number of alternative hypotheses. Furthermore, the inclusion of temporal aspects to an extension of PCT that includes probabilistic information also eliminates the problems of incorrectly rejecting hypotheses if a necessary symptom has not yet occurred.

1 Introduction

Diagnostic reasoning, that is, finding causes that explain observed symptoms, is one of the major application areas for knowledge-based systems. In some domains, time is an important aspect of the diagnostic reasoning itself: knowing when a symptom occurred may be as an important information as knowing just that the symptom did occur. In some medical diagnostic applications, temporal information about the occurrence of the symptoms is vital for a correct diagnostic and some "second generation medical expert systems" [Con89, Ham87] tried to deal with this aspect.

On the other hand, the diagnostic reasoning itself, independently of temporal considerations, does not have an agree upon theoretical foundation. [Pen90] proposed such a theoretical foundation under the name of Parsimonious Covering Theory (PCT). But PCT is still a theory of reasoning about static symptoms, in the following sense. PCT is based on a model that associates to each disease a set of symptoms it may cause. Thus, PCT assumes that, at the moment of diagnostic, all symptoms are observable and that the order of occurrence of these symptoms is irrelevant for the diagnostic.

This work extends the PCT model in such a way that to each disease one associates evolutions of symptoms (or sets of possible histories of symptoms). Thus, at diagnostic time, one will not just describe the symptoms present, as one would in a static diagnostic system, but describe the whole evolution of the symptoms. Even symptoms that are no longer present may be relevant for the diagnostic process.

This paper is organized as follows: section 2 briefly defines the simplest version of PCT. Section 3 extends this theory to incorporate temporal knowledge. Section 4 presents the solution of the problems that may arise when probabilistic knowledge is incorporated into PCT. Finally, section 5 presents the conclusions and the limitations of proposed temporal reasoning.

2 Basics of Parsimonious Covering Theory

First we will briefly introduce the PCT. In the basic version of PCT [Pen90], one uses two finite sets to define the scope of diagnostic problems (see Figure 1). They are the set D, representing all possible **disorders** d_l that can occur, and the set M, representing all possible **manifestations** m_j that may occur when one or more disorders are present.

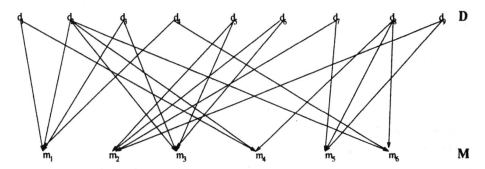

Fig. 1. Causal network of a diagnostic knowledge base $KB = \langle D, M, C \rangle$.

To capture the intuitive notion of causation, one uses the relation C, from D to M, that associates to each individual disorder its manifestations. An association $\langle d_l, m_j \rangle$ in C means that d_l may directly cause m_j; it does *not* mean that d_l *necessarily* causes m_j. The sets D, M, and C together are the knowledge base (KB) of a diagnostic problem.

To complete the problem formulation we need a particular diagnostic **case**. We use M^+, a subset of M, to denote the set of **observations**, that is, manifestations that are present in the case. The set M^+ does not necessarily have to be specified all at once at the beginning of problem-solving; it can be gradually obtained from the answers to questions asked by the diagnostic system.

Definition 1. A **diagnostic problem** P is a pair $\langle KB, Ca \rangle$ where:

- $KB = \langle D, M, C \rangle$ is the **knowledge base**, composed of
  - $D = \{d_1, d_2, \ldots, d_n\}$ is a finite, non-empty set of objects, called *disorders*;
  - $M = \{m_1, m_2, \ldots, m_k\}$ is a finite, non-empty set of objects, called *manifestations*;

- $C \subseteq D \times M$ is a relation called *causation*
- $Ca = \langle M^+ \rangle$ is the case, and $M^+ \subseteq M$ is the set of observations.

For a diagnostic problem P, it is convenient and useful to define the following sets of functions based on relation C:

Definition 2. For any $d_l \in D$ and $m_j \in M$ in a diagnostic problem P

- $effects(d_l) = \{m_j | \langle d_l, m_j \rangle \in C\}$, the set of manifestation directly caused by d_l;
- $causes(m_j) = \{d_l | \langle d_l, m_j \rangle \in C\}$, the set of diseases which can directly cause m_j.

The set $effects(d_l)$ represents all manifestations that may be caused by disorder d_l, and $causes(m_j)$ represent all disorders that may cause manifestation m_j. These functions can be easily generalized to have sets as their arguments.

2.1 Solution for Diagnostic Problems

In order to formally characterize the solution of a diagnostic problem one needs to define the notion of "cover", based on the causal relation C, to define the criterion for parsimony, and to define the concept of an explanation (explanatory hypothesis).

Definition 3. The set $D_L \subseteq D$ is said to be a **cover** of $M_J \subseteq M$ if $M_J \subseteq effects(D_L)$.

Definition 4. A set $E \subseteq D$ is said to be an **explanation** of M^+ for a diagnostic problem iff E covers M^+, and satisfies a given parsimony criterion.

In the following definition we present the possible parsimony criteria:

Definition 5.
(1) A cover D_L of M_J is said to be **minimum** if its cardinality is the smallest among all covers of M_J.
(2) A cover D_L of M_J is said to be **irredundant** if none of its proper subsets is also a cover of M_J; it is **redundant** otherwise.
(3) A cover D_L of M_J is said to be **relevant** if it is a subset of $causes(M_J)$; it is **irrelevant** otherwise.

[Pen90] uses irredundancy as the preferable choice for the parsimonious criteria and in this paper we follow that choice. Acording to the authors, minimality, which is another usual criteria of parsimony, should be seen more as a domain specific heurisic than a general criteria.

In many diagnostic problems, one is generally interested in knowing all plausible explanations for a case rather than just a single explanation because they, as alternatives, can somehow affect the course of actions taken by the diagnostician. This leads to the following definition of the problem solution:

Definition 6. The **solution** of a diagnostic problem $P = \langle KB, Ca \rangle$, designated $Sol(P)$, is the set of all explanations of M^+.

Example 1. In the Figure 1, $\{d_1\}$, $\{d_2\}$, $\{d_3, d_8\}$, and $\{d_4, d_8\}$ are the only plausible explanations (i.e. irredundant covers) for $M^+ = \{m_1, m_4\}$, and therefore they are the solution of the problem.

2.2 Algorithms and Problems of PCT

[Pen90] presents the algorithm `bipartite` which incrementally and constructively compute the set of solutions of a diagnostic problem P. The algorithm processes one observation (m_j) from M^+ at a time, and incorporates $causes(m_j)$ to the set of explanations it has computed so far.

The main problem with the basic version of PCT is that the solution of a problem tends to have many alternative explanations. The reason is that irredundancy is too weak a criteria to significantly reduce the number of alternative explanations. For most practical applications a further processing to filter out some of the explanations based on domain specific heuristics or at least to order the set of explanations so that more "plausible" explanations are presented before less "plausible" ones.

A more complex version of PCT (called probabilistic causal model) is also presented in [Pen90] which incorporates probabilities to the links between a disease and its manifestations, that is, the probability that the manifestation will occur provided that the disease is present. This probabilistic information allow one to rank the explanations. Furthermore, this probabilistic information allows one to filter from the set of all explanation those that contain a disease for which a necessary manifestation was not present in the case. If a disease d_i necessarily causes a manifestation m_j, that is, the probability that m_j is present given d_i is 1, then if m_j is known not to be among the observations of the case, then one can remove explanations that contain that disease. This is called categorical rejection.

3 Parsimonious Covering Theory and Time

The aim of this research is to extend PCT so that instead of associating to each disease a set of manifestation, one could associate an evolution of manifestations. Thus, the database could state that disease d_i causes first m_1 which will last between 2 and 5 days, followed in 2 to 3 days by m_2 which may last an undetermined amount of time, and so on. We accomplish this temporal representation using a graph, where vertices are manifestations and directed arcs between vertices represent temporal precedence. If there is quantitative information about the duration of the manifestation, it is associated with the corresponding node; if there is quantitative information about the elapsed time between the start of two manifestations, it is associated with the corresponding arc. Furthermore, quantitative information are not represented as a single number, but as an interval. Therefore one can state that a manifestation will follow another in 2 to 3 days. To each disease one associates one such temporal graph.

3.1 Dynamic Diagnostic Problem Formulation

Time points will be primitive objects to represent temporal information. *Intervals* are defined as non-empty convex sets of time points (points on the time line), represented by $I = [I^-, I^+]$ such that I^- and I^+ are the extreme points of interval I, respectively (obviously $I^- \leq I^+$; $I^- > I^+$ indicates an empty interval I). We use the following notations for operations on intervals:

- $I + J = [I^- + J^-, I^+ + J^+]$;
- $I \cap J = [max(I^-, J^-), min(I^+, J^+)]$;
- $I \leq p \Rightarrow I^+ \leq p$, where p is a time point.

A temporal graph is a *direct, acyclic, transitive*, and not necessarily connected graph. The existence of an arc from m_i and m_j in a temporal graph denotes the fact that the beginning of the occurrence of manifestation m_i must precede the beginning of the occurrence of m_j.

The *temporal distance* between manifestations and the *duration* of a manifestation are represented by functions on the graph, denoted by $DIST$ and DUR, respectively. The temporal distance function $DIST$ associates an interval $R = [R^-, R^+]$ to each arc of a temporal graph G_l. $DIST(G_l, (m_i, m_j)) = R$ for $(m_i, m_j) \in A_l$, which we will abbreviate as $DIST_l(m_i, m_j) = R$, states that the difference between the time of the beginning of m_j and the beginning of m_i in the temporal graph G_l of d_l must be within the interval R. The duration function DUR associates to each vertex m_i of a temporal graph G_l em G an interval J, that specifies that the duration of m_i must be within the interval J.

The transitivity of the temporal graph must be consistently carried over to the $DIST$ function: if $DIST_l(m_i, m_j) = R_1$ and $DIST_l(m_j, m_k) = R_2$ then $DIST_l(m_i, m_k) = R_1 + R_2$.

Figure 2 illustrates the temporal information about the disorders d_8 and d_9 of the diagnostic problem shown in Figure 1.

Definition 7. The **temporal graph** of a disorder $d_l \in D$, $G_l = (V_l, A_l)$, is a direct, transitive and acyclic graph defined as:

- $V_l \subseteq M \equiv$ set of objects directly caused by d_l, and
- $A_l = \{(m_i, m_j) |$ the beginning of m_i occurs *before* the beginning of m_j when the disorder d_l is said to be present$\}$.

Definition 8. The **knowledge base** of a dynamic diagnostic problem is the tuple $KB = \langle D, M, G, DIST, DUR \rangle$ where D and M are defined as before, G is a set of temporal graph, each one associated with one disease of D, $DIST$ and DUR are the temporal information functions defined above.

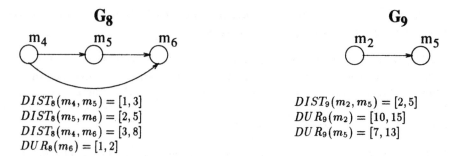

Fig. 2. Temporal graphs of the disorders d_8 and d_9 with their temporal distance functions and duration functions.

In order to represent the case, we will need the set of observations M^+, as before, and the temporal information about these observations. The function BEG^+ associates an interval to some of the observations in M^+. $BEG^+(m_j) = I$, $m_j \in M^+$, states that m_j started at any time within interval I. Similarly, the function DUR^+ associates to some of the observations in M^+ an interval, such that the duration of the observation was anything within that interval.

Definition 9. A **dynamic diagnostic problem** P is a pair $\langle KB, Ca \rangle$ where KB is defined as before, and $Ca = \langle M^+, BEG^+, DUR^+ \rangle$ is the case.

One can define the *effects* and *causes* functions in a similar way to definition 2. For example $causes(m_j) = \{d_l | m_j \in V_l$, for any temporal graph $G_l = (V_l, A_l) \in G\}$, represents the set of diseases that may cause m_j.

It is important to notice that the temporal model allows for many forms of uncertainty and incompleteness of information both at the case and at the knowledge base. For example, temporal information about the case need not to be precise but can be stated as an interval, or can be ommited althogether. In the knowledge base, not all manifestations need to be temporally related to the others: the graph need not to be connected, nor do all arcs need to have intervals associated with them. The theory uses the temporal information if it is available, otherwise it behaves as the basic PCT.

3.2 Solutions for Dynamic Diagnostic Problems

In order to define a solution for a diagnostic problem, we need to define a set of concepts about temporal inconsistency. This will eventually allow one to remove the explanations that contain diseases in which the evolution of manifestations contradicts the evolution of the observations in the case. For example, if for a certain disease m_1 precedes m_2 but in the case, the occurrence of m_1 started after the occurrence of m_2, then one can disregard all explanations that contain such disease, since it contradicts with the temporal information in the case.

Definition 10. For a dynamic diagnostic problem P let $G_l = (V_l, A_l) \in G$, $(m_i, m_j) \in A_l$, $DIST_l(m_i, m_j) = R$, $m_i, m_j \in M^+$, $BEG^+(m_i) = I_{m_i}$ and

$BEG^+(m_j) = I_{m_j}$. The arc (m_i, m_j) **is temporally inconsistent with respect to the case** iff $(I_{m_i} + R) \cap I_{m_j} = \emptyset$.

The resulting interval of operation $(I_{m_i} + R)$ corresponds to a set of valid values for the beginning of m_j. Thus if the intersection of this interval and I_{m_j} ("real" valid interval for the beginning of m_j) is empty, then the arc (m_i, m_j) is temporally inconsistent with the case. The inconsistency criterion defined above is equivalent to one described in [Con93].

Definition 11. For a dynamic diagnostic problem P let $G_l = (V_l, A_l) \in G$ the temporal graph of a disorder $d_l \in D$. The **disorder d_l is temporally inconsistent with the case** $Ca = \langle M^+, BEG^+, DUR^+ \rangle$ iff

- exist at least one arc $(m_i, m_j) \in A_l$ temporally inconsistent with respect to the case , or
- exist at least a vertex $m_j \in V_l$, such that, $m_j \in M^+$ and $DUR_l(m_j) \cap DUR^+(m_j) = \emptyset$.

Finally, based on the above definitions, we formalize the notions of temporally consistent explanation and temporally consistent solution.

Definition 12. A set $E \subseteq D$ is said to be a **temporally consistent explanation of the case** for a dynamic diagnostic problem P iff

- E covers M^+, and
- E satisfies a given parsimony criterion, and
- for any $d_l \in E$, d_l is *not* temporally inconsistent with the case.

Definition 13. The **temporally consistent solution** of a dynamic diagnostic problem $P = \langle \langle D, M, G, DIST, DUR \rangle, \langle M^+, BEG^+, DUR^+ \rangle \rangle$, designated by $Sol(P)$, is the set of all temporally consistent explanations of the case $\langle M^+, BEG^+, DUR^+ \rangle$.

Algorithm Solution: Basic Ideas We implemented an algorithm that solves a temporal diagnostic problem. Due to space limitations, we will only present the basic ideas of the algorithm and briefly discuss an example. The full algorithm can be found in [Rez96]. The important aspect of the algorithm is that temporal consistency is not implemented as a filter, that is, it is not applied after the original **bipartite** algorithm has generated the solutions, but it is incorporated very early into the process of merging the causes on the "new" observation into the set of current explanations. Thus the algorithm has to deal with smaller sets of explanations.

At the beginning of a new cycle, after a new observation has been entered, the disorders evoked by the new observation are checked for temporal consistency with the case information so far. Then hypotheses that contain the temporally inconsistent disorders are eliminated from the set of current hypotheses and the new temporally consistent evoked disorders are used to update the set of hypothesis.

The example below illustrates the basic ideas of the algorithm. For example in Figure 1, we have that $S_1 = \{\{d_1\}, \{d_2\}, \{d_3, d_8\}, \{d_4, d_8\}\}$ is the set of all explanations (irredundant covers) of $M^+ = \{m_1, m_4\}$ temporally consistent with $BEG^+(m_4) = [10, 10]$ and $DUR^+ = \emptyset$. Each time a new observation is discovered and temporal information is available for it, the system verifies the temporal consistency of the hypotheses in S_1, and update the hypotheses in the correct way. Thus, consider m_5 new observation of M^+, and $BEG^+(m_5) = [16, 18]$ and $DUR^+(m_5) = [2, 3]$. First, we obtain the disorders evoked by m_5 (i.e. $causes(m_5) = \{d_7, d_8, d_9\}$) that are temporally inconsistent with $BEG^+(m_5)$ and $DUR^+(m_5)$. As an illustration, consider d_8 and d_9 in Figure 2. Disorder d_8 is temporally inconsistent because the arc (m_4, m_5) with label $[1, 3]$ is inconsistent with $BEG^+(m_4)$ and $BEG^+(m_5)$. On the other hand, disorder d_9 is temporally inconsistent because the duration of m_5 in d_9 is inconsistent with $DUR^+(m_5)$. In the next step, we remove all explanations in S_1 that contain these temporally inconsistent disorders. Thus, $S_2 = \{\{d_1\}, \{d_2\}\}$ is the set of all explanations that are not inconsistent with this new information. Finally, the consistent disorders (only d_7 in this case) are used to update the current explanations. $S_3 = \{\{d_1, d_7\}, \{d_2, d_7\}\}$ is thus the set of all explanations temporally consistent with the case (with m_5 added). If no other manifestation is present than S_3 represents the temporally consistent solution.

4 Categorical Dynamic Diagnostic Problems

We mentioned that the basic PCT can be extended so that probabilities can be associated to each manifestation in a disease. This allows one to eliminate a disease in the absence of an observation if that manifestation is necessary for the disease. But when time is added, this categorical rejection may pose some problems. It may happen that a necessary manifestation was not observed because there was not enough time for it to occur. Thus, some form of temporal reasoning must be performed in order to ascertain whether a disease can be categorically rejected.

4.1 Problem Formulation and its Solutions

In this paper we are not interested in a general probabilistic (numeric) information relating manifestations and disorders, but just some information whether the disorder necessarily causes the manifestation, or whether the causation is only possible. Thus, in the knowledge base KB we have to add a function $POSS$ that attributes to each vertex of each temporal graph either the label N, for necessary, or the label P, for possible. Thus, $POSS(G_l, m_j) = N$, abbreviated as $POSS_l(m_j) = N$, states that disorder d_l necessarily causes the manifestation m_j.

For categorical diagnostic problems, one is interested in manifestations known to be absent in the case, called **negative observations**. Thus we add, M^-, the set of negative observations, and I_{now}, the time point that represents the moment of diagnosis, to M^+, BEG^+, DUR^+ as the components of the case Ca.

Definition 14. Let $P = \langle KB, Ca \rangle$ be an open dynamic diagnostic problem and $G_l = (V_l, A_l) \in G$. The **disorder d_l is categorically inconsistent with the case** iff

- exist an arc (m_j, m_k) in A_l, such that, $POSS_l(m_j) = N$, $m_j \in M^-$ e $m_k \in M^+$, or
- exist an arc (m_i, m_j) in A_l, such that, $POSS_l(m_j) = N$, $m_j \in M^-$, $m_i \in M^+$ and $BEG^(m_i) + DIST(m_i, m_j) \leq I_{now}$.

The definition above has two conditions. For both of them, the disorder d_l is categorically inconsistent due to the combination of two factors: a necessary manifestation is not present ($POSS_l(m_j) = N$ and $m_j \in M^-$) and there has been enough time for it to happen. In the first condition the second factor is warranted because a later manifestation has already occurred ((m_j, m_k) in A_l and $m_k \in M^+$). In the second one, this factor is warranted because all values of a set of valid values (time points) for the beginning m_j are lower or equal than the actual instant ($BEG^+(m_i) + DIST_l(m_i, m_j) \leq I_{now}$). The categoric rejection problem occurs when one considers only the first factor above as a sufficient condition to classify a disorder as categorically inconsistent with the case.

Finally, we define an explanation of a categorical dynamic diagnostic problem.

Definition 15. A set $E \subseteq D$ is said to be a **consistent explanation** of the case for an open dynamic diagnostic problem $P = \langle KB, Ca \rangle$ iff

- E covers M^+, and
- E satisfies a given parsimony criterion, and
- for any $d_l \in E$, d_l is *not* temporally inconsistent, and
- for any $d_l \in E$, d_l is *not* categorically inconsistent.

As with the basic PCT plus time, we developed an algorithm that solves categorical dynamic diagnostic problems. It can be found in [Rez96].

5 Conclusion

This paper presented temporal and categorical extensions of the parsimonious cover theory which could serve as the core of a diagnostic system specially for problems where the temporal evolution of the manifestations is an important aspect.

5.1 Implementation

We developed a small example of a medical diagnostic system as a test for the theory developed herein. This diagnostic system deals with food-borne diseases [Man90] which is a domain of application where temporal information is very important. The domain included 28 diseases and 60 different symptoms. Because of the simplicity of the PCT model of diagnostic, in which no heuristic information needs to be included into the knowledge base, the whole diagnostic system was developed in two days, mainly from textbook information [Man90], with only one consultation to a specialist to resolve ambiguities in the text. The results of diagnostic cases were also verified by the specialist.

With the introduction of the temporal and categorical extension there was a significant reduction on both the number of hypotesis in the solution and the time to compute them, as compared to the basic PCT. In a particular case, the number of hypothesis in the solution was reduced from 73 to 2, and the time to compute the solution was reduced by 70 %.

5.2   Limits of the extension of PCT

The main limitation of the theory refers to multiple simultaneous disorders. The PCT assumes that multiple disorders that cause the same manifestation do not interfere with each other. That is, if both d_i and d_j cause m_k then they can both be part of an hypothesis that explains the observation m_k. Unfortunately, in the presence of temporal information is very unlikely that two disorders will not interfere with each other. As an example, let us suppose that d_i causes m_k with duration I and d_j causes m_k with duration J. Then certainly the presence of both disorders simultaneously will cause some change on the duration of m_k (the same can be true for the temporal relation of m_k with other manifestations in both d_i and d_j). This has been documented in the area of medical diagnostics [Pat81]. PCT, and therefore our extension to it, cannot represent and deal with this interference.

References

[Con89] L.Console, A. J. Rivolin, D. T. Dupré, and P. Torasso, Integration of causal and temporal reasoning in diagnostic problem solving, *in:Proc. 9th International Workshop on Expert Systems and Their Applications (Conference on 2nd Generation Expert Systems)*, (1989).

[Con93] L. Console and P. Torasso, Temporal constraint satisfaction on causal models, *Information Sciences*, 68 (1993) 1-32.

[Ham87] I. Hamlet and J. Hunter, A representation of time for medical expert systems, *Lecture Notes Med. Informatics*, 33 (1987) 112-119.

[Man90] G. L. Mandell, R. G. Douglas and J. E. Bennett, *Principles and pratice of infectious diseases* 3ed. (1990).

[Pat81] R. S. Patil, Causal representation of patient illness for eletrolyte and acid-base diagnosis, *MIT Laboratory for Computer Science*, Technical Report, MIT/LCS/TR-267, (1981).

[Pen90] Y. Peng and J. A. Reggia, *Abductive Inference Models for Diagnostic Problem-Solving*, Springer-Verlag, (1990).

[Rez96] A. de M. Rezende, Uma Extensão Temporal à Teoria das Coberturas Parcimoniosas. *Master Thesis (in portuguese)* Instituto de Computação, UNICAMP, Jul. (1996).

Biological Inspirations in Neural Network Implementations of Autonomous Agents

M. Roisenberg[1], J. M. Barreto[2], F. M. Azevedo[2]

[1] Computer Science Institute, Dept. of Applied Computer Science,
Universidade Federal do Rio Grande do Sul, Porto Alegre, Brazil
e-mail: roisenb@inf.ufrgs.br
[2] Biomedical Engineering Research Group, Dept. of Electrical Engineering,
Universidade Federal de Santa Catarina, Florianópolis, Brazil
e-mail: barreto@gpeb.ufsc.br, azevedo@gpeb.ufsc.br

Abstract. This paper describes the development of an Artificial Neural Network (ANN) architecture that is capable to implement reactive behavior in Autonomous Agents (AAs). We make considerations about biological paradigms, as evolutionary mechanisms and animals' behaviors, trying to find solutions that, once applied to the development of artificial devices, provide more robust and useful AAs to operate in the real world. To have higher survival chances, life beings must have developed more complex behaviors, as reactive and internally motivated, in which the agent's action must depend on the past history of sensory values in order to be effective. This work shows that reactive behaviors can be described through Finite State Machines (FSMs) that requires a recurrent neural network architecture to be implemented, in order to insert dynamics and memory in the system. After the description of such network architecture and a biologically inspired learning algorithm, we make some experiments. Finally, conclusions for future work are given.

Keywords: Autonomous Agents, Behavior-Based Agents, Connectionist Models, Robotics and Artificial Life Systems.

1 Introduction

The study of animal behavior, as well as natural evolution mechanisms, has been the milestone of the development of many works in the AAs area. Biological inspiration could allow the construction of models that, as the animals, could work very well in the real world. This biological inspiration can be the source of mechanisms and solutions that, once implemented, allow to reach high level of autonomy, and so, it is important to verify how these biological paradigms are transformed in AAs construction tools.

In Artificial Intelligence area, the Evolutionary Algorithms (EAs) give the computational model that simulates the natural procedures of reproduction, mutation and selection that allow de evolution of individual structures searching the most capable solution for a given environment. Concerning the modeling aspects of animals behaviors, the Connectionist approach is an appropriate tool to model and simulate AAs behavioral aspects.

This work presents the idea that a series of behavior classes, observed in animals, can be implemented through different Artificial Neural Networks (ANNs) architecture's. We also emphasize that these different architectures can be obtained using EAs. The obtained results should confirm the hypothesis that pure reflexive behaviors could be implemented through simple static neural networks architecture's, like feedforward architectures. More complex behaviors, as reactive and internally motivated behaviors, that persist and develop, even after finished the sensorial exciting stimulus, require more complex neural networks architecture's, like a recurrent one, with dynamic neurons to insert dynamic and memory in the system. In section 2 we present a study about the animal behavior and how it can be used to obtain an AA. The ANNs architecture's as well as a biological inspired learning algorithm capable to implement some previously presented behavior patterns are presented in section 3. In section 4 we describe some experiments and the obtained results. Finally, in section 5 we present some conclusions and make suggestions for future works.

2   Animal Behavior

In their works, Anderson & Donath [1] and Beer et al. [4] make considerations about the animal behavior, trying to list and classify primitive behavior patterns and stimulus that caused it, looking for their implementation in artificial models.

There are a lot of observed animal behaviors, and the nomenclature and classification can vary from different researchers. One way to classify animal behaviors is as: reflexive, reactive and motivated behaviors.

2.1   Reflexive Behaviors

Reflexive is the simplest behavior class, in which a fast, stereotyped response is triggered by a particular class of environmental stimuli [4]. The most remarkable characteristic of reflexive behavior is that the intensity and duration of the response is a direct function of the intensity and duration of the trigger stimulus.

2.2   Reactive Behaviors

A more complex behavior class involves that behaviors called reactive or sequential. This kind of behavior is formed by a series of stereotyped responses as reaction for a given stimulus. The response usually involves a temporal sequence of complex actions that run to completion, even if the triggering stimulus isn't present any more. By their turn, the series of behaviors can be related in an intricate way, in which a new behavior is triggered by the completion of a precedent fixed-action behavior. An example is described by Anderson & Donath [1] that was extracted from [12].

"A female digger-wasp emerges from her underground pupa in spring. Her parents died the previous summer. She has to mate with a male wasp and then perform a whole series of complex patterns connected with digging out a nest hole, constructing cell within it, hunting and killing prey such as caterpillars, provisioning the cells with the prey, laying eggs and finally sealing up the cells. All of this must be completed within a few weeks, after witch the wasp dies."

This complex behavior can be explained as the sequential aggregation of a series of fixed-action behaviors, where the result of a given behavior triggers the next behavior. We can describe this behavior with a Finite State Machine (FSM) in which each compound behavior is a state of the machine. If any behavior triggering signal was removed, that behavior will not be triggered, and this will inhibit the triggering of all the following behaviors. Experiments described in [1] with the female digger-wasp prove it.

This behavior class seems to be innate to animals and genetically transmitted over the generations as a series of neural network hardwired connections, probably generated by evolutionary processes.

2.3 Motivated Behaviors

There are behaviors that don't present a simple or rigid dependence on external stimuli, but instead, are primarily governed by an animal's internal state. These behaviors are known as motivated behaviors [4]. In these behavior class, the animal tendency to present a given behavior, for example, to eat, depends not only on the presence of the triggering stimulus (the food), but also on internal motivational variables (the hungry). It is interesting to notice that the motivated behaviors can occur even in the absence of any evident external stimuli, apparently as a result of some kind of animal "reasoning". We must emphasize that this class of behavior exhibits some form of plasticity or learning process, i.e., future behavior features can be modified as the result of past experiences of the animal with the environment. For example, a rat that avoid to eat a particular food if prior ingestion of that food was followed by sickness [4], or a lion cub that learn how to hunt with his ancestors [1]. The time scale of these modification can vary from seconds to years [2].

3 Implementing Behaviors with Neural Networks

3.1 Behavior-Based Autonomous Agents

An Autonomous Agent can be defined as an artificial device acting in an environment and that continuously runs a task that maps the system sensorial inputs to effector outputs. The environment is everything that is outside the agent, possibly including other agents or human beings. The agent operates in a cycle, receiving environment stimuli through its sensors and making some processing. This processing generates an output to its effectors affecting the environment. Such a mapping from an input stream to an output stream is referred to as behavior [7]. This behavior can be an instantaneous function of the input values, or can have states or memory, allowing that its actions at a given instant potentially depend on all the previously received inputs until that time.

Many researchers, [5][9][11][13], are developing reactive behavior-based techniques as a response to overcome the difficulty to operate in real-time in a real world. But, when searching for biologically inspired approach to implement a reactive behavior- based AAs, the ANNs seems to present many advantages over other behavior-based proposed architectures, as high noise immunity, fault tolerance, processing time, learning capacity, and the capacity of implementing a program without explicit knowledge of the corresponding algorithm.

3.2 Biologically Inspired Learning Algorithm

Relating these aspects to the evolution question, we can suppose that exists a "cost function" associated with neural network complexity, that is, simpler network topologies could be easily obtained than complex ones. So, in an evolutionary scale, primitive beings appeared firstly with purely reflexive behaviors, implemented with simple and small neural networks. Once the survival task becomes harder and competitive, demanding more complex behaviors, an evolutionary process created beings whose the neural networks was bigger and presented cycles, expanding the behavior complexity and repertoire. With closed loops neural networks, we now have a new class of behaviors. Extending the concepts, at that moment we can say that the being can present behaviors that are based in the past history of their sensations.

In this work, the neural network topology, as well as the strength of the connections between the neurons, is induced in a explicit way. However, there are some works [2][14][15] that induce these parameters using evolutionary algorithms, and we intend to use this approach in a future work.

Another important point to be remarked concerns about how to determine the connection strength between the neurons in the proposed neural networks architecture's, i.e., the training procedure. One of the most popular ANN training procedure is the backpropagation algorithm. However, in this work we proposed a biologically inspired procedure to train the neural networks by the following reasons: in first place, researches suggest that the backpropagation is not biologically plausible, because there are scientific evidences that it is impossible to exist error backpropagation circuitry between the brain neurons; the second reason is that when using recurrent neural networks, with dynamic neurons, we can't use any more the standard backpropagation algorithm, that is suitable for feedforward topologies, altough there are versions of the algorithm, like recurrent backpropagation and backpropagation through time, which can be used in a time demanding architecture.

The proposed algorithm can be briefly described as:

1. Initialize randomly with small values the weights of neural network connections and each connection with a "disturbance direction" as +1 or -1;

2. Propagate all training set input vectors through the network, comparing the obtained result with the desired one, calculating a global error value, the mean square error, for example;

3. For each connection of the network:

   (a) Calculate a new weight, adding the current weight with a small delta multiplied with the "disturbance direction" of that connection;

   (b) Propagate again all training set input vectors through the network, obtain a new error value;

      i. If the global error value reduces, than select a new connection and go to step 3a;

      ii. If the global error value increases, reverse the "disturbance direction", restore the previous weight and go back to step 3a; (if in a second loop, the global error value, still doesn't decrease, reduce the "disturbance direction" and go to step 3a.)

4. When all connections had been updated, go back to step 2 until the global error had been reduced to an acceptable value.

3.3 Neural Networks Implementing Behaviors

Regarding an evolutionary point of view, we can imagine a very primitive life being with a very simple sensory-motor nervous system. The only survival requirement for this creature would be the ability to sense the presence of food and to move to the its direction in an environment free of predators and obstacles. Its easy to verify that this kind of simple behavior, purely reflexive can be implemented using feedforward neural networks.

Once the environment becomes more complex and hostile, the capability to survive could not be granted any more by a purely reflexive behaviors repertoire obtained by a combinatorial system implemented in a feedforward neural network. We believe that an evolutionary process created a more complex neural network topology, including cycles between the neurons. This new neuronal architecture allows more complex behaviors, increasing the survival chances.

The next step in this study was the implementation of this nervous system model in an ANN architecture presenting the same features. As a reactive behavior can be described using FSMs, a neural network architecture capable to implement these machines was developed. The proposed neural network architecture is composed by two interconnected neural networks. In the first one, the input neurons acts as sensory organs, receiving the external signals coming from the environment, and the output neurons are dynamic neurons with linear activation function and a unit delay output function. There are connections from these output neurons to hidden neurons with hyperbolic tangent activation function. A simplified diagram of this architecture can be seen in figure 1a.

In this architecture the output neurons map the states of the desired FSM, and each state corresponds to a given behavior of the modeled behaviors sequence. Its still necessary to map each state to the respective effectors values

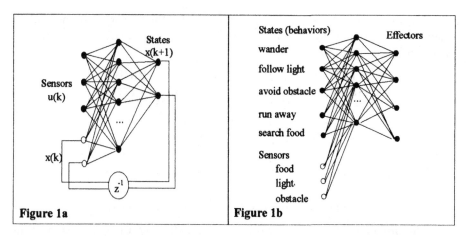

Figure 1a   **Figure 1b**

Fig. 1. Dynamic Neural Network that implements FSM states and the Feedforward one that implements the FSM outputs

capable to produce the behavior. To do that, a static feedforward neural network is used. The input neurons of this second network are the input and output neurons of the first network, as showed in figure 1b.

We can see in Barreto [3] the formal proof that this compound architecture is equivalent to FSMs.

4   Experiments

The carried out experiments aim to confirm both the efficacy of the proposed learning algorithm as well as the capability of the neural network architecture's to implement the described behavior classes.

In a first experiment, a purely reflexive orientation behavior was implemented. A very primitive creature, modeled by a small feedforward neural network with two sensors and two effectors, as can be seen in figure 2, would be capable to feel the presence of food and to move in the right direction to feed itself.

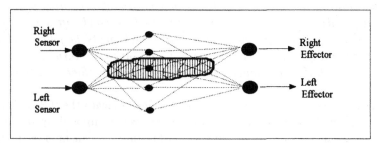

Fig. 2. Primitive creature with a feedforward nervous system

The mapping between the signal captured by the sensory-neurons and the right action executed by the motor-neurons to take the creature up to the food is given by the following table:

LEFT SENSOR	RIGHT SENSOR	LEFT EFFECTOR	RIGHT EFFECTOR
-1 - don't detects food +1 - detects food		-1 - effector off +1 - effector on	
-1	-1	-1	+1
-1	+1	+1	-1
+1	-1	-1	+1
+1	+1	+1	+1

Table 1. Orientation behavior mapping function

The proposed learning algorithm worked well, even though, it some times leads to local minimum points, but the neural network learned the sensory-motor mapping shown in table 1.

The second proposed experiment aims to implement a simple reactive behaviored AA that could be described through a FSM and consequently needed the previously presented recurrent neural network architecture to be implemented. In the proposed AA was implemented the behavior exhibited by the tracker task described by Jefferson et al. and extracted from Angeline [2].

"In this problem, a simulated ant is placed on a two dimensional toroidal grid that contains a trail of food, shown in figure 3a. The ant traverses the grid, collecting along the way any food it contacts. The goal of the task is to discover a controller for the ant that collects the maximum number of pieces of food in a given time period.

Following Jefferson et al., the ant is controlled by a connectionist network with two input nodes and four output nodes, an example of which is shown in figure 3b. The first input node, labeled FOOD in the figure denotes the presence of food in the square directly in front of the ant. The second input node, labeled NO FOOD in the figure, denotes the absence of food in this same square. This restricts the possible legal inputs to the network to (+1,-1) or (-1,+1). Each of the four output units of the network, labeled as MOVE, LEFT, RIGHT and NO-OP in figure 3b, correspond to a unique action by the ant - move forward one step, turn left 90°, turn right 90°, and no-op respectively. At each step, the action whose corresponding output node has maximum activation is performed.

One possible solution for this problem is the FSM handcrafted by Jefferson et al. and shown in figure 4a. This simple system implements the following behavior: "move forward if there is food in front of you, otherwise turn right four times looking for food. If food is found while turning, pursue it, otherwise, move forward one step and repeat".

The recurrent neural network was then trained to learn the states of the FSM that describes this behavior. The training set was composed by the temporal sequence of all possible inputs in each FSM state, as can be seen in table 2. The state 0 was considered the initial state both in the training as during the execution phase.

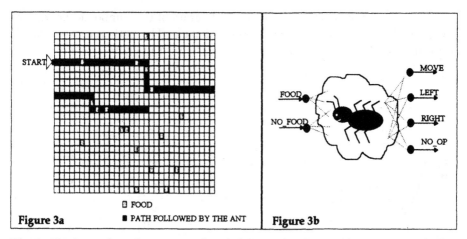

Figure 3a   ▫ FOOD
              ■ PATH FOLLOWED BY THE ANT   Figure 3b

Fig. 3. Tracker task environment and path followed by the ant. Ant sensors and effectors

After that, a feedforward neural network was trained to maps the FSM states given by the first neural network outputs and the sensors inputs to the effectors outputs, as shown in table 3.

Sensor Input		State			
FOOD	NO_FOOD				
+1	-1	-1	-1	-1	(0)
+1	-1	-1	-1	-1	(0)
-1	+1	-1	-1	+1	(1)
+1	-1	-1	-1	-1	(0)
-1	+1	-1	-1	+1	(1)
-1	+1	-1	+1	-1	(2)
+1	-1	-1	-1	-1	(0)
-1	+1	-1	-1	+1	(1)
-1	+1	-1	+1	-1	(2)
-1	+1	-1	+1	+1	(3)
+1	-1	-1	-1	-1	(0)
-1	+1	-1	-1	+1	(1)
-1	+1	-1	+1	-1	(2)
-1	+1	-1	+1	+1	(3)
-1	+1	+1	-1	-1	(4)
+1	-1	-1	-1	-1	(0)
-1	+1	-1	-1	+1	(1)
-1	+1	-1	+1	-1	(2)
-1	+1	-1	+1	+1	(3)
-1	+1	+1	-1	-1	(4)
-1	+1	-1	-1	-1	(0)

Table 2. Training set for the FSM

Sensor Input		State	Effector Output
+1	-1	(0)	MOVE
-1	+1	(0)	RIGHT
+1	-1	(1)	MOVE
-1	+1	(1)	RIGHT
+1	-1	(2)	MOVE
-1	+1	(2)	RIGHT
+1	-1	(3)	MOVE
-1	+1	(3)	RIGHT
+1	-1	(4)	MOVE
-1	+1	(4)	RIGHT

Table 3. Training set for effector outputs

We can see in figure 4b the schematic diagram of the compound neural network capable to implement the desired behavior. The path generated by the trained network after the training phase can be seen in figure 3a.

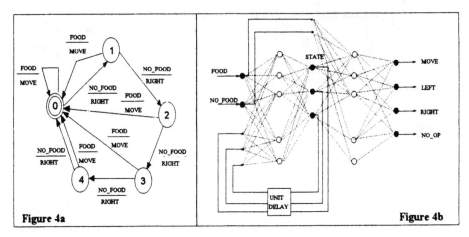

Fig. 4. FSM that describes the ant's behavior and compound neural network that implements it

5   Conclusions and Future Works

This paper has addressed the biological inspiration as a paradigm for the development of AAs implementation tools. Between them, we highlight the studies in the evolutionary mechanisms and animal behavior areas.

We have tried to classify typical animal behavior patterns, featuring the complexity, survival usefulness, and if each behavior is innate and genetically transmitted over generations or is learned and improved during the animals life. We also emphasize how to describe the behavior looking for its implementation using a connectionist approach.

As we are dealing with biologically inspired mechanisms and recurrent neural networks, we discard the backpropagation learning algorithm and proposed an hebbian one, based in the punishment-reward strategy. Its important to note that the training set used to learn the states of the FSM to the network must be a temporal sequence of all possible inputs in each FSM state.

Our experimental results show that, even slow, the proposed algorithm works and converges, even though, it some times leads to local minimum points. The results show that the proposed architecture is an effective alternative to implement reactive behaviors in AAs, using the advantages of the connectionist approach.

As future work perspectives, we must remark that the induction of neural network parameters, as topologies and connection strengths, using evolutionary algorithms and relating with different behavior classes is a very interesting research field.

Another point that will be subject of a future work is how to implement a set of behaviors, some even antagonics and that affect the same effectors, for example, goes toward a food and run away from a predator, using a multi-agents approach.

Finally, we observe that does not exist in the Nature a distinct separation between a learning and execution phase for motivated behaviors. Both occurs in parallel, some times with a teacher, other times alone. The development of AAs that can continuously learns, adapting itself to new situations and environments is a very challenging and fascinating task.

References

1. Anderson, T. L. and Donath, M. Animal Behavior as a Paradigm for Developing Robot Autonomy. In. Maes, P. (ed.) Designing Autonomous Agents. Theory and Practice from Biology to Engineering and Back. MIT Press. 1991. p. 145-168.
2. Angeline, P. J. Evolutionary Algorithms and Emergent Intelligence, Ph.D. Thesis - Ohio State University. USA. 1993. pp. 172.
3. Barreto, J. M. Connectionism in Problem Solving, Titular Professor contest Monograph, UFSC, Florianópolis, March 1996 (in portuguese).
4. Beer, R. D. et al. A Biological Perspective on Autonomous Agent Design. In. Maes, P. (ed.) Designing Autonomous Agents. Theory and Practice from Biology to Engineering and Back. MIT Press. 1991. p. 169-186.
5. Brooks, R. A. Elephants Don't Play Chess. In. Maes, P. (ed.) Designing Autonomous Agents. Theory and Practice from Biology to Engineering and Back. MIT Press. 1991. p. 3- 15.
6. Freeman, J. A. and Skapura, D. M.. Neural Networks, Algorithms, Applications and Programming Techniques. Addison-Wesley. 1991. pp 401.
7. Kaelbling, L. P. Learning in Embedded Systems. MIT Press. 1993. pp 176.
8. Kuperstein, M. Neural Networks that Create their Own Goals with Growth Cycles. In Proc. of the World Congress on Neural Networks. Portland, Oregon. 1993. p.111-122. Vol. 3.
9. Lin, L. Programming Robots Using Reinforcement Learning and Teaching. In. Proc. of the Ninth Nat. Conf. on Artif. Intel. USA. 1991. p.781-786.
10. Maes, P. Guest Editorial. In Maes, P. (ed.) Designing Autonomous Agents. Theory and Practice from Biology to Engineering and Back. MIT Press. 1991. p.1- 2.
11. Mahadevan, S. and Connell, J. Automatic Programming of Behavior-based Robots using Reinforcement Learning. In. Proc. of the Ninth Nat. Conf. on Artif. Intel. USA. 1991. p. 768-773.
12. Manning, A. An introduction to Animal Behavior. 3rd ed. Addison-Wesley, Massachusetts, 1979.
13. Piggott, P. and Sattar, S. Reinforcement Learning of Iterative Behaviour with Multiple Sensors. Journal of Applied Intel., 4, 1994. p.351-365.
14. Vaario, J. An Emergent Modeling Method for Artificial Neural Networks. Doctor Dissertation of Engineering - The Univ. of Tokyo. Japan. 1993. pp. 216.

Intelligent Tutoring Systems Modelled Through the Mental States

Neila Maria Moussalle [†] e **Rosa Maria Viccari**[†]
neila@inf.ufrgs.br   rosa@inf.ufrgs.br

Milton Corrêa[‡]
correa@cos.ufrj.br

Abstrat. This paper aims at presenting part of the work we have developed and its objective as to simulating the functioning of the changes which occur in the following mental states: belief, desire, intention and expectation of two cognitive autonomous agents during a teaching/learning interaction. The objectives of the work are to observe and to analyse the changes that occur in the mental states during an interaction between agents; to develop and to apply teaching strategies; to use the SEM (Sociedade dos Estados Mentais)[1] agents architecture [1] to replace the traditional Intelligent Tutoring Systems (ITS) archicture and to build the agents models from the ITS environment. The major contribuitions of this paper are the use of teaching/learning strategies connected to the local agent's intention, to track down the changes that occur in the mental states which were analysed in certain teaching/learning situations, the use of an architecture of agents to model ITS's, the use of values to determine the urgency to fulfilling the agents'objectives.

Keywords: Architecture for Intelligent Tutoring Systems, Distributed Artificial Intelligence

1. Introduction

Our application is made up of three teaching/learning distinct situations, each one of them with a well-defined objective, where the domain is natural numbers division operation, in Mathematics:

• A situation in which the agents exchange ideas about a problem solution; the student knows how to solve it and teaches the tutor a new solution strategy;

• A situation where the agents have distinct knowledge, the tutor proposes a problem, the student makes a mistake trying to solve it and the tutor corrects him;

• A situation in which the tutor proposes a problem, the student does not know how to solve it and the tutor offers him help.

The SEM architecture is used to substitute an ITS functional archicture allowing the mental states to be treated like local agents or subagents. The architecture models the behavior of each mental state as well as the changes caused by the interaction. With this approach, a greater flexibility, a better visualization of the changes in mental states, a more granular accompanying of the agent's reasoning process and greater facility to detect and follow the changes that occurred in each state, were observed in the interaction between the agents.

[†] CPGCC - Instituto de Informática - Universidade Federal do Rio Grande do Sul
Av. Bento Gonçalves, 9500 - Porto Alegre - Brasil - 91501-970 Phone: +55-51-316-6801
[‡] SERPRO - RJ- Seviço Federal de Processamento de Dados - Rio de Janeiro - Brasil

[1]Sociedade dos Estados Mentais means Mental States Society

1.1 The SEM architecture

The *SEM* architecture [1], is a generic architecture of autonomous, deliberative and cognitive agents whose ultimate characteristic is that the agent's specification is done through the mental states. The agent's behavior theory is based on the fact that the only thing the programmer has to do is to specify the agent's mental states.

One feature of the *SEM* architecture is that the agent's mental states definition are provided according to the Theory of Situations developed in [5],[6]. In [1], this Theory has been used to model Artificial Intelligent Agents. The kernel of this architecture is made up of four autonomous local agents that correspond to the mental states: *belief, desire, intention* and *expectation*. These local agents interact among themselves through messages.

The SEM_A architecture, which maintains the structure of the architecture presented in [7], is described in [1],[8] by an 8-tuple structure representing global agent's:

$$SEM_A = <M_A, S_A, R_A, \alpha_A, \upsilon_A, \Psi_A, BDE_A, I_A > \quad where:$$

$M_A \rightarrow$ is the agent's internal states set.

$S_A \rightarrow$ is the " all possible external states for agent A" set.

$R_A \rightarrow$ is the S partitions set that characterizes the agent's sensory capabilities.

$\alpha_A \rightarrow$ is the set of actions agent A can perform.

$\upsilon_A \rightarrow$ is a sensory function that relates the states in S_A with the partitions in R_A

$$\upsilon_A : S_A \rightarrow R_A$$

$\Psi_A \rightarrow$ is an effectory function that characterizes the effects of the agent's actions on the external world: $\quad \Psi_A : \alpha_A \otimes S_A \rightarrow S_A$

$BDE_A \rightarrow$ is a 3-tuple $< B_A, D_A, E_A >$ where:

    $B_A \rightarrow$ is agent's A belief structure.

    $D_A \rightarrow$ is agent's A desire structure.

    $E_A \rightarrow$ is agent's A expectation structure.

$I_A \rightarrow$ is agent's A intention structure.

The structure of each local agent is defined by an architecture made up of an 8-tuple whose symbolism is similar to that of the global agent. Each one of the so-called local agents have specific functions that result from the definitions, properties, and relations among the mental states:

• Local Agent Belief: it supervises the beliefs and is in charge of creating, changing, inferring, deducing beliefs, building up strategies and plans, and doing everything related to the agent's reasoning.

• Local Agent Desire: it supervises the desire by creating, attributing or changing desires; providing intentions from the desires and verifying whether or not they were satisfied.

• Local Agent Intention: it supervises the intentions by selecting the ones to be satisfied in a certain moment, that is to say, choosing and acting properly so that a specific intention is achieved; interrupting or canceling the achievement of a certain intention; attributing or changing the urgency, intensity and insistence values of intentions.

- Local Agent Expectation: it supervises the expectations. It is in charge of verifying whether a certain expectation is or not satisfied; attributing values to the urgency, intensity and insistence of the expectations and providing beliefs whenever they are necessary.

2. Example of an EBL Application in which the Tutor Learns

The Explanation-Based Learning (EBL) [4],[9] method used in 'Machine-Learning' and adopted by us will be explained here. The student offers himself to explain the tutor a different way to check whether the result of an operation is correct or not, without having to apply the algorithm the tutor considers correct to solve the operation. In the EBL method the situation above is defined as follows:

Goal Concept: to teach the tutor a practical way to check the natural numbers division operation.

Domain Theory: in the student's domain theory there is the *STRATCR* strategy .

Training Instance: a couple of questions and answer and an interaction between tutor and student through a dialogue which is presented in the next paragraph.

Operationality Criterion: the explanation should be given by applying qualities of the tutor's theory which are supplied by the student. For instance, to check whether the result of a division operation is correct or not, the following should be done by dividing a natural number called *dividend(D)* into another rather than zero called *divisor(d)*, we obtain a result called *quotient(Q)* and a *rest(R)*. The result of the operation can be either right or wrong. It will be right if by multiplying the quotient by the divisor, and by adding the rest we obtain the dividend.

Determine: an operational explanation to the student's answer.

The tutor, in order to check whether the result of the operation performed by the student is correct or not, applies the algorithm *STRAT6* (it is a division operation already known by the tutor, see 4.2) which performs the whole operation and then assures that the result presented by the student is correct.

The student discovers through a dialogue with the tutor that it does not have the belief that the inverse operation checks the result, so it decides to explain the tutor how to perform such task.

3. The Agent-Based Architecture for an ITS

Based on the SEM architecture's local and global agents, an Agent-Based Architecture for ITS, made up of local agents, as shown in figure 1, was built.

The global agent tutor, through its local agent desire, sends a message to the global agent student that receives it through its local agent intention. The local agent intention checks the desire connected to it by bringing into action the local agent desire. Intention, however, through an inference process, checks if there is a strategy to fulfill the desire associated to it.

Along with the local agent belief, the local agent intention, that already has the teaching strategy determined, controls the execution and sends to the global agent tutor a message saying that the action requested has been performed (or not) successfuly (or not) and that it has been received by the tutor through the local agent desire, which brings into action the remaining agents to check if the desire has or has not been fulfilled and sends a new message, or waits for a new one that will be sent by the student. The global agent tutor can receive from the global agent student an action which is the answer to the request made by the tutor to the student through a message exchange between the local agents desire (tutor) and intention (student), or an that which is a request made by the student to the tutor.

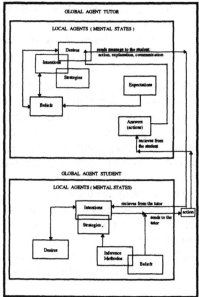

Fig. 1. Agent's Architecture as for Intelligent Tutoring Systems

Figure 2a, ilustrates the interaction cycle which occurs during the application. Action and message exchange among the local agents *desire, belief and intention* occurs, as follows:

(1) Global agent has a desire;

(2) The desire brings into action an intention associated to it and sends a message: 'There is a desire to be fulfilled';

(3) Desire and intention send a message: 'Check if there is a set of beliefs to create and/or execute a teaching strategy in order to fulfill the desire';

(4) Belief sends a message: 'Set of beliefs selected';

(5) Belief determines or selects a teaching strategy;

(6) Intention controls the teaching strategy execution;

(7) Sends message to the local desire agent: 'Desire fulfilled'.

4. Application

A part of the dialogue of the situation in which the student knows how to solve the operation proposed and teaches the tutor a new strategy will be described and analysed here. Figure 2.b shows a complete dialogue. The part pointed out will be presented in detail. The complete dialogue as well as the explanations and their formalism can be found in [10].

The dialogues in this application are written in Portuguese to ease comprehension. These dialogues are messages formated as programs written in Prolog without a steady format. There is a 'manager' in the programs that governs the tutor/student interaction and knows the message structures. This manager filters them whenever it is necessary to assure that the interaction is not broken and is performed successfuly.

In order to perform this tasks, the tutor and the student use beliefs and strategies, as described below.

4.1 Description of the Tutor's/Student's Beliefs

Tutor's Constant Beliefs

From the previous knowledge assumed by the tutor, one may observe its constant beliefs, knowledge about the application domain, and the tutor's beliefs about the student's knowledge, as follows:

1 - It believes all the one-digit operation with natural numbers.

2 - It believes all the two-digit operation with natural numbers.

3 - It believes all the three-digit operation with natural numbers.

4, 5, 6 - It believes the addition, subtraction and multiplication operation.

7 - It believes the meaning of dividing a number made up of two or more digits into another made up of one digit, according to the algorithm discribed in 4.2.

8 - It believes the digit position in a certain number.

9 - It believes the relationship among the digit classes.

10 - It believes that unit is the minor class of the already studied digits.

11 - It believes that each class, except unit, is equal to 10 times the next minor class.

Student's Constant Belief

In the example assumed here, the student's beliefs agree with the tutor's beliefs (from 1 to 11), so they are not to be repeated here. The student has the beliefs above, besides the one below:

12 - It believes that multiplication is the inverse of the division operation.

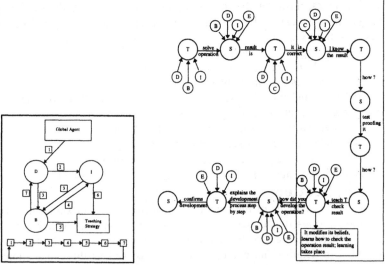

Fig. 2a. Interaction Cycle among the local agents   **Fig. 2b.** Dialogue

4.2 Strategies Used by the Student and the Tutor

The strategies, which are crucial to the ITS's, are dealt with like teaching plans, that is, they are used to promote learning since they define the procedures which will determine the way in which a content should be taught. The teaching strategies are dealt with in a different way from [1], here. In our work, the teaching strategies need to be available to be easily manipulated, selected, treated and executed whenever it is necessary. They are connected to the local agent intention that, among other functions, controls the execution of the teaching plans and constitutes a set of actions that the global agent belief has access to, being applied to fulfill desires, intentions and expectations. When a teaching strategy is necessary, the local agent belief sends a message to the set of strategies and selects the most suitable one based on the global agent's beliefs.

Figure 3 shows the diagram of the strategies used by the student and the tutor.

We will present now the tutor's strategy to solve the division problem of a natural number X into a number Y, with the beliefs associated to its application in this case. The strategy used to divide a number into another, learned previously by EBL, is made as follows:

1) Divide the major class digit A1 into divisor D, quotient Q, rest $R1$;

2) Multiply $R1$ by 10, quotient $R10$;

3) Add $R10$ to the following minor class digit $A2$, quotient $A210$;

4) Repeat steps 1 to 3, up to the unit digit;

5) The operation quotient is the number whose digits are the Q .

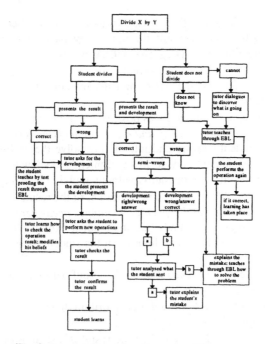

Fig. 3. Agents' Teaching Strategies Diagram

This strategy can be described by a tutor's strategy like below:

STRAT6 |={<<do-if,BS1,AC1,1>>,<<do-if,QS1,ACQ1,1>>,<<do-if,BR1,ACR1,1>>,
        <<do-if,BS2,AC2,1>>,<<do-if,BS3,AC3,1>>,<<do-if,BQSD,ACQ,1>>}

BS1 |=<<completed-division,N,D,0>> &<<major-class-digit,N, A,1>> &
        <<division-not-completed, A,D,1>>

N is of type [NP|SN |=<<division,NP,DV,1>>&<<dividend,NP,1>>] with the numerical parameter NP anchored in N; D is of type DV|SN |=<<division, NP,1>>&<<divisor, DV,1>>] with the numerical parameter   DV anchored in D.

AC1 |=<<divides,AT,A,D,1>>

A is of type [AP|SAP|=<<completed-division,N,D,0>>&<<major-class-digit,N,AP,1>> & <<division-not-completed, AP,D,1>>] where AP is a digit parameter anchored in A.

$QS1$ |={<<bel,A_T,P$_{PQS1}$,1>>} where P$_{PQS1}$ is the proposition:

       PQS1 |=<<division-quotient, A, D,Q1,1>>

$ACQ1$ |=<<set-digit-on-division-quotient, AT, N,D,Q1>>

$BR1$ |={<<bel, A_T,P$_{PR1}$,1>>} where P$_{PR1}$ is the proposition:

       PR1 |=<<division-rest, A,D,R,1>>

$ACR1$ |=<<multiplies, AT,R,10,1>>

$BS2$ |={<<bel,A_T,P$_{PS2}$,1>>} where P$_{PS2}$ is the proposition:

       PS2 |=<<completed-division,N,D,0>>&<<major-class-digit,N,B,1>>

       AC2 |=<<add, AT,PS2,1>> B is of type[BP|SBP|=<<completed-division,N,D,0>>& <<major-class-digit,N,BT,1>>& <<division-not-completed, BP,D,1>>]

  $BS3$ |={<<bel,A_T,P$_{PS3}$,1>>} where P$_{PS3}$ is the proposition:

       PS3 |=<<sum-result, R10,B, C>> ;   AC3 |=<<divide, AT,C,D>>

  $BQSD$ |={<<bel, A_T,P$_{PQSD}$,1>>} where P$_{PQSD}$ is the proposition:

       PQSD |=<<division-result,C,D,QS>>

ACQ |=<<set-digit-on-division-quotient, AT,N,D,QS>>

STRATCR is the student's knowlege regarding the application domain, and the strategy to check the division result through its inverse operation.

4.3 Dialogue Commenting the Changes in the Mental States

- Step 3.Tutor: "The result is correct".

The tutor, so far, has the desire and the intention that the student solves the proposed problem correctly.

- Step 4.Student: "I know, I was positive about the answer".

Desire, intention, strategy and expectation changes occur here.

It was the student's desire and intention to solve the problem proposed by the tutor correctly. The student now desires and intends to show the tutor that he knows how to check the result of an operation without applying STRAT6.

- Step 5. Tutor: "How can you be confident of the result"?

Desire, intention and expectation changes occur here.

The tutor desires and intends that the student explains how he is so confident about the result being correct, and hopes that the student explains how he performed the proofing operation.

- Step 6.Student: "I checked it through a proof before presenting the result".

There is no change occurence.

- Step 7.Tutor: "Was it through the algorithm division"?

There is no change occurence.

- Step 8.Student: "No, I checked the result of the division through its inverse operation".

There is no change occurence.

- Step 9.Tutor: "I did not understand your explanation".

Desire, intention and expectation changes occur.

The tutor desires and intends to learn how to check the division result and hopes that the student teaches it the process he applied to check the division result.

- Step 10.Student: "I will explain it".

Desire, intention, strategy and expectation changes occur.

The student desires and intends to teach the tutor the process and hopes it will learn. To teach the tutor, the student will apply the EBL method (see 2). To explain the process applied the student uses STRATCR.

• Step 11.Tutor: "I could understand it now".

Belief, desire, and intention changes occur.

In this moment, the tutor adds the inverse operation belief to it showing that learning has taken place, that is, it has learned the way to check whether the operation result is correct or not by applying the operation algorythm.

4.4 Dialogue Analysis

The dialogue begins with the tutor sending the student the following message:

- "Represent the division result of 642 into 3".

By sending such message, the tutor has two desires which are: a) Propose problem $p1$ to the student; b) That the student answers problem $p1$ correctly.

In the symbolic representation of such desires, a parameter value was defined as to determine which of the desires has greater priority. Knowing that the values concerning urgency vary from 0.0 (minor urgency) to 1.0 (major urgency), the values chosen were 1.0 for the situation desire (a) and 0.7 for the situation desire (b). This way we have the desires (a) and (b) described, for example, as follows:

$D_a \models \{<< des, A_T, P_{SP1}, EPS1, T, 1 >>\}$ where P_{SP1} is the proposition:

$SP1 \models << proposes, A_T, A_A, p1, 1 >>$ & $p1 \models << divide, 642, 3, 1 >>$

$EPS1 \models << satisfaction, ds, t_1, 1 >>$ & $<< urgency, 1.0, t_1, 1 >>$ $\lor$

$<< satisfaction, dns, t_1, 1 >>$ & $<< urgency, 1.0, t_1, 1 >>$

where ds indicates fulfilled desire and dns indicates non-fulfilled desire.

$D_b \models \{<< des, A_T, P_{RP1}, EPS2, T, 1 >>\}$ where P_{RP1} is the proposition:

$RP1 \models << response, A_T, A_A, p1, 1 >>$ & $<< cor-resp, p1, 1 >>$

$EPS2 \models << satisfaction, ds, t_1, 1 >>$ & $<< urgency, 0.7, t_1, 1 >>$ $\lor$

$<< satisfaction, dns, t_1, 1 >>$ & $<< urgency, 0.7, t_1, 1 >>$

Associated to each one of these desires, we have the intentions and associated to them there are the suitable strategies to fulfill the desires. The strategies are the teaching plans and are built on the tutor's permanent beliefs. Such beliefs are the ones regarding the tutor's knowledge in relation to the domain under study.Besides these beliefs, the tutor has the belief that it knows how to present the student a problem, along with the strategy on how to present the student the problem. Fulfilling desire (a) through a suitable strategy, intention sends desire a message: "Desire (a) has been fulfilled", and awaits for a new message regarding the next desire which is desire (b). Intention proceeds in a similar manner to desire (b) and, knowing it has been fulfilled, sends desire a similar message to item (a). If there are no more desires to be fulfilled, the tutor awaits for a new intervention of the student as for the dialogue to go on.

When the student receives a message from the tutor, he aims at solving the problem and presenting it an answer. The student receives an order and creates the following desire: "Solve the problem proposed by the tutor". The tutor, after receiving the answer from the student, will check it and determine if it is correct or not. In any one of the situations above, the tutor will ask the student to develop the problem step by step so as to test proof it, that is, the tutor would like to conclude, through interactions with the student, if it really knows how to perform the operation (EBL)(see figure 3).

The answer presented by the student in the situation above is correct, but it does not assure the tutor that the student is applying the correct strategy to solve the problem and consequently, find the result. For this reason, the tutor asks the student to present all the steps he applied to find the result. The test proof of the result is done through a strategy defined in the tutor's intention in relation to the result presented by the student. Such intention is associated to the desire that the student's answer is correct, and that such desire is fulfilled through the strategy that has already been mentioned.

The student's affirmation about the result being correct 214 * 3 = 642, means that he wants to show the tutor that by multiplying the result of the division performed by the divisor number, which is 3, in this case, the result obtained is the number which was initially divided - 642 (student's belief). The students is teaching the tutor a way to check the division operation result, which means a change in the student's desire. Linked to such desire there is an intention that calls for the suitable strategy, which along with the student's beliefs, in relation to the defined inverse operation, tries to fulfill the desire mentioned above. The tutor does not have the inverse operation belief and knows how to check the operation result by applying the STRAT6, only. The student holds the belief that the multiplication operation is the division's inverse operation, and uses a strategy STRATCR to teach the tutor that it is possible to check the result of any operation through its inverse one.

Learning is closely related to the beliefs of an agent and according to [2],[3], in the moment in which alterations in beliefs occur, by adding new beliefs or updating some old ones, we can say that learning has taken place since the beliefs of an agent express his knowledge in relation to the domain involved.

In the situation we are describing learning takes place regarding the tutor. The student has his expectations *the tutor accepts his explanation in relation to the inverse operation and its application to check the division result* fulfilled in the moment in which the tutor accepts his explanation and add the new belief to his beliefs.

The dialogue continues with the tutor asking the student to present the operation development step by step, so that it can analyse what is being done, and interrupt the student's work whenever it is necessary. In the sentence in which the tutor closes the dialogue, concluding that the student knows how to perform the operation correctly, a strategy change happens, because besides checking if the student answered the proposed problem correctly by comparing the student's answer with its own answer, it is necessary to compare the strategy presented by the student with its own strategy. The tutor's desires are fulfilled when the tutor ends up with the comparisons and concludes they are similar.

5. Conclusion

A better learning/teaching process understanding is accomplished when the interaction analysis among the agents is done through the mental states *belief, desire, intention and expectation*, by observing the changes that occur in the tutor and student's agent states during the teaching/learning interactions.

We have observed that whenever a desire changes, the intention associated to it also changes. However, the teaching strategies, which are also associated to intentions, can or cannot change.

By adopting the SEM architecture to model the example presented, we checked that parameters influence in the construction of the agents, and also in the simulation of the interaction among them. Our option to the SEM architecture to model the ITS's, besides what has been presented in this work, aims at modelling social aspects of the interaction among the agents such as how the behavior of a certain agent influences the general behavior of a society. Imagine that our society has several students and that the performance of one of them is not as successful as we expected; it is of our interest to model and observe how such individual behavior will influence the behavior of such society as a whole.

The use of the Theory of Situations allowed a more granular representation of the mental states increasing the interaction explanation power promoting a better evaluation of the changes occurred in the teaching/learning process. The various states modelled allowed the agents to act more precisely.

In the case presented, learning has taken place when the tutor agent assimilated the new belief and the new strategy to check the operation result verification whose explanation was presented through an operational explanation created by EBL.

The use of the teaching strategies created to supply explanations about the solution presented by agents to solve the problems proposed were an innovation in relation to the strategies used in [1].

The treatment of an urgency that represents the priority in fulfilling desires and expectations is regarded when there is more than one desire and more than one expectation in a determined phase of the dialogue. This treatment allows the maintanance of dialogues in which the agents have different priorities to be fulfilled.

REFERENCES

1. Corrêa, M.. The Architecture of Dialogues among Distribuited Cognitive Agents. Rio de Janeiro:UFRJ, Rio de Janeiro, 1994. Doctoral Thesis.
2. Oliveira, F; Viccari, R. Equilibration and Belief Revision: Strategies for Cooperative Tutoring and Learning. In:Congresso Chileno de Informática, 1993. Proceedings...
3. Oliveira, F; Viccari, R; Coelho,H. Conceptual Distance and Equilibration in an Intelligent Tutoring Situation. In:SBIA, 10, 1993, Porto Alegre. Anais...
4. Costa, E.; Urbano, P. Machine Learning, Explanation-Based Learning and Intelligent Tutoring Systems. In: Advanced Research Workshop on New Directions for Intelligent Tutoring Systems, Sintra, Portugal. Proceedings... Springer Verlag,1990.
5. Barwise, J.; Perry, J. Situations and Attitudes, A Bradford book, The MIT Press, 1983.
6. Devlin, K. Logic and Information. Cambridge: Cambridge University Press, 1991.
7. Genesereth, M.; Nilsson, N. Logical Foundations of Artificial Intelligence. Los Altos: Morgan Kaufmann, 1987.
8. Corrêa, M.; Coelho, H.. Around the Architectural Approach to Model Conversatinos. In: European Workshop on Modelling Autonomous Agents in a Multi-Agent World, 1993, Neuchatel, Suiça. Proceedings...
9. Baffes, P; Mooney, R. Refinement-Based Student Modelling and Automated Bug Library Construction. Journal of Artificial Intelligence and Education, Apr, 1995.
10. Moussalle, N. Tutor - Student Interactions Analysed Through Their Mental States. Porto Alegre: CPGCC da UFRGS, Dez, 1995. Master Course Essay.

Fundamentals of Fuzzy Logic and Its Hardware Implementation

Kaoru Hirota

Department of Computational Intelligence and Systems Science
Interdisciplinary Graduate School of Science and Engineering
Tokyo Institute of Technology
4259 Nagatsuta-cho, Midori-ku, Yokohama 226, Japan
e-mail hirota@hrt.dis.titech.ac.jp

Abstract. The fundamentals of fuzzy logic and fuzzy logical circuits are introduced with several hardware implementation examples. Fuzzy logic is characterized as an extension of two valued Boo- lean logic, where NOT, AND and OR operators are extended to fuzzy negation, t-norm and s-norm, respectively. The fundamental fuzzy logical circuits are mentioned first and then followed by the most important application, i.e., fuzzy inference circuit or fuzzy inference chip. It is characterized as one of the fuzzy extension of combinatorial circuit in two valued Boolean logic. In the case of AI applications, e.g., fuzzy expert systems, it is necessary to introduce multi stage fuzzy inference. In such a situation, the concept of fuzzy extension of sequential circuit, which is the complex of combinatorial circuit and memory modules, in two valued Boolean logic should be discussed. So the concept of fuzzy flip flop is presented. It is a fuzzy extension of two valued J-K flip flop. The fundamental equations of several types of fuzzy flip flop are derived and their hardware implementations are mentioned. The concept of fuzzy flip flop has been introduced by the presenter who has more than 15 years' carriers to guide company engineers in the field of fuzzy technology mainly in Japan. This is an easily understandable tutorial lecture even for the beginner of fuzzy technology, and audiences will be able to make design or develop various fuzzy hardware circuits toward the realization of fuzzy controllers after finishing this course.

Status & Challenges for Coordination Technology:
An AI Perspective

Mark Klein

Pennsylvania State University, USA.
klein@quark.arl.psu.edu

Abstract. The objective of this tutorial is to critically review the current state of the art of computer-based coordination support technology, and help participants better understand the key challenges and emerging solutions that are being identified by artificial intelligence and related fields. This tutorial will examine the three main classes of technology that have emerged to address coordination challenges in collaborative work settings: process management, rationale capture and conflict management technology. We will review the problems they are designed for, their functionality (e.g. using software demos and video segments), commercial availability and current weaknesses. The key future challenges and emerging solutions for these technologies will be identified from the perspective of basic research on coordination undertaken in distributed artificial intelligence and related fields. The course is designed for researchers, advanced developers and technical managers interested in understanding how coordination technology is likely to evolve in the near to mid-term future.

Combining Natural Language Understanding and Information Retrieval for Flexible Hypertext Navigation

J.G. Pereira Lopes[1]

Departamento de Informática, Faculdade de Ciências e Tecnologia, Universidade Nova de Lisboa, Quinta da Torre, 2825, Monte da Caparica, Portugal. gpl@fct.unl.pt

Abstract. Flexible navigation through huge amounts of textual data, either closed or continuously updated, can not based on links manually encoded within one text pointing to other texts. Though this is common practice in rather small hypertext applications, it is not feasible for large evolving applications. Flexible navigation requires the use of statistical information retrieval techniques (weighted index vectors, clustering, etc.), in order to enable dynamic creation of tables pointing out the most relevant document parts that should fulfill user queries. But, as we all know, even these techniques fail to point out the relevant text parts when the query is too short or when it asks for information that is implicit in the texts. And then the use of more powerful techniques for natural language understanding and for information extraction and retrieval are required. Imagine a user looking for the causes of some known coup d'état, interacting with a newspaper document base. Probab! ly, the most interesting document
So, this tutorial is divided into five parts. First, a short motivation will be presented. Then, the current practice in the Information Retrieval area will worked out. Then I'll go through the work by Salton and Allan in order to show how statistical Information Retrieval techniques can be used for helping the navigation task in the hypermedia field. Then, I'll overview the techniques currently used for robust understanding of texts. Finally, it will be shown how statistical information retrieval and robust text understanding techniques can interact and give rise to better navigational tools for enabling one to mine the information s/he is looking for.

References

1. Frakes, W. and Baeza-Yates, R.: Information Retrieval: Data Structures and Algorithms. Prentice Hall, 1992.
2. Jacobs, P.: Text-Based Intelligent Systems. Lawrence Erlbaum Associates, 1993.
3. Salton, G., Allan, J.: Selective text utilization and text traversal. In International Journal of Human-Computer Studies, 43 (3), 1995.

Numerical Models for the Treatment of Imperfect Information in Knowledge-Based Systems

Sandra Sandri

National Space Research Institute (INPE), Brazil

Abstract. Already in the construction of the first knowledge-based systems, an important issue has been the modeling of imperfect information. In a general piece of information contained in a knowledge base, usually described by a production-rule, some kind of imperfection is expected due exactly to its generalization. In other words, the more applicable is a rule, the less informative its conclusions are bound to be. In a specific piece of information, usually called a fact, imperfection of information arises when one is uncapable of obtaining good measurements or judgements.

Information imperfection is usually known as uncertanty. This term is, however, too restrictive; what is conventionally called uncertainty treatment may in fact be addressing other kinds of imperfection like imprecision, conflict, partial ignorance, etc...

A knowledge based system should model and process each piece of imperfect information in its most suitable model. For instance, for each piece of information above, there is a formal model that can treat it. Imprecise information can be treated by fuzzy sets theory, by rough sets theory or by the manipulation of reference classes. Fuzzy sets theory can also treat vague information. Uncertain information with a probabilistic flavour can be treated by probability theory or by evidence theory (also known as Dempster-Shafer theory), whereas uncertain information with a possibilistic flavour can be treated by possibility theory. Uncertainty is also regularly treated by ad-hoc models. Inconsistent and incomplete information can be treated by non standard logics, like paraconsistent and 4-valued logics in the first case, and non-monotonic logics in the second case, like default logic or circumscription.

In this tutorial we compare some numerical models for the treatment of imperfect information, namely, fuzzy sets theory, possibility theory, probability theory and Dempster Shafer theory. We then present some implementations based on those theories, like Mycin, Fril, fuzzy control and a proposal of the implentation of possibilistic logic PL1 in the knowledge-based system FASE.

Intelligent Tutoring Systems:
Functional Approach x Agents Approach

Rosa Maria Viccari and Lúcia Maria Martins Giraffa

Instituto de Informática, Universidade Federal do Rio Grande do Sul, Caixa Postal 15064, 91501-970 Porto Alegre - RS, Brazil. {rosa, giraffa}@inf.ufrgs.br

Abstract. This work presents an ITS-Intelligent Tutoring Systems' overview using functional and agents approaches. The ITS modular architecture is based on a student model, a domain module, a tutorial module, and a communication module on functional approach. The modular architecture takes place to an agent's society wich works on a co-operative way, considering belives and mental models (intentions, desires, and expectation), where each state of mental models is represented by an agent, on agents approach.

We have the following purposes, on both approaches: to present some basic concepts of each one, at a conceptual level; to discuss the possibilities of using belief systems for student modelling; and to discuss, also at a conceptual level, the consequences of including an automatic learning module in the ITS architecture.

The Case-Based Reasoning Paradigm: Perspective, Technology and Impacts

Agnar Aamodt

Trondheim University, Norway

Abstract. Case-based reasoning (CBR) is an integrated approach to problem solving and machine learning, emphasizing the learning and reuse of case-specific rather than generalized knowledge. The talk presents foundational issues of case-based methods, classification of method types illustrated by existing systems, and a state-of the art description of the CBR field. Specific problems related to case representation, case contents, and indexing methods, will be discussed. Different types of learning, such as adding new cases, modifying existing cases, learning of indexes, will be described. Recent developments of integrated methods are also included, i.e. methods that combine case-specific and other knowledge types, both for learning and problem solving. This also includes the combination of CBR and sub-symbolic methods such as neural networks and genetic algorithms.

Qualitative Models for Interactive Articulated Learning Environments

Bert Bredeweg

University of Amsterdam
Department of Social Science Informatics
The Netherlands

Abstract. It is a generally held position that the process of learning will improve when learners are given computer-based tutoring programs that allow for interactive access tuned to the specific knowledge state of each individual learner. Computer artefacts for learning should therefore be both interactive and articulated. Interactive learning environments can be seen as a specific type of tutoring artefacts. They are engines for education that try to facilitate learning by having learners interact with a simulation of the subject matter. Designing, diagnosing and controlling the behaviour of "physical" systems is an important feature of daily human activities, both in professional and non–professional situations. Interacting with physical systems requires comprehension of their behaviour, in particular how manipulations of some aspect of the system will effect its behaviour. In order to teach these behavioural characteristics, quantitative simulations of these systems are often used in computer-based learning environments. However, some behavioural features are hard to communicate by a computer program that is based on such a quantitative simulation. Among others, generating causal explanations of the systems' behaviour, reasoning from structure (e.g., deriving the behaviour of a given structural description), and qualitativeness in general (e.g. a vocabulary for reasoning about behaviour in qualitative terms) cannot be dealt with adequately. A large part of the research on qualitative reasoning originated from efforts trying to cope with the limitations that followed from using quantitative simulators for teaching purposes. This talk will first discuss the idea of interactive learning environments. In particular, it will focus on the idea of learning by interacting with a simulation model. Next, the talk will present ideas on how qualitative models can be used for this purpose. During the past 10 years a large number of promising results have been achieved by the qualitative reasoning community, whereas at the same time the limitations of the current techniques are well understood. The talk will particularly focus on the use of causal models for curriculum planning, cognitive diagnosis and explanation. Finally, the use of digital multimedia technology provides opportunities to broaden the scope of communication between learner and computer. As such multimedia related issues are important for the construction of interactive articulated learning environments. Interesting is the notion of knowledge-based multimedia: automated generation and adaptation of a certain medium and its contents by a computer program in order to optimise the interaction with a learner or a trainee. The idea of automatic visualisation of qualitative models will be discussed.

H-Computation

N. C. A. da Costa and F. A. Doria

Universidade de São Paulo (USP), Brazil

Abstract. We develop the theory of H-computability, which is strictly more powerful than Turing computability. ("H" stands for "Hilbert", since we can decide Peano Arithmetic in H-computation theory). H-computation is Turing computation plus an intuitive principle which goes back to Euclid and is called here the "Geometric Principle". Turing degrees are shown to be a natural complexity measure for H-computable objects.

Is Computer Vision Still AI?

Robert B. Fisher

Department of Artificial Intelligence, University of Edinburgh

Recent general AI conferences show a decline in both the number and the quality of vision papers, whereas there is a great growth and specialization of computer vision conferences. Many of the vision papers themselves are considerably more mathematical than commonly encountered in AI papers and are often based on a lot of physics. By contrast, AI is most active in areas of formal representations, knowledge-based systems, heuristics and uncertainty based reasoning systems. Hence, one might conclude that CV is parting, or has parted, company from AI.

We propose that the divorce of CV and AI suggested above is actually an "open marriage", and while CV is developing through its own research agenda, there are many shared areas of interest and many of its key methodologies, goals, domain assumptions, and characteristics are shared with AI. We will examine these interrelationships to demonstrate that there is actually still a close relationship.

What is central to Computer Vision are issues of how to represent what is known and observable, how to reason with this represented information and how to act on that knowledge (controlling both internal and external behavior). As these will always be three of the main foundations of Artificial Intelligence, there is no chance that Computer Vision will ever drift far. In the past decade, much Computer Vision research has concentrated on developing competences that reliably extract useful low-level descriptions of the world. As this research phase matures, there will then be a major increase in research that relates those descriptions to stored representations of objects and situations, and this will again make clear the association with Artificial Intelligence.

Fuzzy Robotics and Fuzzy Image Understanding

Kaoru Hirota

Department of Computational Intelligence and Systems Science
Interdisciplinary Graduate School of Science and Engineering
Tokyo Institute of Technology
4259 Nagatsuta-cho, Midori-ku, Yokohama 226, Japan
e-mail hirota@hrt.dis.titech.ac.jp

Abstract. Two topics, i.e., fuzzy robotics and fuzzy image understanding, are introduced in this order. The author's group developed various types of fuzzy robots from early 1980s. Several typical examples are shown in this talk. The first one realizes a grasping and putting operation in industrial line based on fuzzy if then rule based control and fuzzy image decision tree techniques. Then a flower arrangement robot is introduced. It realizes the human artistic skill in the robot task based on fuzzy rules. The third one is 2D Ping-Pong robot that demonstrates the realtime control with image process- ing using a simple 16-bit personal computer. The forth is con- cerned with an irregular moving object shooting based on fuzzy chaos prediction method. Finally a group of autonomous mobile robots is presented. It realizes various group movements such as line formation and triangular shaped movement, where fuzzy neuro techniques are introduced. There exist several advantages in these approaches to robotics. Fuzzy technologies made it possible to introduce humans' skill in a human friendly manner and to design the system easily. In most application examples presented here it took for a few weeks for a few graduate students to implement the fundamental part of the system including the knowl- edge acquisition process. The costeffectiveness of these technol- ogies is another noteworthy point. Even a very small personal computer realized the real time control or the real time image understanding for these robotics examples. Some of the techniques presented have been applied to Japanese robotics applications in real industrial lines. Then various image understanding techniques based on fuzzy technology developed by the authors group have been surveyed. First fuzzy clustering is applied to the remote sensing images. It is a modified version of the well known FCM. Then a shape recognition algorithm is presented for a robotics assembling line. It is a fuzzy discriminant tree method for a real time use. Finally a fuzzy dynamic image understanding system is presented. It can understand the dynamic images on general roads in Japan, where a fuzzy frame based knowledge representation and a special kind of fuzzy inference engine are introduced. Experimental results are shown by an OHP and a slide projector.

Toward a Theory of Molecular Computing

A. F. Rocha

RANI - Research on Artificial Intelligence
R. Tenente Ary Aps, 172
Jundiai - SP CEP 13207-110, Brazil
email: eina@turing.ccvax.unicamp.br
http://www.fem.unicamp.br/ rani

Abstract. Many recent papers have foccused attention on a very new topic called molecular computing aiming to discuss how to develop intelligent computers using biological molecules as computational devices.

The theory of formal languages was introduced as a formalism to support the analysis both of the human language as well of those artificial languages used in computers. Any attempt to develop a strong theory for molecular computing will require, therefore, the translation of the knowledge about genetic networks into this or a similar formalism. This is a necessity because of the precise and complex analysis to be performed to create any consistent and practical artificial machine mimicking the cellular problem solving capabilities.

Many AI techniques have been proposed to help analysis in molecular biology and formal language was proposed as a tool to help DNA parsing. The key issue in these approaches is to use the AI tool to analyse experimental results, but not to take the formalism as a representational and reasoning technique to help the understanding of the biological phenomena underlying the experiment.

The purpose of the present paper is to discuss the theory of formal language as an adequate formalism to support the development of any theory of molecular computing, aiming both to furnish a strong reasoning tool about data collected by biology concerning the molecular systems subserving life, as well as to allow the creation of computing artificial systems founded over similar concepts. The paper has the following organization. the FFL theory is briefly introduced in the first section. In the sequence, some basic biological concepts are discussed preparing the reader to accept Fuzzy Formal Languages (FFL) as an adequate formalism to deal with genetic networks. The third section shows how to construct a biochemical language upon the concepts previously discussed. Finally, distributed cellular systems are proposed as the adequate formal tool to control the ambiguity of the FFL supporting the molecular computing, in order to reduce the identification process cost.

Index of Authors

Springer
and the
environment

At Springer we firmly believe that an international science publisher has a special obligation to the environment, and our corporate policies consistently reflect this conviction.

We also expect our business partners – paper mills, printers, packaging manufacturers, etc. – to commit themselves to using materials and production processes that do not harm the environment. The paper in this book is made from low- or no-chlorine pulp and is acid free, in conformance with international standards for paper permanency.

 Springer

Lecture Notes in Artificial Intelligence (LNAI)

Lecture Notes in Computer Science